A Space of Anxiety

Dislocation and Abjection in Modern German-Jewish Literature

AMSTERDAMER PUBLIKATIONEN ZUR SPRACHE UND LITERATUR

in Verbindung mit

PETER BOERNER, BLOOMINGTON; HUGO DYSERINCK, AACHEN;
FERDINAND VAN INGEN, AMSTERDAM; FRIEDRICH MAURER†,
FREIBURG; OSKAR REICHMANN, HEIDELBERG

herausgegeben von

COLA MINIS†
und
AREND QUAK

138

AMSTERDAM - ATLANTA, GA 1999

A Space of Anxiety

Dislocation and Abjection in Modern German-Jewish Literature

by

Anne Fuchs

∞ The paper on which this book is printed meets the requirements of "ISO 9706:1994, Information and documentation - Paper for documents - Requirements for permanence".

ISBN: 90-420-0797-4
©Editions Rodopi B.V., Amsterdam - Atlanta, GA 1999
Printed in The Netherlands

For Helen

Contents

Acknowledgements	VII
Introduction	1

Freud's Jewishness: Opposing the "Compact Majority"

Marked Territories: "Aryan" and "Jew" in Fin-de-Siècle Discourse	19
Freud's Position of Difference	28
Freud's *Der Mann Moses* and the Creation of the Jew	31
Freud's *Moses*: A Narrative of Anxiety?	34
Reading *Moses*: A Story of Jewish Self-Hatred?	37
Reading *Moses*: A Story of Adoption and Abjection	43

The Longing to Belong: Dislocation and Abjection in Kafka's *Der Verschollene (Amerika)*

Setting the Scene: Two Arrivals in America	49
Labyrinths and Linguistic Whirlpools	51
Kafka on the Couch?	55
Uncle Jakob's "Matter of Discipline"	60
A Suitcase, a Passport and a Photograph	63
Food Nausea	68
Of Animals and Hunger Artist	71
Encroaching Women and a "Mother in the Distant"	75

Roth's Ambivalence: The Logic of Separation in His Writings on Eastern Jewry

Abjection and the Denial of Kinship	81
The World of the *Shtetl*	87
"Ich bin mit Wonne ein Abtrünniger": The Pleasure of Being Abject	96

Roth's *Hiob:* A Jewish Story of a Simple Man, a Simple Story of a Jewish Man   101
A Systemic View of the Family   105
Ritual and Abjection in *Hiob*   109
Women and the "Place of Rot"   112

Files against the Self : The Case of Albert Drach

When a Jew from Brody sits under a Plum Tree   123
Schmul goes West   128
File Style   135
Mimicry of Power: A Figure of Uncertainty   137
Dissecting Women: >>Z.Z.<< *das ist die Zwischenzeit*   142
A Pedlar who may be God   147
Mastering the Mob   151
Reality as Labyrinth: From Sterne's *Sentimental Journey* to Drach's *Unsentimentale Reise*   154

Bad Boys and Evil Witches: Gender and Abjection in Edgar Hilsenrath's *Der Nazi & der Friseur*

Hansel and Gretel Revisited: *Der Nazi & der Friseur*   163
Humour in Holocaust Fiction   165
The Scandal of Mimicry: A Nazi Imitates a Jew   168
Eating Monsters and Waste Factories: Female Abjection   172

Summary: A Space of Anxiety   177
Bibliography   185
Index   197

Acknowledgements

Many people have helped me in the preparation of this book. I would especially like to thank Michael Kane and Jeanne Riou for their enormous contribution. Their eagle-eyed proof-reading and useful comments were invaluable towards completion of this volume. I also want to thank Florian Krobb who read the entire manuscript and responded with his usual thoroughness and care. Hugh Ridley's astute comments on sections of this study assisted me greatly in completing the book. I would also like to thank Torsten Flüh for his commentary. Thanks are especially due to Helen Doherty for her continued support and encouragement. Finally, I would like to thank the Department of German, University College Dublin for the attempt to maintain a research-friendly atmosphere in an otherwise pressurised educational context. Last but not least, I want to thank my M.A students whose keen interest in courses on German-Jewish themes has fuelled my own enthusiasm over the years.

The volume is addressed to students of German literature, comparative literature and students involved in Jewish studies. Due to the interdisciplinary nature of this study I felt it necessary to provide English translations of all longer German quotations in the footnotes; shorter quotations are frequently translated in the main body of the text. Unless otherwise stated, all translations were made by the author. Details of abbreviations are given in footnotes and in the bibliography.

Dublin, June 1999

Introduction

Travel — Maze-walking

This study engages with a body of German-Jewish literature that, from the beginning of the century onwards, explores notions of identity and kinship in the context of migration, exile and persecution. Migration, exile and persecution all involve a loss of the connection with what one might call the "space of homeliness", commonly considered the locus of identity. Severing the link between the self and its environment, all the authors included in my study employ, to varying degrees, the travel paradigm to explore those borders and boundaries that define the space between self and other. In clear contrast to travel writings of the Enlightenment and Eurocentric kind where travel, with its pitfalls, dangers and challenges, acts as a positive catalyst, allowing the self to undergo a process of self-formation (*Bildung* in German), the travel narratives under discussion in this study fundamentally challenge the notion that such "positive" appropriation of the world is tenable in a modern context. Here the suspension of intimacy, one of the hallmarks of travelling, points to the fragility and instability of subjectivity in a largely unreadable and hostile environment. The travelling self we encounter in these narratives is therefore no longer the "seeing man" who, as Mary Louise Pratt's study of eighteenth and nineteenth century travel writing, *Imperial Eyes*, suggests, looks out in order to possess.[1] Instead he is a blinded maze-walker whose experience of the world remains disorientating and fragmented.

A summary mapping of the territory covered by the German-Jewish writings under discussion in this volume starts with the exodus of the Jews from Egypt and their repatriation under Moses's leadership in Palestine and ends with the image of a ship called "Exitus" carrying Shoah-survivors to Palestine in 1947. Framed by these "imaginings"[2] of a homecoming and a Jewish identity are images of exile, emigration and persecution. These include the image of a sixteen year old boy who arrives in America at the beginning of this century, that of a Jewish family from Eastern Europe who

---

[1] Mary Louise Pratt, *Imperial Eyes. Travel Writing and Transculturation.* London and New York: Routledge, 1992: 7.
[2] I am using this term in the sense defined by Benedict Anderson in *Imagined Communities. Reflections on the Origin and Spread of Nationalism.* London: Verso, revised ed. 1991: 5-7.

leaves the *shtetl* in search of a new life in the new world, and finally the image of a man who finds himself stranded in Vichy France on a journey of exile. Instead of a ship awaiting him, there is a train travelling to a concentration camp in Eastern Europe.

Against this background I propose to explore how at moments previous and subsequent to the Shoah the travel paradigm is used to relate the experience of estrangement, the precarious boundaries between self and other, the heterogeneity of modern subjectivity, and, what Kristeva terms the *jouissance* of writing. The German-Jewish travel writings under discussion here propel the protagonists into what I shall call "a space of anxiety" which is mapped out by a socially engendered paranoia and phobia. I argue that this space does not only reflect the protagonists' individual disposition, their personal anxieties, concerns and fears, but also the phobic underside of the social order which tries to protect its boundaries through mechanisms of exclusion. The main protagonists of these travelling narratives are therefore not tourists or travellers in the traditional sense, hungry to explore the riches of the world, but migrant maze-walkers trapped in a labyrinth where all movement is disorientating and dangerous. Driven by the longing to belong, these characters stray through a territory where their longing is always misplaced and evidence of their otherness.

Modernity — Jewishness

Many of the texts included here articulate this experience of displacement and otherness from a Jewish perspective, or rather from the viewpoint of German Jews who, from the turn of the century onwards, were increasingly confronted with the aggressive rhetoric of anti-Semitism and the tribal spirit of *völkisch* nationalism, a point to which I will return. Freud, Kafka, Drach, Roth and Hilsenrath all approach the problematic of self and other, identity and alterity, belonging and displacement from a particularly "Jewish" angle which reflects their own experience of alienation from the dominant German culture. However, although a certain degree of "Jewishness" is inscribed in these texts, it is a Jewishness that defines itself primarily through its relationship with modernity. Modernity is such a contested term that it requires some brief definition for the purpose of this study.

I agree with Zygmunt Bauman who in *Modernity and Ambivalence* analyses modernity as a "historical period that began in Western Europe with a series of profound social-structural and intellectual transformations of the seventeenth century and achieved its maturity (1) as a cultural project — with the growth of Enlightenment; (2) as a socially accomplished form of life — with the growth of industrial [...] life."³ Unlike modernism, which can be defined as an intellectual and aesthetic practice that, by reflecting upon the project of modernity, paves the way for the postmodern condition, modernity is a political, legislative, administrative and discursive practice whose overriding aim is the production of a rationally designed order. This quest for order does not tolerate anything that eludes classification, for this reason modernity strives for the elimination of all categories that defy definition, above all ambivalence. As the threatening other of modernity's ordering activity, ambivalence thus became the "unwanted waste" of the modern quest for order.[4] Bauman continues that:

> intolerance is, therefore, the natural inclination of modern practice. Construction of order sets the limits to incorporation and admission. It calls for the denial of rights, and of the grounds, of everything that cannot be assimilated — for delegitimation of the other.[5]

In the context of this increasingly intolerant and *völkisch* quest for order, German Jews began to realise from the turn of the century onwards that in spite of their assimilatory efforts discussed below they continued to be haunted by the stigma of difference.

In the chapters that follow I want to show that the "demon of ambivalence" that characterises the position of German-Jewish writers in society provided them with a starting point for a critical investigation of the foundations of the social order. The writers discussed here therefore present their Jewish experience as a problematic that highlights the repressed underside of the modern social order.[6] At some point in their intellectual journey they used the travel paradigm to explore paradigmatically the limits of incorporation and admission that Bauman mentions above. This study intends to demonstrate that the physical, psychological and epistemological

---

[3] Zygmunt Bauman, *Modernity and Ambivalence*. Cambridge: Polity Press, 1991: 4.
[4] Ibid., 15.
[5] Ibid., 8.
[6] In his recent study *Von Kafka bis Celan. Jüdischer Diskurs in der deutschen Literatur des 20. Jahrhunderts* (Göttingen: Vandenhoek & Ruprecht, 1998) Dieter Lamping rightly challenges an understanding of German-Jewish literature which confines itself to outlining the great contribution of Jewish authors to German culture. Instead he attempts to trace the transformation of German-Jewish literature into a specifically Jewish literature in the German language. However, while it is undoubtedly correct that German-Jewish literature after 1945 focuses on Auschwitz and the themes of persecution and extermination, it is important to note that the experience of dislocation and abjection are voiced long before the Shoah. For Lamping Jewish literature in German gives voice to a Jewish identity (27). He suggests that this involves the author's "Zugehörigkeit zum Judentum", affiliation with Jewishness (28). In contrast to Lamping's approach my study argues that modern German-Jewish literature questions and undermines all notions of stability and identity. It is not so much identity but abjection, ambivalence and difference that characterise modern German-Jewish literature.

dislocation articulated in this body of German-Jewish travel writing maps out the position of the modern subject as a split and "abject" self.

Abjection — Jews

This leads me to an important theoretical cornerstone of this study. I draw upon Julia Kristeva's *Powers of Horror. An Essay on Abjection* together with post-colonial theories to explore the ontological and psychological displacement articulated in these (post-) modern German-Jewish texts.

To be abject is to be misplaced, astray and without identity. Abjection is a terrifying borderline state which estranges the individual from all social relations. It is the stigma of the modern subject that cannot locate itself via another object. The sphere of abjection is the in-between, the ambiguous, that which does not respect borders, rules and systems. In Kristeva's words it is "a threat that seems to emanate from an exorbitant outside or inside, ejected beyond the scope of the possible, the tolerable, the thinkable. It lies there, quite close, but it cannot be assimilated."[7] Kristeva's evocative description of the threat that is posed by abjection also indicates a connection that is of particular interest in the context of the German-Jewish experience, namely that abjection seems to be the reverse side of assimilation. Or, to put it differently, all that which defies assimilation is abjected. Looked at from this angle, this poses the question as to whether the drive towards Jewish assimilation in the nineteenth century did not already carry the seed of the *völkisch* abjection of "the Jew". The most horrific expression of this is the Shoah.

Abjection is also a founding moment in the archaeology of subjectivity. The boundaries between self and (m)other, inside and outside, the proper and improper, the clean and unclean, all of which structure sociality, are mapped out on the basis of abjection. Before we are speaking subjects in a world of coherent objects we all inhabit a space without proper boundaries and borders. Kristeva refers to this space as the *chora*, "a self-contemplative, conservative, self-sufficient haven" which is shared by mother and child and precedes the mirror-stage.[8] Abjection is that important moment in the journey towards subjectivity when the young child begins to demarcate boundaries between self and (m)other. The emerging subject needs to free itself from the mother's body which in this process becomes abject. The child in the pre-oedipal phase engages in expelling the unclean and improper

---

[7] Julia Kristeva, *Powers of Horror. An Essay on Abjection*. Translated by L. S. Roudiez. New York: Columbia University Press, 1982: 1.
[8] Ibid., 14.

such as faeces, food, urine, tears, saliva and so on, and by doing that, begins to claim the body as its own. The abjection of the unclean is quite obviously based on natural cycles of incorporation and evacuation, processes that help to designate bodily zones as erotogenic ones (genitals, anus, mouth, eyes, ears etc). A good example of abjection is the child's rejection of the food offered by the mother, an act which in a paradoxical double motion serves to establish and abject the self:

> 'I' want none of that element, sign of their desire; 'I' do not want to listen, 'I' do not assimilate it, 'I' expel it. But since the food is not an 'other' for 'me', who am only in their desire, I expel myself, I spit myself out, I abject myself within the same motion through which 'I' claim to establish myself.[9]

This example shows that the abjection of the "improper" and "unclean" is not caused by a lack of hygiene or health but by those elements which threaten borders, positions and the subject's boundaries. And, with reference to the archaeology of the subject, the food example illustrates that abjection is one of the infant's earliest attempts to break away from the maternal hold — Kristeva calls it a "clumsy breaking away" which runs the constant risk "of falling back under the sway of a power as securing as it is stifling."[10] In actual fact, it needs a third party, the father or the "paternal metaphor", to pursue this struggle to demarcate and divide and to ensure that the subject will find its place in the symbolic order. The paternal metaphor enables the struggling "not-yet-I" to make the transition and to give up the "good maternal object"[11] in favour of finding its place within the symbolic order. The implication here is that the symbolic order as the domain of language, reason, positions and rules etc. functions only because of the repression of the maternal. Elizabeth Grosz comments that "civilization, the symbolic order, the coherent text, then are possible only at the cost of the silencing, the phallicisation, of the maternal *chora*."[12]

The rule of the symbolic order is never guaranteed or fully stable, since from its banished place the abject continues to threaten the subject. If in the subject's archaeology, this space between inside and outside, self and other has not been properly demarcated we are in the presence of the borderliner who is constantly invaded by the abject and therefore incapable of proper object relations. Torn between the desire for the mother and the brutal separation from her, the abject self has lost his power to identify with the other: "Where objects are concerned he delegates phantoms, ghosts, 'false

---

[9] Kristeva, *Powers of Horror*, 3.
[10] Ibid., 13.
[11] Ibid., 45.
[12] Elizabeth Grosz, *Sexual Subversions. Three French Feminists*. Sydney etc.: Allen & Unwin, 1989, 49.

cards': a stream of spurious objects, seeming egos that confront undesirable objects. [...] No subject, no object."[13] As a result of this lack, this wanting self cannot answer the question "who am I?" any longer but only "where am I?". Kristeva refers to the abject also as a "deject who places (himself), separates (himself), situates (himself), and therefore strays instead of getting his bearings, desiring, belonging, or refusing."[14] Without a sense of orientation the abject character glides through a space of anxiety where the boundaries between inner and outer world are constantly threatened by the invasion of the abject and where no true objects of desire can exist.The abject is thus the terrifying abyss into which the subject may fall when language and the symbolic sphere fail.

The symbolic order tries to prevent this failure by modes of exclusion that position the abject at a safe distance from the symbolic. Kristeva discusses the incest taboo as a universal example of how the symbolic tries to protect itself from the return of the abject by, for instance, demarcating a border between the clean and unclean, the proper and improper etc. This raises the question as to whether Kristeva's analysis of the interplay between the symbolic and the abject does not ultimately ontologise and normalise the exclusion of the other. After all in Germany's history, phobic modes of exclusion resulted in a policy of extermination. It is not difficult to show, however, that this would be a serious misunderstanding of Kristeva's theory of abjection, which, in my view, provides the basis for an analysis of the pathology of the Third Reich. Looked at from a Kristevean angle, the crisis of the Jews' abjection and the Nazis' policy of extermination can now be read as a breakdown of the symbolic order and a psychotic unleashing of drives. Remember that abjection is normally kept at bay through the *integrity* of the signifying practice of the symbolic order. In clear contrast to this, the Nazis' hatred of "the Jew" is evidence of a *phobic* configuration in which the Jew is turned into the abject other and stabilises a symbolic order that had, from the demise of the *Kaiserreich*, become increasingly fragile. Anti-Semitism is the disease of the German male who responded to the weakening of the phallic signifier (experienced as the defeat in the First World War and a threat to male dominance by women's ascent in society) by plunging into an empty identification with an "Aryan" maleness for which the notion of "the Jew" became the only violent link to the world. The Nazis' so-called "Final Solution" resembles the psychotic's phobic attempt to literally kill that which he perceives as a threat to his subjectivity.

---

[13] Ibid., 47.
[14] Ibid., 8.

Jew — Woman

I now want to return to the "normal" role abjection plays in the constitution of the subject. We have previously seen that —paradoxically — abjection is both a threat to subjectivity and its very pre-condition. Anna Smith explains the impossibility of mastering abjection in the following words:

> What the symbolic system expels as waste or defilement becomes abject, but its very persistence indicates the ongoing difficulties of any final exclusion. The threat of abjection comes from a maternal entity that is neither 'us' nor 'not us', but somewhere in between [sic] that summons up an archaic state in the development of the subject [...].[15]

This leads me to a brief discussion of Kristeva's negative treatment of the maternal in *Powers of Horror*. While Kristeva's discourse generally tends to oscillate between valorising and denigrating the feminine, in *Powers of Horror* she aligns the maternal body *literally* with the abject. Smith criticises Kristeva for the horrific place she accords to the maternal function thus:

> In the same way that psychotics believe the mother to have the power of castration, and in the same way that they acquiesce to the negativity of the drives over symbolisation, we could say that Kristeva mimics their dissociated condition, and mimics Céline in the horrific place she accords to the maternal function.[16]

Although Smith suspects that Kristeva's fascination for Céline is the reason why she elevates "his narrative of hatred and fear into a universal condition", she comes to the conclusion that Kristeva ultimately moves beyond an identification with Céline when she suggests that women have an investment in the imaginary that allows them to *imagine* rather than experience abjection.[17]

This is an important point since nearly all the texts under discussion here create a link between the threat of abjection and the maternal body. I shall argue that they articulate a libidinal economy which turns woman *literally* into the abject other of the symbolic order. Implicitly these texts encode abjection as a gender-specific problematic that engages the male characters in repetitive gestures of separation. Trying to escape from a devouring interior, namely the "first natural mansion"[18] of the maternal body, these male anti-heroes frantically set up their own boundaries through loathing women. It is therefore hardly surprising, from Kafka to Hilsenrath,

---

[15] Anna Smith, *Julia Kristeva. Readings of Exile and Estrangement*. Houndsmills: Macmillan, 1996: 149f.
[16] Ibid., 153.
[17] Smith, *Julia Kristeva*, 155. See also Kristeva, *Powers of Horror*, 144.
[18] Smith, *Julia Kristeva*, 151.

that the signifier "woman" is aligned with images of waste, defilement and decaying body parts. My thesis therefore is that although these texts engage on one level in the deconstruction of the Aryan-Jew opposition and, by implication, the rhetoric of race, on another, perhaps less conscious level, these narratives translate the signs of difference attributed to the male Jew into the gender paradigm, thus turning woman into the site of abjection. This economy allows the male characters (and writers) to transfer abjection from the male Jewish body onto woman, thus ratifying the cross-stitching of racial and sexual difference inherent in the scientific discourse of the nineteenth century.

The writers discussed here, from Sigmund Freud, Franz Kafka, Joseph Roth and Albert Drach to Edgar Hilsenrath, are undoubtedly extremely divergent in terms of genres, styles, registers and generation; they share however a German-Jewish background at moments before and after the Shoah. They all came from assimilated families who had largely rejected Jewish traditions in favour of assimilation to German culture. This absence of a living link with Judaism is explicitly dealt with in Kafka's famous letter to his father written in 1919, in which he reproaches his father for having failed to initiate him into a meaningful connection with Judaism.[19] But Kafka was not alone in this: to a varying degree all the authors discussed here are involved in this quest for a sense of Jewishness that was not primarily religious.

East — West

In addition, most of the writers included in this book were Austrian Jews, for whom Vienna was the metropolis and intellectual centre of the Habsburg Empire, and after the demise of the Empire, of Austria.[20] For instance, Roth, who was born in Brody, the Eastern outpost of the Empire (now the Ukraine), was drawn to the magnet of Vienna. In Freud's case, the family had moved from Freiberg in Moravia to Vienna when Freud was only three. Drach was born in Vienna, to which he returned after the end of the Second World War.

The move of the Freud family to Vienna is paradigmatic for thousands of Jews in the Empire who, from the 1850s onwards, migrated from the Eastern provinces to the West. Robert S. Wistrich describes these large scale migration movements in the following words:

---

[19] Cf. Franz Kafka, *Brief an den Vater*. Frankfurt: Fischer, 1992: 44-50.
[20] One exception is Edgar Hilsenrath who was born in Leipzig in Germany.

once the gates of the Imperial capital were open to mass migration in the 1850s, the *Ostjuden* from the Polish provinces began slowly to abandon this economically backward region and to converge on Vienna or else emigrate overseas. They were joined and initially, at least, outpaced by a steady stream of Jewish immigrants from Bohemia, Moravia, and above all Hungary, which swelled the Viennese Jewish community from less than 10,000 in the 1850s to a high point of 175,318 by 1910.[21]

The geographical division between the East and the West and their respective definition as periphery and centre mapped out an economic, cultural and ideological system according to which the East, and by implication the Eastern Jew, was backward and unenlightened. In his pioneering book *Brothers and Strangers*, Steven Aschheim analyses the discourse on the Eastern Jew and its popularity in the early twentieth century. According to Aschheim, this discourse is the immediate by-product of the modernisation of Jewish life and consciousness. "Once German Jewry itself became modernized", writes Aschheim, "unemancipated Eastern Jewry served as a constant reminder of the mysterious and brooding ghetto presence."[22] One good example of this is the body of writing by Karl Emil Franzos, a fervent supporter of assimilation and a strong opponent of Eastern European *Hasidism*. In 1876 he published *Aus Halb-Asien* [From Half-Asia] which was a collection of "Kulturbilder" [cultural vignettes] from Galicia, the Bukovina, Southern Russia and Romania, in other words, from areas of the Habsburg Empire where traditional forms of Jewish life were still prominent. The orientalist stance adopted by Franzos is exemplified in his preface where he stigmatises the East as a space of semantic ambiguity:

> Im allgemeinen herrscht im Osten oder doch mindestens in dem Teile des Ostens, von dem diese Blätter Kunde geben, weder heller Tag, noch dunkle Nacht, sondern ein seltsames Zwielicht, im allgemeinen sind Galizien, Rumänien und Südrußland weder so gesittet, wie Deutschland, noch so barbarisch, wie Turan, sondern eben ein Gemisch von beiden — Halb-Asien!²³

Franzos was not alone in dissociating himself from a stigmatised background: Aschheim's study shows that Jews, German liberals and anti-

---

[21] Robert S. Wistrich, *The Jews of Vienna in the Age of Franz Joseph*. Oxford: Oxford University Press, 1989: 41.
[22] Steven S. Aschheim, *Brothers and Strangers: The East European Jew in German and German Jewish Consciousness, 1800-1923*. Madison, Wisconsin: University of Wisconsin Press, 1982: 58.
[23] Karl Emil Franzos, *Aus Halb-Asien. Kulturbilder aus Galizien, der Bukowina, Südrußland und Rumänien*. Berlin: Concordia Deutsch Verlags-Anstalt, 4th ed. 1901, I: xvi [Generally speaking, the East, or at least those parts which these pages describe, is characterised neither by bright daylight nor by dark night but rather by a strange twilight; Galicia, Romania and Southern Russia are generally neither as civilized as Germany nor as barbaric as Turan; instead it is a mixture of both — it is indeed Half-Asia!]

Semites alike "appeared to repudiate the physical and spiritual characteristics associated with the ghetto".[24]

Reacting to this stereotype of the Eastern Jew, a new generation of writers began to emerge from the beginning of the twentieth century, among them Franz Kafka, Arnold Zweig, and Joseph Roth, who attempted a positive reappropriation of the image of the Eastern Jew. While chapter three specifically analyses Roth's discourse on the Eastern Jew, it is noteworthy that all the writers discussed in this study had to position themselves in relation to a system of representation which stigmatised the Eastern Jew and the East as inferior. Chapters four and five explore how this theme resurfaces in the novels of two post-Shoah writers, namely Albert Drach and Edgar Hilsenrath.

German — Jewish

The five authors included in this study all produced their seminal writings in the German language. But although German served as a substitute for a Jewish sense of belonging, this does not mean that their identification with German culture was straightforward. German Jews of the early twentieth century could no longer share the optimism of their grandparents' generation which saw assimilation as the Jewish entry-ticket to German society.

It may be useful here to introduce the basic tenets of the great project of assimilation. In the nineteenth century assimilation was largely guided by the universalist (and Eurocentric) assumption that a perceived otherness had to be given up in favour of a uniform national culture. According to Florian Krobb, the de-ghettoisation of Jews and the process of assimilation can also be viewed in terms of Jewish de-colonisation:

> It is not surprising that the first de-colonising step of the Jews was an assimilatory one, an attempt to become like the dominant group in terms of looks, dress, habit, and language, to participate in their professions and excel in their philosophy, art and writing in order to demonstrate the entitlement to equal status with the privileged majority group.[25]

From the viewpoint of German Jewry in the early twentieth century, it was far from certain that assimilation had really been a successful step on the

---

[24] Steven Aschheim, *Brothers and Strangers*, 59.
[25] Florian Krobb, 'Reclaiming the Location: Leopold Kompert's Ghetto Fiction in Post-Colonial Perspective'. In: Anne Fuchs and Florian Krobb (Eds.), *Ghetto Writing: Traditional and Eastern Jewry in German-Jewish Literature from Heine to Hilsenrath*. Columbia: Camden House, 1999: 44.

road to de-colonisation. While German Jews of the nineteenth century felt confident that a unified Germany would also show her human face, this optimism had considerably faded by the beginning of the twentieth century. Instead of experiencing the humanistic spirit of German *Kultur*, which, in the eyes of nineteenth-century German Jewry, was also the guarantor of equality, writers from Freud onwards were faced with the sad reality of politically organised anti-Semitism and the racist rhetoric of the *völkisch* nation. Bauman argues that the real result of assimilation was merely the conversion of pre-modern segregation in the ghetto of old into the sublimated category of alienation and social isolation in the modern world. "Trapped in ambivalence", assimilated German Jewry was now a non-category, "prised from the traditional Jewish community as much as from the native German elites."[26]

Bauman's findings are echoed in Jakob Wassermann's autobiographical study *Mein Weg als Jude und Deutscher* [My Path as a German and a Jew, 1921] which describes the trap of alienation thus:

> Ich wurde als Mensch nicht als zugehörig gefordert, weder von dem einzelnen, noch von einer Gemeinschaft, weder von den Menschen meines Ursprungs, noch von denen meiner Sehnsucht, weder von denen meiner Art, noch von denen meiner Wahl.[27]

The widespread stereotyping of "the Jew" is demonstrated in Sander Gilman's studies of the discourse of the medical science of the nineteenth and early twentieth centuries. According to Gilman medical discourse identified Jewish circumcision as a signifier of difference and, in addition, the figure of "the Jew" with a threatening form of sexuality.[28] Another negative marker of difference was the language of the Jew, "jüdeln", "mauscheln", or *Jargon* (that is the use of a slightly changed syntax, the insertion of Hebrew words, and a different intonation), which was perceived to capture the Jews' "true" essence as liars, swindlers and the like.[29] In his recent study *Die Sprache jüdischer Figuren in der deutschen Literatur (1750– 1933)* [The Language of Jewish Characters in German Literature from 1750 to 1933], Matthias Richter compares the treatment of Yiddish with that of German dialects. He shows that while the German dialects experienced a positive re-evaluation from the early nineteenth century on, the same does

---

[26] Ibid., 120.
[27] Jakob Wassermann, *Mein Weg als Deutscher und Jude*. Munich: Deutscher Taschenbuch Verlag, 1994: 34. [I was not accepted as a human being in my own right, neither by the individual nor by the community, neither by the people of my origin nor by those to whom I longed to belong, neither by the people of my own kind nor by those whom I had chosen.]
[28] Cf. Sander L. Gilman, *Freud, Race, and Gender*. Princeton, New Jersey: Princeton University Press, 1993: 49ff.
[29] Sander L. Gilman, *Jewish Self-Hatred: Anti-Semitism and the Hidden Language of the Jews*. Baltimore and London: John Hopkins University Press, 1986: esp. 68-86 and 139-147.

not apply to Yiddish which continued to be regarded as a corrupt and degenerated idiom.³⁰ In his research, Richter did not come across a single German source which evaluated Yiddish in positive terms.

Yiddish or *Jargon* was rejected by Germans and assimilated Jews alike. Most prominent in the Jewish camp is Moses Mendelssohn, the philosopher of the Enlightenment period, who considered the adoption of standard High German as inseparable from Jewish emancipation. He dismissed *Jargon* as impure, arguing that it had contributed not a little "zur Unsittlichkeit des gemeinen Mannes. [...] [Gesprochen werden sollte] nach Beschaffenheit der Umstände, rein deutsch oder rein hebräisch [...] Nur keine Vermischung der Sprachen!"³¹ In a recent article on 'German versus *Jargon*: Language and Jewish Identity in German Ghetto Writing' Gabriele von Glasenapp comments that:

> Mendelssohn's brusque verdict, announced at the beginning of the period of Jewish emancipation, had far-reaching consequences for the language used by German Jews. Up to the end of the nineteenth century the eradication of Yiddish was seen as necessary for social integration into German society. In the nineteenth century, when the Jews understood the term assimilation to include full secularisation and to exclude Jewish idiosyncrasies, they were, quite understandably, particularly determined to avoid any conspicuous linguistic peculiarities in order to reduce the risk of being cast onto the social and cultural scrapheap.³²

Both the negative evaluation of the Jews' language and the medical discourse on "the Jew" are two great themes of Albert Drach's *Das große Protokoll gegen Zwetschkenbaum* [The Massive File against Zwetschkenbaum, 1964] which I analyse in detail in chapter four.

---

³⁰ Matthias Richter, *Die Sprache jüdischer Figuren in der deutschen Literatur (1750-1933): Studien zu Form und Funktion.* Göttingen: Wallstein, 1995: 55-60.
³¹ Cited in Jacob Toury, "Die Sprache als Problem der jüdischen Einordnung im deutschen Kulturraum," in *Jahrbuch des Instituts für deutsche Geschichte Tel Aviv*, Beiheft 4 (1982), 77. [to the immorality of the common man. Depending on the situation, pure German or pure Hebrew should be spoken. But no mixing of the languages!]
³² Gabriele von Glasenapp, 'German versus *Jargon*: Language and Jewish Identity in German Ghetto Writing'. In: Anne Fuchs and Florian Krobb (Eds.), *Ghetto Writing*, 55.

Identity — Difference

Using some of the theory which has been developed to deal with the issues of colonisation, de-colonisation and post-colonial experience, this study proposes that modern German-Jewish writers engage (like the post-colonial subject) in revising an ideology that sets up the relation between Aryan and Jew exclusively in a binary structure of opposition. In what follows I argue that the German-Jewish writers under discussion here turned their experience of estrangement into a vantage point from which they challenged precisely those narratives of origin and identity that are at the heart of the *völkisch* imagining of the nation state. Freud, Kafka, Roth, Drach and Hilsenrath all inhabit a borderline position which allows them to challenge and contest the national imagining of an originary subjectivity and tradition in favour of the ongoing articulation of difference. They were especially susceptible to the recognition that the binary opposition between self and other, Aryan and Jew, coloniser and colonised ultimately silences the experience of cultural ambivalence and difference. This difference must, however, not be understood in essentialised ethnic terms but as a performative category that is produced through cultural engagement. The critic of the post-colonial condition, Homi Bhabha, warns against the danger of essentialising difference in the following words:

> The representation of difference must not be hastily read as the reflection of *pre-given* ethnic or cultural traits set in the fixed tablet of tradition. The social articulation of difference, from the minority perspective, is a complex, on-going negotiation that seeks to authorize cultural hybridities that emerge in moments of historical transformation.[33]

Drawing upon post-colonial and psychoanalytic theories this study suggests that, by embracing their position of difference, German-Jewish writers from Freud to Hilsenrath reacted to and destabilised a system of representation and a discourse characterised by those binary oppositions that suggest an ontological polarisation between Jew and Aryan, East and West, centre and periphery.

Chapter one analyses aspects of the discourse on "the Jew" around the turn of the century and Freud's understanding of his own Jewishness. This prepares the ground for a detailed reading of Freud's last book *Der Mann Moses und die monotheistische Religion* [translated as *Moses and Monotheism*, 1939] which occupies a special position in Freud's œuvre in that the work is surprisingly fragmented and repetitive. Freud was aware of the scholarly shortcomings of his study and considered publishing *Der Mann*

---

[33] Homi K. Bhabha, *The Location of Culture*. London and New York: Routledge, 1994: 2.

Moses as a historical novel. He dropped this idea because, in his view, the publication of a novel would have jeopardised his scientific reputation. However, what Freud presents here in an unusually hesitant style turns out to be not a scientific study but a narrative of adoption and abjection that highlights what is repressed in the national imagining of a people. Although Freud appears to be only concerned with the figure of Moses, his leadership and the homecoming of the Jewish people, I hope to show that his narrative implicitly responds to the paranoid logic of the Third Reich. In *Der Mann Moses* Freud undermines the notion of a stable national identity once and for all by placing the drama of abjection at the birth of nationhood. In many ways, *Der Mann Moses* also provides a summary of Freud's life-long engagement with cultural constructs. For this reason, this study departs from the chronology and begins with an analysis of Freud's book on Moses.

Commensurate with this theme is that of the individual's quest for identity. In many of the narratives under discussion here passports play a significant role. The passport is an official document allocating the individual an identity within the framework of the nation state. In chapter two we will see how the protagonist of Franz Kafka's *Der Verschollene* [Missing Person, 1912] relies on his passport to attest to a sense of identity that he does not have in his own right. Here the official document has usurped the place of individual identity.

Der Verschollene is not a narrative with an explixitly Jewish theme. The chapter focuses on the novel because, as a narrative of exile, it highlights some of the phobic mechanisms of exclusion which are pertinent to the drama of abjection. Kafka's Jewishness has been discussed in many other studies and will therefore not be one of the main themes of this chapter.[34] Instead I will examine the way in which Kafka encodes the interplay between abjection and the social order in *Der Verschollene* and some of Kafka's short prose.

Chapter three focuses on abjection and the denial of kinship in Joseph Roth's writings. Analysing the ambivalence that characterised Roth's attitude to his Eastern Jewish origin, I then discuss Roth's *Juden auf Wanderschaft* [Jews on their Wanderings, 1927] and *Hiob* [Job, 1930] as two prominent examples of an imaginary resolution of the crisis of abjection. In Roth's novel *Hiob* the question whether one holds a "proper" passport is also raised. The Eastern European Jew Mendel Singer finds the world of officialdom so frightening that he eventually resolves to bribe an intermediary to get hold of passports which allow him and his family to emigrate to the United States.

---

[34] For a brief survey of the question of Kafka's Jewishness cf. Hartmut Binder, *Kafka-Handbuch*, vol. 1, *Der Mensch und seine Zeit*. Stuttgart: Kröner: 491-509.

Chapter four examines Albert Drach's analysis of the abjection of "the Jew" in his novel *Das große Protokoll gegen Zwetschkenbaum* [The Massive File against Zwetschkenbaum, 1964] and in his autobiographical novels. While in *Das große Protokoll* Drach analyses the discourse of power and, in particular, the mechanisms of exclusion that the modern state applied to the Eastern Jew before the Shoah, in his autobiographies >>Z.Z.<< *das ist die Zwischenzeit* [>>I.P.<< that is the Interim Period, 1968] and *Unsentimentale Reise* [Unsentimental Journey, 1966] he explores the individual's experience of abjection in the context of the Shoah. *Unsentimentale Reise* focuses on what happens if one does not hold a "proper" official identity but instead a German passport with the "J"-stamp that stigmatises the Jew as outcast and other. In Drach's autobiographical novel, the central character is forced to forge his papers and disavow his Jewish family background in order to survive. While this forgery saves him from death in Auschwitz, it ultimately undermines his sense of belonging and identity. Here the National Socialist abjection of the Jew results in the protagonist's self-abjection.

A forgery of an outrageous kind plays an important role in Hilsenrath's novel *Der Nazi & der Friseur* [The Nazi & the Barber, 1977] in which the main protagonist is an SS-man who adopts the identity of one of his Jewish victims. The implications of this role reversal for my theme are discussed in chapter five. Chapters three, four and five also discuss the transfer of abjection onto the female signifier which is a characteristic shared by many of the texts under discussion here.

The book is written in such a way that each of the chapters can be read as a single case study. However, the chapter outline above already suggests that the theme of abjection creates an important link between the chapters. I will explore how, from Freud to Hilsenrath, German-Jewish literature emerges from an ambivalent space of enunciation which challenges the great narrative of an historical identity authenticated by an "originary" past. In Homi Bhabha's terms modern German-Jewish writers inhabit a "Third Space" which poses an alternative to an understanding of culture as a homogeneous tradition based on (national) unity.[35]

By endeavouring to explore this "third space" in examples of modern German-Jewish literature, the following study also aims to contribute to recent efforts to rewriting literary history. Moving away from an unproblematic descriptiveness that largely ignores the ambivalence of the Jewish experience in favour of the supposed "universality" of the modern subject, this study examines instead the social articulation of difference.[36]

---

[35] Ibid., 37.
[36] A similar point has been made recently by Bryan Cheyette and Laura Marcus who argue for a recognition "that the Jewish other is both at the heart of western metropolitan culture and

It is beyond doubt that recent years have witnessed a dramatic revival of German-Jewish studies within "Germanistik". Despite this new interest, it seems to me that this revival has been largely characterised by a socio-historical methodology which has remained unaffected by the theoretical discourses and reflections on modernity and subjectivity. In retracing the inherent ambivalence in how German-Jewish literature situates itself in cultural discourse, this study focuses on how this literature subverts received notions of identity and racial boundaries.

---

is also that which is excluded in order for ascendant racial and sexual identities to be formed and maintained." Cf. Bryan Cheyette and Laura Marcus, 'Introduction; Some Methodological Anxieties'. In: Bryan Cheyette and Laura Marcus (Eds.), *Modernity, Culture and the 'Jew'*. Cambridge: Polity Press, 1998: 3.

Freud's Jewishness: Opposing the "Compact Majority"

Marked Territories: "Aryan" and "Jew" in Fin-de-Siècle Discourse

"The intimate relationship between psychoanalysis and the 'Jewish spirit' is so obvious that few of those who refer to it stop to define the 'Jewish spirit' or to ask how it has been transmitted from generation to generation."[1] When Marthe Robert made this opening statement in her book *D'Oedipe à Moise*, published in 1974, she aptly summarised the notable lack of in-depth analyses of Freud's connection with Judaism and the "Jewish spirit". Since then this gap has been widely addressed. This is reflected in Sander L. Gilman's extensive bibliography on Freud's Jewish identity which documents research carried out in this area until 1992.[2] Arguably, this dramatic upsurge of interest in Freud's Jewishness is only surpassed by feminist critiques of Freud's phallocentricity, that is his theoretical privileging and idealisation of patriarchy and the complementary construction of femininity as deficient.[3] It seems to me that this co-emergence of new studies of Freud's Jewishness and of the feminist critique of basic psychoanalytic concepts is not entirely coincidental; it reflects and imaginatively responds to the crisis of western Eurocentricity that has been the focal point of the postmodernist debate of the past two decades. In addition, this co-emerging interest in both Jewish studies (particularly in contemporary Germany) and the feminist critique of phallocentricity echo the very themes that surfaced in the

---

[1] Marthe Robert, *From Oedipus to Moses. Freud's Jewish Identity*. Translated by Ralph Manheim. London and Henley: Routledge, 1977: 3.
[2] Cf. Sander L. Gilman, *Freud, Race, and Gender*. Princeton, New Jersey: Princeton University Press, 1993: 201ff. In the following argument I am particularly indebted to Marthe Robert, Sander L. Gilman and, above all, Jacques Le Rider who traces and analyses Freud's Jewish identity in great detail: Cf. Jacques Le Rider, *Modernity and Crisis of Identity. Culture and Society in Fin-de-Siècle Vienna*. Transl. by Rosemary Morris. Cambridge: Polity Press, 1993.
[3] A good overview over both American and French feminist critiques of Freud can be found in Naomi Segal's essay *Freud and the Question of Women*. In: Edward Timms and Naomi Segal (Eds.), *Freud in Exile. Psychoanalysis and its Vicissitudes*. New Haven and London: Yale University Press, 1988: 241-253. Also see Madelon Sprengnether, *The Spectral Mother, Freud, Feminism and Psychoanalysis*. Ithaca and London: Cornell University Press, 1990. This book offers an excellent analysis of the preoedipal mother as a figure of subversion haunting Freud's theorising.

literature of the turn of the century. In his study *Modernity and Crisis of Identity — Culture and Society in Fin-de-Siècle Vienna*, Jacques Le Rider examines the themes of the modernist identity crisis and the attempts to overcome it, the very challenges to the polarization of male and female, and the crisis of Jewish identity towards the close of the nineteenth century. He treats these not as distinct but closely linked aspects of the same problem and shows that in the debate of the fin-de-siècle the categories of the masculine (which is seen to be jeopardised), feminine and the Jew are omnipresent:[4]

> Alongside visions of a culture becoming dominated by the female, we find visions of a culture becoming dominated by the Jew; the anti-feminism of certain critics of modernism is expressed through a logic analogous to that of anti-semitism. This analogy in fact points to a deep-rooted dimension of culture in the 1900s: the emerging relationship between the masculine identity crisis — the redistribution of male and female roles — on the one hand, and the confrontation between Jews and non-Jews, on the other.[5]

Looked at from this angle, it is only logical that the current debate concerning Freud's Jewish identity engages with and revolves around the same cultural signifiers which dominated the modernist crisis: the binary opposition of Aryan/masculine as against Jew/feminine. It has to be stressed, however, that any critical engagement with this discourse has to be aware of its potential pitfalls. Engaging with the binary opposition of Aryan-Jew, the critic runs the risk of unwittingly reproducing those cultural stereotypes which s/he had initially set out to deconstruct. In a different, although not unrelated context, Homi K. Bhabha, analyses the stereotype as "a form of knowledge and identification that vacillates between what is always 'in place', already known, and something that must be anxiously repeated [...]".[6] That this definition reads like a comment on the stereotyping of both gender and race in the discourse of the nineteenth and early twentieth century is hardly surprising. But Bhabha's observation also says something about the language of the post-colonial or poststructuralist critic who must question the way in which he or she employs conceptual categories such as gender, class or race. In Bhabha's analysis the cultural critic is asked to move into a utopian location of difference which undermines the cultural straightjacket of binary oppositions.

> What is theoretically innovative, and politically crucial, is the need to think beyond narratives of origin and initial subjectivities and to focus on those moments or processes that are produced in the articulation of cultural differences. These 'in-between' spaces provide the terrain for elaborating strategies of selfhood — singular

---

[4] Le Rider, *Modernity and Crisis of Identity*, 1f.
[5] Ibid., 3.
[6] Homi K. Bhabha, *The Location of Culture*. London and New York: Routledge, 1994: 66.

or communal — that initiate new signs of identity, and innovative sites of collaboration, and contestation, in the act of defining the idea of society itself.[7]

But Bhabha also warns of the pitfall of using difference merely as a deconstructionist fantasy which implicitly reproduces a relation of domination by turning difference into the 'good object of knowledge'. He argues that deconstruction, with its emphasis of the other, ironically tends to depoliticise this other by showing it to be the passive effect of discourse.[8] This note of warning seems to me to be particularly important in the context of fin-de-siècle culture which is, after all, wrought with stereotypical fantasies of Jewish otherness. Traces of such unwitting stereotyping can be found in the current debate, concerning the nature of Freud's Jewishness. As a first example of the pervasiveness of stereotypes I want to analyse the recent debate of the connection between Freud's theory of femininity and his Jewishness. We will see that this debate unwittingly repeats the geographical and ideological division between East and West which, in Freud's own times, was used to stigmatise the Eastern Jew as inferior.

In his book *Freud, Race and Gender* Sander L. Gilman takes issue with the feminist critique of Freud's analysis of gender, arguing that it neglects the important connection between stereotypical representations of race and gender in both Freud's work and in his times. Where this analysis has taken place it has been in the shadow of the presupposition that Freud had a fundamentally negative image of "the female". He quotes Judith van Herik's study *Freud on Femininity and Faith*, which suggests that Freud identified with Judaism because the religion offered an ideal of masculinity and male power. Gilman disputes her claim, arguing that Freud rejected all religious values. For Gilman it is unlikely that Freud could not abandon identification with the " masculinity" of Judaism.[9] He finds equally unconvincing Esthelle Roith's book *The Riddle of Freud — Jewish Influences on his Theory of Female Sexuality,* which analyses Freud's construction of the feminine in terms of the psychodynamic of the Eastern European Jewish

---

[7] Ibid., 1f.
[8] Bhabha writes: "Montesquieu's Turkish despot, Barthes' Japan, Kristeva's China, Derrida's Nambikwara Indians, Lyotard's Cashinahua pagans are part of this strategy of containment where the other text is forever the exegetical horizon of difference, never the active agent of articulation [...]." Ibid., 31.
[9] Gilman, *Freud, Race, and Gender,* 7. I tend to agree with van Herik's analysis according to which in Freud's theory as a whole, gender-specific male renunciation of wishes is seen to be the source of high cultural and mental achievements. With reference to *Moses and Monotheism* van Herik states righly that "the psychical situation of Jewish believers is possible only within Freud's masculine developmental schema. The father figure is not emphasized in his procreative, nurturant functions. Instead he appears from the outside and chooses his people, placing restrictions on them [...]." Van Herik, *Freud on Femininity.* Berkeley, Los Angeles and London: University of California Press, 1982: 193.

family and its rabbinical values. According to Gilman this presupposes that "Freud was an Eastern European Jew rather than a highly acculturated Western Jewish physician-scientist with Eastern Jewish roots whose knowledge of the Eastern European rabbinical tradition was probably limited to what he read in the German-language journals of his day."[10] I am, however, less inclined to reject Freud's knowledge and first-hand experience, not of orthodoxy, but of "traditional everyday Judaism" which would have comprised those attitudes to women upon which Freud, the scientist, implicitly draws in constructing the feminine. Indeed, Freud's parents practised "a Judaism without religion" and "Jacob Freud had emancipated himself from the Hasidic practices of his ancestors: his marriage to Amalie Nathanson was consecrated in a reform ceremony. In time he discarded virtually all religious observances, mainly celebrating Purim and Passover as family festivals."[11] This secularisation did, however, not amount to a denial or even eradication of the family's Judaic roots in Freud's upbringing which is implied in Gilman's statement.[12] Undoubtedly, Freud's own Jewishness was fiercely secularised as has been convincingly shown by Marthe Robert, Peter Gay and Jacques Le Rider.[13] Despite Freud's widely discussed secularism it seems hard to dismiss Roith's argument that Freud's view of the "authentic" woman, who seeks compensation for the wound of castration through children, was influenced by Judaism's exclusion of women from any ritual or communal role outside the home.[14] Freud's belief that a woman's relationship with her son is the only relationship which gives her "unlimited satisfaction" and that is entirely "free from ambivalence"[15]

---

[10] Gilman, *Freud, Race, and Gender*, 7.
[11] Peter Gay, *Freud. A Life for Our Time*. London: Papermac, Macmillan, 1993: 6.
[12] Yosef H. Yerushalmi comments on Freud's Jewish education which, in his view, was far from trivial. Cf. Yosef H. Yerushalmi, *Freud's Moses: Judaism Terminable and Interminable*. New Haven and London: Yale University Press, 1991: 64. With reference to the Ludwig Philippsohn Bible that Freud studied, Yerushalmi comments that in spite of the illustrations, a violation of the prohibition of images, the attitude of the bible's commentary towards biblical and Jewish tradition "is nothing if not reverent, indeed conservative." (Ibid.) He also argues that Jakob Freud taught Sigmund to read it in Hebrew (ibid.). Yerushalmi quotes Judith Bernays Heller according to whom Jakob Freud could recite the entire text of the Passover Haggadah by heart (ibid., 67). The Jewishness of Freud's upbringing is also emphasised in Emanuel Rices study *Freud and Moses. The Long Journey Home*. New York: State University of New York Press, 1990.
[13] David Bakan attempts to trace psychoanalysis back to the Jewish Mystical tradition, claiming that psychoanalysis is Kabbalistic in orientation. Cf. David Bakan, *Sigmund Freud and the Jewish Mystical Tradition*. New York Schocken, 1969: 71. This approach is problematic in the light of both Freud's fierce rationalism and atheism. For a critique of Bakan's approach see Marthe Robert, *From Oedipus to Moses*, 171 and Le Rider, *Modernity*, 213.
[14] Esthelle Roith, *The Riddle of Freud — Jewish Influences on His Theory of Sexuality*. New Library of Psychoanalysis 4. London and New York: Tavistock Publications, 1987: 106f.
[15] Sigmund Freud, 'Femininity'. In: *The Standard Edition of the Complete Psychological Works of Sigmund Freud*, transl. and ed. by James Stratchey. London: Hogarth Press, 1964, XXII: 133.

reflects the traditional Jewish woman's compensatory investment in her relationship with her son:

> With the 'embourgeoisement' of Jewish society in Vienna, which devolved on the successful achievement of the upwardly aspiring males of her family, and her own confinement by the norms and values of nineteenth-century secular society, the ambitious Jewish woman found herself with a truly enormous investment in her son's achievements.[16]

In support of her argument, Roith quotes Ernest Jones's description of Amalie Freud's confidence that her son was destined for greatness and her pride in this respect.[17]

We can now see to what extent the discussion of Freud's Jewish origins revolves even today around a geographical division between East and West. Despite their opposing views, both Gilman, who foregrounds Freud's scientific thinking within a Western tradition, and Roith, who diagnoses Freud's devaluation of women with reference to the specific constraints of the Eastern Jewish family dynamic, share an implicit belief in the significance of a geographical distinction which, at Freud's own time, elaborated and mapped out ideological and political interests. This close relationship between geography and ideology translated itself into the binary opposition between the unassimilated, unenlightened "Ostjude"[18] [Eastern Jew] on the one hand and the assimilated, enlightened "Westjude" on the

---

[16] Roith, *The Riddle of Freud*, 109.
[17] Ernest Jones, *Sigmund Freud. Life and Work*. London: Hogarth, 1965, I: 5f.
[18] One example of this bias towards the Eastern Jew is the propaganda specifically directed against the Eastern Jewish immigrants in Vienna who, at the end of the First World War, were blamed for all the consequences of the war, from the black market economy to revolutionary tendencies. Cf. Leopold Spira, *Feindbild 'Jud'. 100 Jahre politischer Antisemitismus in Österreich*. Vienna and Munich: Löcker, 1981: 75. Spira quotes police reports from this era according to which "(d)ie Erbitterung gegen die entweder Schleichhandel oder Wucher treibenden oder ganz untätigen Ostjuden wächst von Tag zu Tag, wie der Haß gegen die jüdischen Kommunisten." (Ibid.) [The anger against the Eastern Jews, who are either involved in the black market or practice usury, grows daily, just as the hatred of Jewish communists.] However, prejudice against Eastern European Jewry was not confined to the language of open anti-Semitism, it could also be traced in the Western Jewish socialist discourse from the turn of the century onwards. In his study *Socialism and the Jews*, Robert S. Wistrich shows that even in the International Socialist Movement, which addressed the Jewish question in Eastern Europe as a class problem, the view prevailed that Eastern European Jewry had to give up their backwardness and unite with the proletariat of all nationalities. Rosa Luxemburg's views are a case in point: "In her view there were no prospects for an independent Yiddish culture in Eastern Europe. The Jewish 'nationality' in Tsarist Poland was a product of social backwardness, the petty-bourgeois mode of production and the narrowness of the shtetl existence." Robert S. Wistrich, *Socialism and the Jews. The Dilemmas of Assimilation in Germany and Austria-Hungary*. Rutherford, Madison, Teaneck: Fairleigh Dickinson University Press; London and Toronto: Associated University Press, 1982: 144.

other.[19] Against this background, one might ask whether a discussion of Freud's Jewishness along such exclusionary lines does not unwittingly continue a discursive tradition which constructs selfhood on the basis of the abjection of otherness. For the discourse about Jewishness at Freud's own time banished Eastern European Jewry outside the boundaries of Western civilisation. It suggested that Eastern European Jewry's unenlightened darkness could not be assimilated into the tradition of Western Enlightenment. "The Western Jew saw himself or herself as a German or Austrian nationalist, culturally German, as well as commanding German, the language of high culture."[20] The adolescent Freud is no exception to this: in a letter, dated 18 September 1872, to his childhood friend Emil Fluss he echoes the language of anti-Semitism when describing his Eastern Jewish travelling companions on a train journey from Freiberg to Vienna:

> Now this Jew talked the same way as I have heard thousands of others talk before, even in Freiberg. His face seems familiar — he was typical. So was the boy with whom he discussed religion. He was cut from the cloth from which fate makes swindlers when the time is ripe; cunning, mendacious, kept by his adoring relatives in the belief that he is a great talent, but unprincipled and without character. A cook from Bohemia with the most perfect pug-face I have ever seen put the lid on it. I have enough of this lot. In the course of the conversation I learned that Madame Jewess and family hailed from Meseritsch: the proper compost-heap for this sort of weed.[21]

Later in this chapter Freud's understanding of what it means to be Jewish will be discussed. This prepares the ground for a detailed analysis of his last book *Der Mann Moses und die monotheistische Religion* [Moses and Monotheism, 1939] which is Freud's final response to fascism. In direct contrast to those critics who read Freud's book on Moses as an "overt expression of self-hatred", I want to show that Freud's *Der Mann Moses* challenges the Aryan-

---

[19] Edward Said's analysis of orientalist discourse springs to mind here. He defines orientalism as "a distribution of geopolitical awareness into aesthetic, scholarly, economic, sociological, historical and philological texts; it is an elaboration not only of a basic geographical distinction [...] but also of a whole series of 'interests' which, by such means as scholarly discovery, philological reconstruction, psychological analysis, landscape and sociological description, it not only creates but also maintains [...]." Said, *Orientalism. Western Conceptions of the Orient*. London: Penguin, 1991: 12.

[20] Sander Gilman, *Freud, Race, and Gender*, 13. See also Emanuel Rice, *Freud and Moses — The Long Journey Home*. New York: State University of New York Press, 1990. Rice traces this prevalent attitude among second and subsequent generations of Viennese Jews in Martin Freud who had great difficulty accepting the Galician origins of the paternal side of the family. Apparently, Martin Freud created a Sephardim origin of the Bernays side of the family to compensate for the "tainted" Galician background of the paternal family. Cf. Emanuel Rice, *Freud and Moses*, 11.

[21] Cf. 'Some Early Unpublished Letters of Freud'. In: *International Journal of Psychoanalysis* 50 (1969): 419-427.

Semite dichotomy which defines Nazism.²² Arguably, *Der Mann Moses* is Freud's most political book.

Freud's radical departure from any attempts to essentialise Jewishness, be it through negative or positive stereotyping, can be best assessed in the light of the anti-Semitic discourse of the fin-de-siècle. While in this discourse Jewishness was exorcised into the realm of an intolerable difference, it simultaneously provided a source of fascination for Western rationality. An example of this titillating fascination is Otto Weininger's *Geschlecht und Charakter* [Sex & Character] which maintained its status as a best-seller from 1903, when it was first published, well into the late twenties.²³ In this book, which was accepted by the University of Vienna as a doctoral thesis, Weininger, who was himself Jewish, places both women and Jewry outside the realm of Western male rationality and morality. He posits a substantialised stereotype of "the woman" and "the Jew" and propels these into an absolute beyond, outside the realm of culture. Basing his supposedly scientific investigation on an essentialised typology which is immune to any empirical data, Weininger defines "the female principle" as "nothing more than sexuality" while the "male principle is sexual and something more."²⁴ What follows from there is a diatribe and an exercise in paranoid negation: on the basis of his definition of the female principle as nothing but sexuality, he denies "woman" consciousness (100), a continuous memory (146), the *principuum rationis* (148), the ability to make ethical and logical distinctions (186), a soul (186), a supersensual personality and, finally, an ego: "The inference that she is wanting in supersensual personality is fully justified. The absolute female has no ego." (186) Weininger's treatise is characterised by a logic of paranoia which reaches its triumphant climax in the very denial of the existence of the phenomenon he set out to analyse in the first place. He declares hysterically: "Women have no existence and no essence; they are not, they are nothing. Mankind occurs as male or female, as something or nothing." (286) By equating woman with nothingness, Weininger produces a fantasy that seems to have been shared by a generation of men which felt increasingly uncertain about gender boundaries. In this context it does not come as a surprise that Weininger's paranoid misogyny goes hand in hand with anti-Semitism.

In a chapter on Judaism (301-330) he applies the same typological principle to his analysis of Jewishness, arguing that it is "a psychological

---

²² Emanuel Rice, *Freud and Moses*, 22.
²³ By 1923 the 25th edition had appeared and *Sex & Character* had been translated into eight languages. Cf. Rainer Stach, *Kafkas erotischer Mythos. Eine ästhetische Konstruktion des Weiblichen*. Frankfurt am Main: Fischer, 1987: 61.
²⁴ Otto Weininger, *Sex & Character*. Authorised Translation from the 6th German edition. London: William Heinemann, 1906: 90. Page numbers in brackets refer to this edition.

constitution which is a possibility for all mankind, but which has become actual in the most conspicuous fashion only amongst the Jews." (303) At first sight this seems to suggest that Weininger goes beyond the racism of his time. However, Weininger's departure from a racial definition of Jewishness is not in any sense progressive as is Freud's radical deconstruction of Zweig's essentialising of both Jewish- and Germanness; on the contrary, Weininger's typological starting point simply enables him to denounce Jewishness along the same lines as the female principle. It is therefore hardly surprising that he arrives at the following conclusion: "Judaism is saturated with femininity." (306) And: "In the Jew and the woman, good and evil are not distinct from one another. [...] Jews, then, do not live as free, self-governing individuals, choosing between virtue and vice in the Aryan fashion." (306) He then moves on to a discussion of assimilated Western Jewry and claims that the converted Jew "has the fullest right to be regarded by the Aryan in his individual capacity" (312). However, Weininger fails to address the question as to what enables the non-moral, soulless and egoless Jew to make a transition to the domain of Aryan male rationality.

Weininger's *Geschlecht und Charakter* is an example of a discourse which saw women and Jews as equally encroaching on Aryan male rationality in order to deterritorialise and thus undermine male identity.[25] The precursors of this discourse were the biological and medical sciences of the nineteenth century as, for instance, studied by Sander Gilman in *Freud, Race and Gender*. Gilman shows that the core of Jewishness for medical science in Freud's time was the practice of infant circumcision, which was seen to mark the Jewish male body as unequal to that of the Aryan.[26] Although all physiological and psychological categories of difference, such as colour of skin, shape and size of skull, systematically developed by the ethnological discourse of the eighteenth and nineteenth centuries, were employed to mark the difference of "the Jew", infant male circumcision became the major signifier of difference for the scientists of the nineteenth century.[27] For example, a body of literature discussed the transmission of syphilis to newly circumcised infants and suggested that no male Jew was free from becoming infected with the disease as part of his becoming a Jew.

> The linked dangers of sexuality, syphilis, and madness were constantly associated with the figure of the male Jew. The Jew, who had become identified with his circumcised state, came to personify this threat. Central to the definition of the Jew was the

---

[25] The history of Weininger's identification of Jews as essentially feminine has recently been traced by Ritchie Robertson in 'Historicizing Weininger: The Nineteenth-Century German Image of the Feminized Jew'. In: Bryan Cheyette and Laura Marcus (Eds.), *Modernity, Culture and 'the Jew'*. Cambridge: Polity Press, 1998: 23-39.
[26] Gilman, *Freud, Race, and Gender*, 49f.
[27] Ibid., 51.

image of the male Jew's circumcised penis as impaired, damaged, or incomplete, and therefore threatening to the wholeness and health of the male Aryan.[28]

The discussion about the nature of the Jew's body as inherently different rested on the Lamarckian idea of the inheritance of acquired traits. Gilman's analysis of the anti-Semitism of nineteenth-century medical science shows that this discourse, which aimed at positivistic scientificity, carried the same metaphors of madness and disease which had been part of the stereotype of Jewishness for centuries.

What was Freud's position in this? Gilman argues that although Freud accepts the difference of the Jewish circumcised genital, he does not see this difference but the response of the Aryan as pathological. While the anxiety about castration is universal, the anxiety about circumcision is specifically Aryan. Anti-Semitism thus became "the disease of the uncircumcised".[29] The downside of Freud's enlightened analysis of anti-Semitism is his projection of the stereotype of male Jewishness onto the category of the female. Undoubtedly, Freud's image of woman as a dark force which is biologically, intellectually and psychologically impaired displays conventional Victorian notions of the inferior role of women in society.[30] It also reflects those stereotypes about male Jewishness which Freud had otherwise so cleverly exposed as based on anxiety. Freud's construction of the inferiority of the clitoris echoes the anti-Semitic discourse according to which the circumcised penis is inferior to the uncircumcised male organ. While Freud, in a radical revision, turned the anti-Semitic category of "the Jew" of the discourse of his time into a positioning which enabled him to destabilise the concept of identity per se, he fell somewhat short of this radicalism when it came to women.[31]

---

[28] Ibid., 61.
[29] Ibid., 81.
[30] For an analysis of the Victorian notions that informed Freud, particularly a discussion of the stereotype of the hysterical woman within the socio-historical context of fin-de-siècle Vienna see Hannah S. Decker, *Freud, Dora, and Vienna 1900*. New York: The Free Press, Macmillan, 1991.
[31] In her essay 'Rethinking Freud on Women', Nancy J. Chodorow points to both Freud's limitations as regards his view of femininity (such as the almost complete absence of the maternal or his view of mature female desire as inhibited at best) as well as an "emphatically plural account of women". In: Nancy J. Chodorow, *Femininities, Masculinities, Sexualities. Freud and Beyond*. London: Free Association Books, 1994: 2. She emphasises Freud's defence of homosexuality in *Three Essays on the Theory of Sexuality* and *The Psychogenesis of a Case of Homosexuality in a Woman* where Freud argues that homosexuality is on a continuum with heterosexuality and where he differentiates between gender identity and object choice. She writes: "Rethinking Freud on women then leaves us with a normative theory of female psychology and sexuality, a rich account of masculinity as it defines itself in relation to women, and several potential openings toward more plural conceptions of gender and sexuality." Ibid., 32. Although Chodorow's statement aptly summarises the ambivalence

Freud's Position of Difference

Unlike Otto Weininger or Karl Kraus, Freud did not suffer from the Jewish self-hatred which seems to be implied in the adolescent letter quoted before. On the contrary, it is a well-known fact that Freud not only never disowned his Jewishness[32] but that he saw a strong, albeit dangerous connection between a specifically "Jewish turn of mind" and psychoanalysis. Writing to Karl Abraham on 3 May 1908 after some serious disagreement between C. G. Jung and Abraham, Freud admonishes the latter:

> Please be tolerant and do not forget that it is really easier for you than it is for Jung to follow my ideas, for in the first place you are completely independent, and then you are closer to my intellectual constitution because of racial kinship, while he as a Christian and a pastor's son finds his way to me only against great inner resistances. His association with us is the more valuable for that. I nearly said that it was only by his appearance on the scene that psychoanalysis escaped the danger of becoming a Jewish national affair.[33]

A few months later, Freud still insisted on a reconciliation between Abraham and Jung. Commenting on Jung's suppressed anti-Semitism, which, in Freud's own analysis, was latently directed against himself and thus only deflected upon Abraham, he maintains, however, that "we as Jews, if we wish to join in, must develop a bit of masochism [...]. Otherwise there is no hitting it off. Rest assured that, if my name were Oberhuber, in spite of everything my innovations would have met with far less resistance."[34] While for the sake of the cause, Freud felt "it incumbent on me not to concede too much to racial preference and therefore neglect the more alien Aryan",[35] the Aryan became even more alien over the years. Against the backdrop of a tidal rise of anti-Semitism in Germany and Austria, he repudiated the very assumption of a superior German culture and intellect which his offhand dismissal of Eastern Jewry in the adolescent letter quoted above may be read to have implied. In a much-cited statement Freud said in 1926, "My language is German. My culture, my attainments are German I considered myself German intellectually, until I noticed the growth of anti-

---

of Freud's position it seems to me that these potential openings remained undertheorised because they would have challenged the patricentric basis of his oedipal model.

[32] Since I do not wish to repeat at length what is much-covered ground I would like to refer the reader to Yerushalmi, 38-55; Jacques Le Rider, 205-250. Cf. Ivar Oxaal's good overview of the various positions towards Freud's Jewishness: 'The Jewish Origin of Psychoanalysis Reconsidered.' In: Edward Timms and Naomi Segal (Eds.), *Freud in Exile. Psychoanalysis and its Vicissitudes*. New Haven and London: Yale University Press, 1988: 37-53.

[33] Hilda Abraham and Ernst L. Freud (Eds.), *A Psychoanalytic Dialogue. The Letters of Sigmund Freud and Karl Abraham 1907-1926*. London: Hogarth Press, 1965: 34.

[34] Ibid., 46.

[35] Ibid., 54.

Semitic prejudice in Germany and German Austria. Since that time, I prefer to call myself a Jew."³⁶ Looking back on his student days in the 1870s, Freud writes in his autobiographical sketch, entitled 'Selbstdarstellung' [An Autobiographical Study, 1925], about his shock when he experienced anti-Semitism first-hand at the University of Vienna: "Die Universität, die ich 1873 bezog, brachte mir zunächst einige fühlbare Enttäuschungen. Vor allem traf mich die Zumutung, daß ich mich als minderwertig und nicht volkszugehörig fühlen sollte, weil ich Jude war. Das erstere lehnte ich mit aller Entschiedenheit ab."³⁷ [When, in 1873, I first joined the University, I experienced some appreciable disappointment. Above all, I found I was expected to feel inferior and an alien because I was a Jew. I refused absolutely to do the first of those things.³⁸] But he goes on to say that he turned this experience of abjection into a positional advantage:

> Aber eine für später wichtige Folge dieser ersten Eindrücke von der Universität war, daß ich so frühzeitig mit dem Lose vertraut wurde, in der Opposition zu stehen und von der 'kompakten Majorität' in Bann getan zu werden. Eine gewisse Unabhängigkeit des Urteils wurde so vorbereitet.³⁹

Freud speaks here of a position of difference which is echoed in Bhabha's search for an "in-between space"; it is a position which undermines all narratives of a stable origin and location of self and, instead, provides a terrain of productive instability. Freud returns to this subject in 1926 in a letter addressed to the members of the Jewish society B'nai B'rith which had celebrated Freud's seventieth birthday. Honouring the society as a circle of distinguished men who paid "wohlwollende Aufmerksamkeit" [benevolent attention] to Freud's ideas when nobody else in Europe wanted to listen to him and when he had no pupils in Vienna, he distances himself in the same letter once more explicitly from both a religious as well as national identification with Judaism arguing that, as a Jew, he would have been particularly attuned to the warning examples of the peoples among whom the Jews live.⁴⁰ Instead he appeals to "die klare Bewusstheit (sic) der inneren Identität" [the clear consciousness of inner identity] and "die Heimlichkeit

---

³⁶ Cited in Gay, *Freud*, 448.
³⁷ Sigmund Freud, 'Selbstdarstellung'. In: Sigmund Freud, *Gesammelte Werke*. Ed. by Anna Freud et al. London: Imago, 1941: XIV: 34.
³⁸ Sigmund Freud, 'An Autobiographical Study'. In: *The Standard Edition*, XX: 14f. All translations into English are cited in square brackets.
³⁹ Sigmund Freud, 'Selbstdarstellung', 35. [These first impressions at the University, however, had one consequence which was afterwards to prove important; for at an early age I was made familiar with the fate of being in the opposition and of being excommunicated by the "compact majority". The foundations were thus laid for a certain degree of independence of judgement.] Sigmund Freud, 'An Autobiographical Study'. In: *The Standard Edition*, XX: 14f.
⁴⁰ Sigmund Freud (1926), 'Ansprache an die Mitglieder des Vereins B'nai B'rith'. In: Sigmund Freud, *Gesammelte Werke*. Ed. by Anna Freud et al. London: Imago, 1941, XVII: 52.

der gleichen seelischen Konstruktion" [the secretiveness of the same mental construction].[41] Freud's choice of the word "Heimlichkeit" is very telling here. It suggests that, in spite of a clear consciousness of Jewish inner identity, this shared mental construction cannot be discursively analysed.[42] And it is precisely this non-discursive, incommensurable dimension of his Jewishness which frees him in his own analysis from those prejudices that inhibit other people's intellect. This prepares him "in die Opposition zu gehen und auf das Einvernehmen mit der 'kompakten Majorität' zu verzichten" [to go into opposition and to do without the agreement of the compact majority].[43] In marked contrast to the discourse of his time, Freud refuses to essentialise or analyse his Jewishness in terms of racial traits, psychological profile, religious or national allegiance; his Jewishness is incommensurable and non-definable because it does not refer to a racial essence but to a positioning which is marked by difference. We can see how Freud turned the painful experience of rejection in his own youth into a radical positioning at the boundaries of both Austrian society and Judaism.

Freud's scepticism towards any such allegiance is particularly prominent in his correspondence with Arnold Zweig. When Zweig appealed to Freud in a letter, dated 29 May 1932, to recognise that they both shared an identifiable Germanness, Freud replied that he would like to free Zweig of his delusion that one had to be German. And he adds: "Sollte man dies gottverlassene Volk sich nicht selbst überlassen?" [Shouldn't one leave this godforsaken people to themselves?].[44] In the same breath Freud makes it clear that he felt equally distanced from an identification with Palestine: "Palästina hat nichts gebildet als Religionen, heiligen Wahnwitz, vermessene Versuche, die äußere Scheinwelt durch die innere Wunschwelt zu bewältigen, und wir stammen von dort [...]." [Palestine has produced nothing but religions, holy lunacies, ill-conceived attempts to overcome the outer world of sham via the inner world of fantasy, and we come from there.][45] Clearly, Freud rejects the cultural allegiance that Zweig sought. Any strong identification would have to be based on precisely those fictitious boundaries between self and other which psychoanalysis questions. Here

---

[41] Strachey translates "Heimlichkeit" as "safe privacy" which, in my view, misses out on the secretiveness which is implied in "heimlich" as opposed to "heimisch". Cf. *Standard Edition*, XX: 273.

[42] See Marthe Robert who also points to the incommensurable quality of Jewishness for Freud: "The mysterious thing 'which makes the Jew' and is 'inaccessible to analysis' — including Freud's psychoanalysis — is manifested primarily in a certain quality of human relations: it is a common bond which cannot be expressed in words and requires no definition." Robert, *From Oedipus to Moses*, 35.

[43] Freud, 'Ansprache', 52.

[44] Sigmund Freud — Arnold Zweig, *Briefwechsel*. Ed. by Ernst L. Freud, Frankfurt am Main: Fischer, 1968: 56.

[45] Ibid., 51.

and elsewhere, Freud defines himself as an intellectual borderliner whose locus of articulation on the periphery of two cultures enables him to oppose any "compact majority" and to expose all constructions of a well-defined self as fictitious.

Psychoanalysis provided an answer to the question why the banished other always returns to haunt the self. Freud's radical thinking thus deconstructs the boundaries between self and other by placing otherness within the self as its repressed·subconscious. In the words of Jacques Le Rider: "After Freud there was not much point in pursuing the identity of the subject, except to confirm its illusionary nature. Or rather, it was better thereafter to substitute for the idea of identity the idea of *identification, Identifizierung* — or even better, of *identifications.*"[46]

Freud's *Der Mann Moses* and the Creation of the Jew

Freud returned to the question of Jewishness towards the end of his life in his last book *Der Mann Moses und die monotheistische Religion* which was published in Amsterdam in 1939 during Freud's exile in London and only a few months before his death.[47] The English translation of Freud's book appeared in London in the same year under the shortened title *Moses and Monotheism*.[48] With his last book Freud revisited a theme that had preoccupied him a good twenty years before in his short essay on Michelangelo's Moses statue 'Der Moses des Michelangelo'.[49] This essay had contested the common interpretation of Michelangelo's famous statue as depicting Moses dropping the tablets after seeing the Israelites worshipping the golden calf. Instead, Freud suggested that Michelangelo's Moses was actually clutching the tablets, thus exercising immense self-control when faced with apostasy. This scenario mirrors an incident in Freud's own life when he was faced with Jung's "heresy" and defection from psychoanalysis after the Congress in Munich in 1913. Thus the Moses of the earlier essay served as an identificatory model for Freud who feared that his cause was threatened by Jung's defection. Clearly, the same fear intensified more than twenty years later when the old and ill Freud returned to the Moses figure in

---

[46] Le Rider, *Modernity*, 42.
[47] Sigmund Freud, 'Der Mann Moses und die monotheistische Religion'. In: Sigmund Freud, *Gesammelte Werke*. Ed. by Anna Freud et al. London: Imago, 1946, XVI: 101-246.
[48] Sigmund Freud, *Moses and Monotheism*. In: *The Standard Edition*, ed. by James Strachey. London: Hogarth, 1964, XXIII: 7-137.
[49] Sigmund Freud, 'Der Moses des Michelangelo'. In: Sigmund Freud, *Gesammelte Werke*. London: Imago, 1946: X: 172-201.

the wake of the threat the Nazis posed to European Jewry (and to psychoanalysis).

Faced with the Nazi persecutions, Freud returned to the subject in 1934. In a letter to the writer Arnold Zweig, dated 30 September 1934, Freud mentions that he was working on a new study called 'Moses, ein Ägypter?'[50] [Moses, an Egyptian?] and he explains that, in the wake of the latest persecutions, he wanted to provide an answer to the question "wie der Jude geworden ist und warum er sich diesen unsterblichen Haß zugezogen hat" [how the Jew came into being and why he has attracted this immortal hatred].[51] The same letter states: "Moses hat den Juden geschaffen, und meine Arbeit bekam den Titel: Der Mann Moses, ein historischer Roman." [Moses created the Jew, and my study received the title: Moses, the man, a historical novel.[52]] Outlining the structure of his historical novel, Freud concludes that he could not publish the piece since the Catholic Church was too hostile to psychoanalysis and would pose a real threat to the new discipline if his *Moses* was published. Freud was to elaborate on this fear three years later in the first preface, dated "before March 1938", of the third part of the published book, 'Moses, sein Volk und die monotheistische Religion' [Moses, his People and Monotheism]. Here he reflects on the historical irony that, in the wake of Nazi barbarism, such a reactionary institution as the Catholic Church had become the unwitting guardian of cultural progress. Although the Church was still strongly opposed to psychoanalysis and — in particular — to the psychoanalytic interpretation of religion as cultural neurosis, it had, as the guardian of cultural progress, become, to an extent, the guardian of psychoanalysis. However, Freud suggests that the strained nature of the relationship between the Church and psychoanalysis would not allow him to publish *Der Mann Moses*.[53]

This was followed by a second preface, dated June 1938, which was written after the "Anschluß" [annexation of Austria] and Freud's emigration to England. Expressing his gratitude for the friendly reception he and his family experienced in England, Freud finally announced the publication of his last piece of work. Although the two prefaces are clearly contradictory in content as well as hesitant and apologetic in style, Freud left them

---

[50] 'Moses, ein Ägypter?' was first published in *Imago*, No. 1, 1937.
[51] Sigmund Freud — Arnold Zweig, *Briefwechsel*, 102.
[52] Ibid.
[53] Yosef Yerushalmi has recently traced a reference of Freud's to Pater Schmidt, who was fiercely opposed to psychoanalysis. In a lecture entitled 'Der Ödipus-Komplex der Freudschen Psychoanalyse und die Ehegestaltung des Bolschewismus' (1928) Schmidt propagated the view that both psychoanalysis and Bolshevism had the destruction of the family in mind. Yerushalmi shows that Pater Schmidt was one of the church's most renowned ethnologists and an influential figure in the Vatican. Thus for example he suggested to the Vatican to put an end to psychoanalyis in Italy. In other words Freud's worries about the publication of *Moses* were more than justified. Cf. Yerushalmi, *Freud's Moses*, 28.

unchanged in the published version in order to document the enormous historical pressure he had been under since the Nazis' rise to power in 1933 and the real threat fascism posed to the continued existence of psychoanalysis. After all, his worst fears were more than justified: the liquidation of psychoanalysis had been rapid in Germany, and it was immediately carried out after the annexation of Austria.

Freud's hesitation over the publication of *Moses* was in no small measure due to the controversial nature of the subject matter of his final work. In the above-mentioned letter to Arnold Zweig he not only refers to external considerations preventing him from publishing, but also to his fear that this work is not scientifically substantiated.[54] By the same token in a letter, dated 16 December 1934, Freud admonishes Zweig: "Mit dem Moses lassen Sie mich in Ruhe. Daß dieser wahrscheinlich letzte Versuch, etwas zu schaffen, gescheitert ist, deprimiert mich genug."[55] [Leave me alone with the Moses project. I find it depressing enough that what is probably my last effort to create something new has failed.] And yet he admits in the same breath "Der Mann und was ich aus ihm machen wollte, verfolgt mich unablässig."[56] [The man and what I wanted to make of him is haunting me all the time]. Again he concludes that publication was not possible due to the fundamental difficulty of his project: "daß ich genötigt war, ein erschreckend großartiges Bild auf einen tönernen Fuß zu stellen, so daß jeder Narr es umstürzen kann" [that I was constrained to put such a frighteningly splendid statue on a clay pedestal in such a fashion that any fool could topple it].[57] However, a few months later, on the 2 May 1935, he writes: "Der 'Moses' gibt meine Phantasie nicht frei."[58] ['Moses' will not leave my imagination alone.] And, finally, on 20 December 1937, Freud states that before the end of the year he would be able to send Zweig a copy[59] and announces: "Er wird großes Aufsehen machen in einer nach Sensation lüsternen Welt."[60] [He (Moses, A.F.) will cause quite a stir in a world hankering after sensations.] Exiled in London, he brings up the subject once more, declaring "Ich schreibe hier mit Lust am dritten Teil des Moses." [I am enjoying writing here the third part of Moses.][61]

---

[54] Sigmund Freud — Arnold Zweig, *Briefwechsel*, 103.
[55] Ibid., 108.
[56] Ibid., 108.
[57] Ibid., 108.
[58] Ibid., 117.
[59] This refers to the second part of the book, entitled 'Wenn Moses ein Ägypter war ...' [If Moses was an Egyptian], which was first published in *Imago*, No. 4, 1937.
[60] Sigmund Freud —Arnold Zweig, *Briefwechsel*, 163.
[61] Ibid., 172.

Freud's *Moses*: A Narrative of Anxiety?

Freud's correspondence with Zweig reflects the battle Freud fought with himself over the wisdom of his final project. His fascination with Moses "the man, and what I wanted to make of him", clearly collided with his scientific integrity which warned him of the danger of erecting a statue on sand. Initially, Freud sought to resolve his dilemma by writing not a scientific treatise but a historical novel, a solution which he elaborated on in some detail in an introduction to the manuscript draft of 1934. He later dropped this along with the subtitle in the published version. In this suppressed preface[62] Freud explains that a character study would require reliable material but that nothing that was known about the man Moses could be called reliable. All the available sources were extremely tendentious and intricately linked up with the religious and national myths of a people, namely the Jewish nation. Any attempt to write a study of Moses would therefore be hopeless "wuerde [sic] nicht die Grossartigkeit der Gestalt ihrer Entlegenheit ein Gegengewicht bieten und zu erneuter Bemuehung [sic] auffordern"[63] [were it not for the fact that the greatness of the figure makes up for his remoteness and invites our renewed efforts]. In other words, in Freud's argument, scientific and scholarly reservations concerning the virtual impossibility of reconstructing the man Moses are eclipsed by the greatness of the figure. Quite clearly, Freud was hooked on Moses almost against his scientific instinct. He tries to deal with his own reservations by suggesting a method of speculative investigation based on probability:

> Man unternimmt es also, jede einzelne der im Material gegebenen Moeglichkeiten [sic] als Anhaltspunkte zu behandeln und die Luecken zwischen einem Stueck und dem naechsten, sozusagen, nach dem Gesetz des kleinsten Widerstandes auszufuellen, das heißt, jene Annahme zu bevorzugen, der man die groessere Wahrscheinlichkeit zuschreiben darf.[64]

And he concludes that this technique would result in a type of historical novel: "es hat keinen oder nur einen unbestimmbaren Wirklichkeitswert, denn eine noch so große Wahrscheinlichkeit faellt nicht mit der Wahrheit zusammen"[65] [it has no or only an undefinable truth value, for a probability, however probable, is not the same as the truth].

---

[62] Yosef Yerushalmi published a transcription of it in an appendix of his book *Freud's Moses — Judaism Terminable and Interminable*, 101-103.
[63] Yosef Yerushalmi, *Freud's Moses*, 102.
[64] Ibid., 102. [So one attempts to treat each possibility which is inherent in the material as a starting point for closing the gaps between one piece and the next by observing the "law of least resistance", which means that one prefers the assumption which has the highest probability.]
[65] Ibid., 102.

The published book *Der Mann Moses* included neither the subtitle "a historical novel" nor this explanatory introduction of the manuscript draft. Since publication the book's lack of scholarship has been widely commented on — many critics have set out to demolish Freud's speculative exploration of Moses, the man.[66] However, I am less interested in the precise nature of the scholarly shortcomings[67] of *Der Mann Moses* than in the anxiety that seeps through the text and draws attention to itself. For what Freud presents here is, according to the editor of the historical-critical edition of Freud's works, Ilse Grubrich-Simitis, "ein Dokument der Überforderung und des partiellen Scheiterns, und zwar im Kanon des Freudschen Werks einzigartig, sowohl formal als auch inhaltlich"[68] [a document showing how he over-reached himself and partially failed which is unique in the canon of Freud's works both as regards form and content]. In other words, although Freud dropped the subtitle 'a historical novel' he could not and — maybe — *would* not conceal the fragmentary, speculative and repetitive character of the book.

On the formal level there are a number of striking anomalies such as the different lengths of the three essays and the absence or presence of introductions: while for example the first essay 'Moses ein Ägypter?' is not prefaced by an introduction, the third part, 'Moses, sein Volk und die monotheistische Religion' [Moses, his People and Monotheism], includes the two aforementioned prefaces with the second effectively cancelling the first. In addition, the third part contains lengthy repetitions of previous arguments. It is as if Freud was driven both by an anxiety to fill out gaps and obvious inconsistencies as well as by a constant awareness that he was unable to produce a seamless argument that would stand up to scholarly investigation. In the context of my argument, these formal inconsistencies are interesting not so much because they unravel Freud's argument but because they unwittingly produce a symptomatic narrative which bears witness to the overwhelming need Freud must have felt during his last years to write his book on Moses against the grain of his scientific integrity. So why did Freud publish these highly speculative and contentious essays?

---

[66] Peter Gay argues that Freud would have done better if he had stuck with his original intention to publish the book as a work of fiction. Cf. Gay, *Freud*, 648. Similarly, Marthe Robert suggests: "If Freud had stuck to his original idea of a 'historical novel', he might have avoided a good deal of regrettable or acrimonious criticism." Robert, *From Oedipus to Moses*, 160. However, I am not so sure that a mere fictionalisation of his Moses study would have resolved the issue since Freud's basic assumptions about Moses and Judaism even presented as fiction would have been just as offensive to pious Jews, particularly in the 1930s.
[67] Emanuel Rice's book *Freud and Moses. The Long Journey Home*, 123-177, offers a thorough analysis of the scholarly shortcomings of Freud's study.
[68] Ilse Grubrich-Simitis, *Freuds Moses-Studie als Tagtraum. Ein biographischer Essay*. Sigmund-Freud Vorlesungen, ed. by Dieter Ohlmeier, vol. 3. Weinheim: Verlag Internationale Psychoanalyse, 1991: 17.

Some psychoanalytic critics have tried to answer this question with reference to Freud's own "family romance", particularly his complex relationship with his father Jakob. According to Marthe Robert, Freud's study did not really respond as much to historical events as to Freud's own remote past, namely his need to liberate himself from his Jewish father Jakob, whom he had already disavowed in his dreams of the *Traumdeutung* [Interpretation of Dreams, 1900]. There he appears as a tenderly loved but ultimately weak and mediocre figure, in short a father who the son had to overcome. Although the older Sigmund Freud was in an entirely different position from that of the writer of the *Traumdeutung* in that he could rank himself amongst the most illustrious men of his time, Robert argues that he still had to revolt against "the inexorable fatality of filiation, which so narrowly limits every man by burdening him with an origin, a race and a name. Frightened by his increasingly marked resemblance to Jakob Freud, he fought with all his strength against this 'return of the repressed' which, beginning in middle life, foreshadows the slow extinction of a man's individuality."[69] And she concludes that, with *Moses,* Freud severed all ties so that he was not Solomon, son of Jakob, "neither a Jew, nor a German, nor anything that still bore a name; for he wished to be the son not of any man or country, but like the murdered prophet only of his life work."[70]

Although I find Robert's interpretation of Freud's family romance, particularly of his ambivalent relationship towards his father generally convincing, I do not agree with her conclusion that in this last book he disavowed his Jewishness. We have seen that Freud's affiliation to his Jewish roots became stronger and more pronounced over the years. With *Der Mann Moses* Freud returned to the very essence of Judaic self-definition, and to the question that he expressed in his letter to Arnold Zweig: "Angesichts der neuen Verfolgungen fragt man sich wieder, wie der Jude geworden ist und warum er sich diesen unsterblichen Haß zugezogen hat."[71] [Faced with the latest persecutions one wonders yet again how the Jew came into being and why he has attracted this eternal hatred.]

Yosef Yerushalmi's argument runs along lines similar to those of Robert's but he arrives at almost the opposite conclusion. Emphasising the significance of Jakob Freud's gift of the famous Philippson Bible with an inscription in Hebrew[72] to his son on his thirtyfifth birthday, Yerushalmi argues that this gift was Jakob's call for Freud to return to those values that

---

[69] Marthe Robert, *From Oedipus to Moses,* 166.
[70] Ibid., 167.
[71] Ernst L. Freud, *Sigmund Freud —Arnold Zweig,* 102.
[72] The original inscription in Hebrew as well as a translation into English can be found in Yerushalmi, *Freud's Moses,* 104ff.

they had originally shared.⁷³ Looked at from this angle, *Der Mann Moses* represents a fulfilment of Jakob's mandate — Yerushalmi calls it an example of "deferred obedience" — which allowed Freud both to carry out his father's wish, i.e. turn his attention to Judaism, and to maintain his independence by focusing his critical attention on the religion of his father.⁷⁴

It seems to me, however, that the significance of Freud's *Der Mann Moses* is not fully recognised if one reads it exclusively with reference to Freud's own family romance. In contrast to this approach, I hope to demonstrate the *political* significance of Freud's book on Moses.

Reading *Moses*: A Story of Jewish Self-Hatred?

In order to show this, it is is useful to analyse the way in which Freud unfolds the plot of his narrative. In the first part of his study, Freud argues that Moses is not really the Jewish child of a Levite family as biblical tradition has it, but that he is of Egyptian origin since the name "Mose" is Egyptian, meaning "child". He then contends that the biblical story of Moses, according to which Moses was abandoned by his Jewish parents, found among the bulrushes and then adopted by the Egyptian princess, operates on the level of a family romance, albeit a distorted one which concealed Moses's Egyptian origin.

Freud's notion of the family romance⁷⁵ is based on the observation that, during the first few years of his or her life, a child is likely to perceive his or her parents as virtually omnipotent, imagining particularly the father as noble and great. This period of ennoblement is followed by the child's realisation that the real father is far less omnipotent and great than he or she thought, a disillusionment which eventually results in a more realistic assessment of the family. However, this typical scenario now faced Freud with the problem that the Moses myth contradicts the typical progress from imagining a high to accepting a low and more realistic family background because, according to the myth, Moses's first family is of humble Jewish

---

⁷³ Ibid., 74f.
⁷⁴ Ibid., 77f. Another important psychoanalytic critic, Ilse Grubrich-Simitis, highlights the importance of Freud's childhood acquaintance with the Bible. For her, *Der Mann Moses* is effectively a daydream and thus the product of the traumatising conditions of extreme distress. In Grubrich-Simitis's view, the Moses-figure and the fate of monotheism served Freud as a paradigmatic example of how demanding teachings can survive even in an hostile environment. Freud's identification with Moses helped him to fantasise about immortality when his own death and the deliberate mass murder of millions of his fellow Jews was imminent. We can see that even as a fantasy the text responds to the concrete historical threat which the Nazis posed to both the survival of European Jewry and psychoanalysis. Cf. Grubrich-Semitis, *Freud's Moses-Studie*, 26.
⁷⁵ See S. Freud, 'Der Familienroman der Neurotiker', *Gesammelte Werke*, VII: 227-231.

origin while the second one is noble, representing Egyptian royalty. This would imply a reversal of the family romance's logic. Freud solves this problem with reference to the common myth of the hero who is abandoned by his natural parents and then adopted by a second family. Freud now claims that in all such cases the first family, which abandons the child, is a fantasy while the second one in which the hero grows up is the real family. He concludes that Moses was probably an Egyptian nobleman who was turned into a Jew by a tendentious myth. This is where the first essay ends.

Freud begins the second essay entitled 'Wenn Moses ein Ägypter war ...' [If Moses was an Egyptian] with a series of warnings concerning the highly speculative nature of his argument, reminding his reader that it was based on psychological probability rather than on objective proof. He concludes that in spite of these grave misgivings he wanted to continue his exploration of this subject matter. Freud now addresses the key question of what would have motivated an Egyptian of high birth to lead an immigrant and culturally underdeveloped people out of Egypt. He answers this question by reconstructing the source of Jewish monotheism: for Freud it originated in the Egypt of the 18th dynasty when Amenopis IV (later called Akhenaten) introduced the monotheistic worship of the sun god Aten.[76] Fighting polytheism, this pharaoh forbade the making of any image of Aten in the same manner as Moses would later forbid the making of graven images. However, since the Aten religion was too relentless it was soon abandoned and the old polytheism was reintroduced. This leads Freud to the assumption that Moses was an Egyptian in the close circle of Akhenaten, who, after the defeat of the Aten religion, satisfied his own ambition by adopting the Jewish people: he imposed a strict monotheism, introduced the custom of male circumcision which, according to Herodotus, also originated in Egypt, and led his new people to Canaan. Again Freud concludes, somewhat tautologically, that Moses was an Egyptian giving monotheism and the custom of circumcision to the Jewish people.

But Freud's plot is not over yet: quoting the biblical scholar E. Sellin who had interpreted some verses of Hosea[77] as implying that Moses was actually killed by his people, Freud suggests that the Jews who were returning from Egypt after they had murdered this father-figure joined up with related tribes and accepted the worship of the midianite Yahweh, a crude and blood-

---

[76] Freud was not the first to point out the resemblance between the worship of Aten and Jewish monotheism. As early as 1912, Karl Abraham had written an article on the subject which was published in the first number of *Imago* in 1912. Esthelle Roith explains Freud's omission of Karl Abrahams's essay with reference to Freud's patriarchal bias: unlike Freud, Abraham interpreted Amenhotep's mother as the instigator of Egyptian reform. She concludes that Freud's need to believe that monotheism was inspired by a masculine hero was so great that he attempted to erase Abraham's thesis altogether. Roith, *The Riddle of Freud*, 173.

[77] For a critique of Freud's reading of Selin's findings see E. Rice, *Freud and Moses*, 149f.

thirsty God, of whom the Egyptian Moses had never heard. Although Moses's doctrine was submerged for generations after the murder, his memory survived amongst the Levites, the people of Moses, who, by keeping Moses's tradition alive, tried to forget and repress their feelings of guilt for his murder. For generations, the Mosaic tradition survived only in a repressed form, but it continued to exercise latent influence over the cult of Yahweh until he became the Mosaic God.

Much of Freud's speculative plot concerning the survival of Moses's teachings draws upon the theory of the latency period of neuroses. It is in his third and final part, 'Moses, sein Volk und die monotheistische Religion' [Moses, His People and Monotheism], that he makes this explicit by comparing ontogeny (the individual's development) to phylogeny (the species' development). Explaining the origin of individual neurosis in early childhood — the child's only way of dealing with a traumatising event is its denial, as a result of which this trauma enters a latency period where it is stored until it eventually resurfaces as the return of the repressed during puberty, expressing itself as obsessional neurosis (compulsion to re-experience the same event) or phobia — Freud then leaps from ontogeny to phylogeny, arguing that something similar happened in the history of mankind. The killing of Moses constituted such a traumatic event which the Israelites repressed for some time through their worship of Yahweh. After a lengthy latency period, Moses and his doctrines, which had survived as repressed memories among his people,[78] re-emerged and became even more powerful and obsessive. Freud then argues that this series of events with its three steps, the killing of Moses followed by a latency period followed by the return of the repressed in an obsessional form, was in actual fact part of an earlier trauma concerning all mankind: the killing of the primal father by his sons in the primal horde.

This argument refers back to *Totem und Tabu* [Totem and Taboo, 1912] where Freud used Darwin's model of the primal horde to analyse the functioning of primitive taboos and totemism: according to Freud, the primal horde was led by a primal father who oppressed his sons by, for example, not allowing them to have sex with his women. Eventually the oppressed sons rebel against the primal father's position of total power by killing him and devouring him in an act of cannibalism. After satisfying their hatred in this manner, tender impulses towards the slain primal father emerge which express themselves in feelings of remorse. This results in the denial of the deed through the introduction of the totem, a replacement of the primal father, which must not be killed and which is surrounded by a

---

[78] Freud's model is based on the Lamarckian assumption that historical events can be inherited by members of the same group. For a critique of the Lamarckian aspect of the model see Yerushalmi, *Freud's Moses*, 30.

number of taboos. Freud emphasises that the primal sons' attitude to the primal father is as ambivalent and as complex as that of the child and later the neurotic who is entangled in the oedipal triangle. Having summarised the basic hypotheses of *Totem und Tabu*, Freud then argues that the killing of Moses is an example of the obsessional return of the repressed, in this case the return of primal guilt of having killed the father. Instead of remembering the primal deed, the Israelites got caught up in the neurotic acting out of the same deed towards Moses.

So far Freud has explained "how the Jew came into being", he now turns to the second part of his question as formulated in his letter to Arnold Zweig, namely "why he has attracted this eternal hatred." And this is where he introduces Christianity into his argument: according to Freud, it was Paul who effectively picked up this repressed guilt by tracing it back to its primal source via the notion of original sin. The Christians did not remember the deed itself either; instead, they fantasised that the primal murder of the primal father had been atoned for in Christ's sacrificial execution, a fantasy which allowed wish fulfilment on the basis that an innocent individual, Christ, could take over and atone for collective guilt. While Christianity is thus a wishful fantasy, Judaism does not allow for such atonement: Freud argues that, as a result of both the repressed guilt as well as the sense of being the chosen people, Judaism became an orthodox religion, demanding utmost moral asceticism, harsh renunciations and rigorous sublimation. For Freud, these renunciations are the very precondition of the great cultural achievement of the Jewish people. And this in turn helps to explain anti-Semitism for Freud: the Christians, who, due to their fantasy of collective atonement, have not experienced the same renunciations, reproach the Jews for denying that they have murdered God (the disguised image of Moses). Freud concludes that this failure on the part of the Jews to admit this murder has burdened the Jews with tragic guilt, and that, throughout history, they have had to pay dearly for this:

> Das arme jüdische Volk, das mit gewohnter Hartnäckigkeit den Mord am Vater zu verleugnen fortfuhr, hat im Laufe der Zeiten schwer dafür gebüßt. Es wurde ihm immer wieder vorgehalten: Ihr habt unsern Gott getötet. Und dieser Vorwurf hat recht, wenn man ihn richtig übersetzt. Er lautet dann auf die Geschichte der Religionen bezogen: Ihr wollt nicht zugeben, daß ihr Gott (das Urbild Gottes, den Urvater, und seine späteren Reinkarnationen) gemordet habt. Ein Zusatz sollte aussagen: Wir haben freilich dasselbe getan, aber wir haben es zugestanden und wir sind seither entsühnt.[79]

---

[79] Sigmund Freud, *Der Mann Moses und die monotheistische Religion*. In: Sigmund Freud, *Gesammelte Werke*, London: Imago, 1950, XVI: 196. [The poor Jewish people, who, with their usual stubborn resistance, continued to deny the murder of the father, have, in the course of history, paid dearly for this. Time and again they were reproached: You have killed our God.

Clearly, this would have been volatile stuff at the best of times but even more so in the late Thirties. Freud was aware of this himself: writing to Zweig on 28 June 1938, he mentions a letter he received from a young American who urged him "den armen, unglückseligen Volksgenossen nicht den einzigen Trost zu rauben, der ihnen im Elend geblieben ist [...]"[80] [not to deprive his poor, unhappy fellow Jews of their last remaining comfort which they were left with in their misery]. But Freud concludes that he did not believe that it was in his power to upset an orthodox believer.

Freud's excuse comes across as a rather lame one: he was well aware of the offensive nature of the implication of his study, namely that by turning Moses into an aristocratic Egyptian who imposed monotheism on an underdeveloped Jewish population he effectively undermined the very foundations of Mosaic teaching. In Freud's view it is not God any more who chooses his people but Moses, the man, whose primary motivation is not so much the liberation of the Jewish people but the fulfilment of personal ambition. Furthermore, in Freud's narrative, Moses appears as an authoritarian figure demanding total submission. Bluma Goldstein points to this in her critique of Freud's last portrait of a great father-figure: "I find it disturbing that from the late 1920s until his death in 1939 Freud should adhere so assiduously to a model of group dynamics that juxtaposes the absolute authority of a powerful leader with a group subjected to his rule."[81] Goldstein's critique leads to another striking aspect of Freud's last book: *Der Mann Moses* is ultimately a book about male power, or according to Emanuel Rice, "a book of men"[82] and, as one might add, for men. It is a story in which cultural achievement is exclusively described as a top-down process with the patriarchal aristocrat passing down his teachings to an unenlightened and passive people. This model does not only marginalise women, it simply ignores them. In this sense, Freud's narrative is also a fantasy of a world without women.

But it is one additional implication which made Freud's Moses study particularly volatile in the context of the Thirties and the "latest persecutions" which, as Freud explicitly stated, had actually triggered his investigation. We have seen how, at the very end of his third essay, Freud claimed that the lack of atonement for the primal murder in Judaism was partly to blame for the anti-Semitic excesses that had occurred throughout

---

And this reproach is right if one translates it correctly. With reference to the history of religions it means: You do not want to admit that you have murdered God (the archetypal God, the archetypal father and his later re-incarnations). An addition should say: We have of course done the same thing but we have admitted it since and are therefore atoned.]
[80] Sigmund Freud — Arnold Zweig, *Briefwechsel*, 172.
[81] Bluma Goldstein, *Reinscribing Moses. Heine, Kafka, Freud and Schoenberg in a European Wilderness*. Cambridge, Mass. and London, England: Harvard University Press, 1992: 125.
[82] E. Rice, *Freud and Moses*, 130.

history. From a Jewish as well as Judaic perspective, the implication of this conclusion was a very grave and offensive one indeed: for Freud was actually suggesting here that the roots of anti-Semitism were not so much to be located in the neurotic psyche of the perpetrator, but rather that they had a real historical foundation. This was a position that had been taken by the anti-Semites all along. Furthermore, Freud's claim that the Jews had repressed their murder of Moses was dangerously close to the anti-Semitic claim that Jews engaged in ritual murders. Bluma Goldstein is just one example of those critics who take strong exception to Freud asking the victims of persecution "to explore their own unconscious for traces of a prehistoric repressed murder and to seek liberation in the recesses of their psyche, while anti-Semitic perpetrators, be they individuals or the state, are spared the full moral responsibility for their acts."[83]

Undoubtedly, there is something disturbing about the final part of Freud's Moses-study: his deliberations concerning the supposed underlying historical reality of anti-Semitism were extremely ill-timed and, within the context of the late Thirties, crude and insensitive. Although Freud, the scientist, tried to brush considerations concerning the question of Jewish solidarity aside, as the above-quoted letter to Arnold Zweig testifies, the fragmentary and repetitive structure of his last book points to the fact that this inner conflict had remained unresolved: Freud could not reconcile his image of the objective scientist with his responsibilities as a prominent Jew. And this explains the illocutionary force of Freud's many repetitions of previous arguments in part three: on the speech act level, these tedious repetitions indicate that Freud was engaged in an act of self-persuasion which barely concealed his own sense of guilt. Looked at from this angle, it does not come as a surprise when some critics read Freud's last book as "an overt expression of self-hatred".[84]

---

[83] Bluma Goldstein, *Reinscribing Moses*, 135.
[84] E. Rice, *Freud and Moses*, 22.

Reading *Moses*: A Story of Adoption and Abjection

Although I share these reservations about Freud's analysis of anti-Semitism, I still believe that Freud's *Der Mann Moses* can be read differently: in spite of its argumentative and scholarly shortcomings and its conflict-laden nature, the book can be read as a story which ultimately destroys all national mythologies and narratives of ethnic belonging and indeed undermines the essentialism of racism in an exemplary fashion. In order to show this, it may be useful to return briefly to the question of which of Freud's hypotheses was really novel and therefore particularly urgent from the viewpoint of the exiled Freud, who knew that his own death was imminent. Clearly, it could not have been the theme of primal parricide because Freud had developed this theory a good twenty years previously in his *Totem und Tabu*. His analysis of religion as a compulsive neurosis equally does not fit the bill,[85] nor does his view of cultural achievement as a process based on renunciation of wishes and drive sublimation. Freud had tackled this topic in 1930 in *Das Unbehagen in der Kultur* [Civilisation and its Discontents]. Although Freud's reformulation of these earlier positions certainly added a contentious edge to his theory of cultural progress, ultimately they contained nothing new.

What was really challenging in *Der Mann Moses* was the very foundation of his argument, namely the contentious claim that Moses was an Egyptian of aristocratic origin, a claim which, as Freud knew, undermined the common image of Moses as the Jewish liberator of God's oppressed but chosen people.[86] I disagree with Ritchie Robertson's view according to which the question "Why did Freud want Moses not to have been a Jew?" is wrongly phrased: "Instead, the question should be why Freud did not consider the obvious and plausible solution, that Moses was a Hebrew largely assimilated to Egyptian society, who recovered his loyalty to his people when he saw them being persecuted."[87] The fact that Freud never considered this possibility, I would argue in response to Robertson's question, simply demonstrates that he did not want Moses to be Jewish. In other words, Freud wanted Moses to be an outsider, someone with no Jewish tribal affiliation.

---

[85] Freud had put forward this theory in *Die Zukunft einer Illusion* [The Future of an Illusion] in 1927.

[86] Jan Assmann's book *Moses der Ägypter. Entzifferung einer Gedächtniskultur* (1998) traces a long tradition which supported the hypothesis that Moses was an Egyptian. Writers in this tradition include John Spencer, William Warburton, Karl Leonhard Reinhold and Freud.

[87] Ritchie Robertson, 'Freud's Testament: *Moses and Monotheism*.' In: Edward Timms and Naomi Segal (Eds.), *Freud in Exile*, 84.

This explains for instance Freud's somewhat contradictory argument concerning the analysis of the family romance and of the heroic myth. As we remember Freud stated that the two families in the family romance represented two stages in a child's life: a period in which the child fantasises that his father is omnipotent and noble is then followed by a more realistic and humble assessment of his real position in life. However, the very logic of the family romance leaves Freud with the problem that it clearly points to a humble family background of Moses, thus agreeing with biblical tradition. In order to resolve this dilemma, Freud refers to Otto Rank's 'Der Mythus von der Geburt des Helden' [The Myth of the Birth of the Hero] which allows him to move from the logic of the family romance to the sequencing of events in heroic myths. Freud now contends that of the two elements constituting the heroic myth, i. e. the hero's abandonment by his first family due to paternal rivalry and his ensuing adoption by a second family, the first element is a common fantasy which helps to magnify the hero's achievement since it shows that he has fate on his side. Only on the basis of this sequencing of events does it become possible for Freud to conclude that the first family of the biblical Moses story, i. e. the Jewish Levites are the product of such a shared and tendentious fantasy and that the second, aristocratic Egyptian one was Moses's real family. Clearly, this spiral of Freud's hypotheses does not really substantiate his claim any better; on the contrary, by moving more and more into the realm of mere speculation, it unwittingly accentuates the urgency this topic had acquired for Freud towards the end of his life. Freud wanted Moses to be a leader without tribal affiliation — the question remains: why?

At this juncture it may be useful to remember that Freud's last book, written in exile, is a book about the *end* of the Egyptian exile of the Jewish people who were returning to Canaan under Moses's leadership. However, Freud's version of the Moses story radically departs from biblical tradition not only in terms of biblical exegesis but also on the level of plot. Although he superficially bases his plot on the sequence exile - homecoming, he ultimately subverts the biblical assurance that goes with this sequence by inscribing two opposing elements in this plot, namely Moses's adoption of the Jewish people and his ensuing murder. These additional moments result in the following pattern: while the Jewish exile coincides with Moses's adoption of the Jewish people, the homecoming is concurrent with Moses's assassination. This is an important point since this pattern undermines any sense of stability in Freud's narrative and effectively rewrites the common myth of a homecoming and of a shared identity founded on faith and race. According to Freud's new myth, the Jewish nation is not chosen by God any longer, a straightforward act of adoption, but ultimately it established itself only through the second move of the sequence adoption - murder. In other words: Freud's *Moses* suggests that it is above all the violent breaking away from this overly demanding paternal figure which defines the Jewish fate.

But parricide, as a self-defining moment, is intricately bound up with the problematic of abjection as studied by Julia Kristeva in her book *Powers of Horror*.[88] Julia Kristeva analyses abjection in terms of a pre-oedipal drama that takes place between the child who is not yet an "I" and its mother who sustains the child through her care and nourishment. In order to establish itself the child has, at some point, to reject this nourishment so that the boundaries between the self and the other can be built up. If abjection occurs in the pre-oedipal phase one must ask whether it is legitimate to apply this concept to Freud's *Moses* in which the maternal does not even play a marginal role. Unlike Kristeva, who locates abjection in the pre-oedipal phase and describes it as the child's first attempt to break away from the maternal hold, Freud presents his drama of abjection as an entirely male affair, in fact as an "oedipal conflict" in which the maternal object of oedipal rivalry is completely eradicated. Freud's last cultural narrative thus silences the feminine effectively.

Indeed, all the key players in his Moses-story are male. But this only points once more to Freud's undertheorising of both the pre-oedipal sphere as well as the feminine, a deficit which should not prevent us from applying a concept to his book which, in any case, is inherent in his narrative, irrespective of its maternal or paternal reference. Both Freud in his *Der Mann Moses* and Kristeva in her *Powers of Horror* tell a story of origin in which the defining moment is a violent breaking away from a bond that constitutes self: it is an act in which the 'not-yet-I' clumsily tries to establish boundaries between the self and the other.

While in Kristeva's analysis the key moment occurs in the pre-oedipal phase of the individual's development, in Freud's version an analogous moment defines the beginning of Jewish identity. If one were to translate the logic of abjection into an overt speech act, it would read along the following lines: "In order to be myself I reject the nourishment you offer to me, although it sustains me." With regard to Freud's Moses plot this would mean that, upon their return from Egypt, the Jewish people killed Moses, who had given both monotheism and male circumcision to his adopted people, in order to establish themselves against the father's overwhelming demands. This twisted logic has far-reaching consequences: abjection as the rejection of that which is offered to define the self (be it individual or collective) constructs and undermines the individual's or collective's stable sense of identity at one and the same time. While the breaking away from

---

[88] Julia Kristeva, *Powers of Horror. An Essay on Abjection.* Translated by L. S. Roudiez. New York: Columbia University Press, 1982.

the authoritarian father-figure serves to construct identity, it undermines it at the same time because as an abject act of violence it has to be repressed.

It could be argued that Freud's drama of abjection could have been perfectly staged with a Jewish paternal figure since the internal logic of abjection, that is self-establishment via the rejection of that which sustains me, requires a breaking away from the maternal (Kristeva) or the paternal (Freud). This is certainly true with regard to the internal dynamic of the drama of abjection. However, it seems to me that by placing an outsider without tribal affiliations at the very heart of his "narrative of origin", Freud effectively destabilises the assumption of a homogeneous national or racial identity from the very start. Thus when Freud posited an Egyptian Moses at the very origin of Jewish identity he did not only provoke adherents of orthodox Judaism but also aimed at the fascist discourse and its paranoid insistence on an absolute difference between self and a demonised and dehumanised other.

In his last book, Freud deconstructs the Aryan-Semite opposition of the Third Reich by strategically placing a non-Semite at the origin of Judaism. Freud's *Der Mann Moses* is thus an anti-myth to all national mythologies which fantasise stories of a stable and homogeneous origin, in that it highlights the permeability of the boundaries between self and other as well as their constructed nature. His *Moses* demonstrates that all such boundaries can only be precariously maintained on the basis of the collective repression of the memory of the silenced other, and it also establishes once more that it is in the very nature of repression to succeed at best temporarily.[89] And this of course implies that Freud's analysis of the process of civilisation as a neurotic acting out of repressed material also implicitly contains the promise that the silencing of all otherness, which is at the heart of fascism, was doomed to failure.

Freud presented his bold re-reading not only of the Mosaic myth but also of the entire process of civilisation in a style that called attention to itself. The structure of Freud's last narrative may well reveal Freud's latent anxiety that the publication of his *Moses* was after all untimely. The book could be interpreted as robbing his people of their sense of a shared identity at a time when they needed to uphold a positive sense of Jewishness against the barbarity of the Third Reich and the paranoid logic of the concentration camps where the other was not simply excluded any longer but systematically exterminated. On the other hand, Freud's Moses-study was very timely indeed: for with this testament Freud demonstrated once more that the category of otherness cannot be permanently banished into a

---

[89] Similarly, Jan Assmann concludes that it was Freud's specific achievement to have highlighted the role which guilt, memory and repression play in the history of religion. Cf. Assmann, *Moses der Ägypter*, 235.

deterritorialised no-man's land or completely silenced since it will always return and haunt the self, thus breaking down the boundaries between self and other.

The Longing to Belong: Dislocation and Abjection in Kafka's *Der Verschollene*

Setting the Scene: Two Arrivals in America

Consider this: a photograph, *Immigrants going down gangplank*.[1] It is a title which denotes the space between two symbolic territories. When people leave a country they are emigrants, when they enter another they are immigrants. Going down the gangplank they are neither; they are in-between these two stages. This photograph by Lewis Hine, taken in New York in 1905, depicts two women dressed in long dark skirts with white woollen shawls wrapped around their shoulders and matching head scarves. Crossing the gangplank, the first one carries a suitcase, the second one lifts up her skirt. On the right edge of the picture we see the dark silhouette of a man with a hat who carries a bag under his right arm: facing the onlooker he too seems to be ready to step on the gangplank to follow the women and go ashore. This young man is akin to Karl Roßmann, the central character in Kafka's unfinished novel *Der Verschollene* [Missing Person, 1912], which is better known under the title *America*. It is a novel which explores the artifice of the American myth through the continuum of Karl's abjection, a symbolic gangplank stage between self and other.

Hine's arrival scene and its caption suggest the beginning of a narrative which lies outside the actual photograph and is informed by a complex intertext consisting of historical facts, texts, fantasies, stereotypes and other images of European emigration. This narrative could be called "The American Dream", "Self-made Man", "The Land of Boundless Opportunities" or simply "America". Such stories and fantasies always reach beyond the actual photograph which in the words of cultural theorist Annette Kuhn "figures largely as a trace, a clue: necessary, but not sufficient to the activity of meaning-making — always signalling somewhere else."[2] A few details in Hine's photograph are particularly powerful iconographic

---
[1] The photograph is reproduced in Victor Burgin, 'Looking at Photographs'. In: Victor Burgin (Ed.), *Thinking Photography*. Houndsmills and London: Macmillan, 1994: 89.
[2] Annette Kuhn, 'Remembrance'. In: Jo Spence and Patricia Holland (Eds.), *Family Snaps — The Meaning of Domestic Photography*. London: Virago, 1991: 19.

clues when it comes to European emigration around the turn of the century: the women's Eastern European appearance suggests a traditional rural background in stark contrast to the urban context of modern New York awaiting them, the gangplank symbolises transition and all the hopes and anxieties of the unknown. It seems to me that it is above all the suitcase and the bag which are especially evocative. They point to the European belonging which the immigrants carry around with them in terms of tradition, culture and language, a baggage which stigmatises and marginalises those concerned as first-generation immigrants. On this level the bag is a burden, symbolising otherness. And yet, on a second level, the bag, bundle or suitcase is also an expression of the immigrant's only available sense of identity as it contains his or her last belonging(s): some clothes, a little money, a passport, and perhaps some family photographs, in short: a few items or rather relics which point to a European home, but a home that lies elsewhere in the far distance and in the past. Once the suitcase has been carried ashore, its contents, the few belongings the immigrants own, turn into the longing not only to have a home but to be at home. Thus the suitcase is a powerful symbol of the immigrants' dislocation: not yet arrived, they do not belong any more. Belong — to be and to long could be considered a universal characteristic.

Kafka's protagonist in *Der Verschollene*, Karl Roßmann, is such an immigrant who is driven by the longing to belong. But in contrast to the ordinary immigrant with his bundle of belongings Karl's burden turns out to be somewhat heavier since he suffers from an acute sense of abjection that shapes his longing. As a character who has never constructed his being he wanders through a space of anxiety where his longing is always misplaced and evidence of his abjection. This chapter argues that Kafka's *Der Verschollene* articulates this threat of abjection through Karl Roßmann's continued displacement in America. As a character who is beset by abjection he strays through an alien territory in which all object relations are constantly destabilised and undermined.

Returning to Hine's photograph, one could take the man in Hine's picture for Karl Roßmann who has just viewed the silhouette of New York with the Statue of Liberty in the distance and who is getting ready to leave the ship with all the other immigrants. But in contrast to the Hine photograph Karl's arrival in New York stops short of a Hine-like immigration scene. When Karl is about to disembark (like the man in the picture) Kafka sends his protagonist on a journey through the ship in search of his umbrella leaving his suitcase on deck with a fellow passenger — one may rightly wonder how on earth could an immigrant abandon his only belongings like this? This search turns into a labyrinthine journey where he completely loses his sense of orientation. At the end of the chapter Karl's confusion is only resolved when his uncle Jacob identifies Karl as his nephew and adopts him as his kin and kind. With this surprising turn of events Kafka alludes to the myth of America as the land of boundless opportunities, of man as the creator of his own destiny, of Liberty and Justice, in short a narrative that reflects those stereotypical European fantasies and desires which he calls up in chapter one in order to deconstruct them in the ensuing novel.

Labyrinths and Linguistic Whirlpools

In his recent study, 'Kafka in America: Notes on a Travelling Narrative', Mark M. Anderson refers to Kafka's *Der Verschollene* as an "anti-tourist guide" as the novel sets out to deconstruct and disfigure America's identifying icons.[3] Anderson argues that this deconstruction and erasure of America's icons is primarily achieved through the way in which Kafka employs the notion of "Verkehr" [traffic] throughout his narrative.[4]

Each chapter sets the protagonist, Karl Roßmann, in motion through a new form of traffic: he moves from the steamship of the opening chapter to the complexity of New York's automobile traffic, to walking along the highway, to the traffic of the lifts in the Hotel Occidental, the monetary and sexual traffic in Brunelda's apartment and, finally, to the train that takes Karl to the Oclahama [sic] Theatre. Kafka's novel is a narrative in motion in which the protagonist Karl is an exceptionally mobile character moving not only horizontally through an imaginary American space but also vertically up and down the social ladder. Nevertheless, the novel lacks what is traditionally associated with travel literature: the protagonist's accumulation of experience on the basis of movement through time and space. On the contrary: one could argue that Karl is immune to experience because he is caught up in a cycle of adoption and expulsion which he fails to interpret in a meaningful way. Karl registers reality as a series of accidents that occur in an American labyrinth which he is unable to read. He is a maze-walker who never quite realises that he is trapped in a labyrinthine movement without progression.[5]

---

[3] Mark Anderson, 'Kafka in America: Notes on a Travelling Narrative'. In: Mark Anderson, *Kafka's Clothes. Ornament and Aestheticism in the Habsburg Fin de Siècle*. Oxford: Clarendon, 1992: 105. The first and widely noted example of this disfiguring of icons is the Statue of Liberty which in Kafka's world carries a sword instead of a torch, thus from the outset poignantly undercutting the American myth.
[4] Ibid., 103.
[5] Penelope Reed Doob has identified the following features as closely linked with the idea of the labyrinth: enforced circuitousness, disorientation, planned chaos, inextricability and

This labyrinthine quality of his American experience is already introduced in the first chapter: upon his arrival in New York, when he is on the point of disembarking from the steamer, Karl leaves his suitcase with a fellow passenger in order to pick up an umbrella that he has left in the lower deck. His walking down the deck turns into a labyrinthine journey that ends with Karl's complete loss of orientation:

> Unten fand er zu seinem Bedauern den Gang, der seinen Weg sehr verkürzt hätte, zum erstenmal versperrt, was wahrscheinlich mit der Ausschiffung sämtlicher Passagiere zusammenhieng, und mußte sich seinen Weg durch eine Unzahl kleiner Räume, fortwährend abbiegende Korridore, kurze Treppen, die einander aber immer wieder folgten, ein leeres Zimmer mit einem verlassenen Schreibtisch mühselig suchen, bis er sich tatsächlich, da er diesen Weg nur ein oder zweimal und immer in größerer Gesellschaft gegangen war, ganz und gar verirrt hatte.[6]

The labyrinthine quality of the ship's interior, with branching off corridors and short staircases that follow each other, anticipates the physical and epistemological disorientation Karl experiences throughout the narrative. Here it leads him into the dead end of the Stoker's cabin where he seems somewhat surprisingly to lose all sense of alienation when taking up the Stoker's invitation to lie down on his bed: "Er hatte fast das Gefühl dafür verloren, daß er auf dem unsichern Boden eines Schiffes an der Küste eines unbekannten Erdteils war, so heimisch war ihm hier auf dem Bett des Heizers zumute." (12) [He had almost lost the feeling that he was on the uncertain boards of a ship, beside the coast of an unknown continent, so much at home did he feel here in the stoker's bunk. A: 16] This feeling of homeliness points to Karl's subconscious identification with the Stoker, a point which I will return to, as well as Karl's acute longing to belong, a desire which characterises Karl's structure of feeling throughout the

---

complexity. It simultaneously incorporates order and disorder, clarity and confusion, unity and multiplicity, artistry and chaos. Cf. Reed Doob, *The Idea of the Labyrinth from Classical Antiquity through the Middle Ages*. Ithaca and London: Cornell University Press, 1990: 1f. Central to the idea of the labyrinth is its ambivalent nature: from an outsider's perspective it is a magnificent design while from the insider's viewpoint it is experienced as a chamber of horrors. Furthermore, some labyrinths are teleological and a metaphor for learning while others are conceived as a prison with no progression. Ibid., 31. Kafka's protagonist is trapped in such a labyrinth "in malo" whose design and goal remain unknown to him.

[6] Franz Kafka, *Der Verschollene*. Ed. by Jost Schillemeit, Frankfurt am Main: Fischer, 1993: 7. Further page references refer to this edition. Translations are taken from Franz Kafka, *America*. Introduced by Edwin Muir, London, Auckland etc.: Minerva, 1992. Cited as A with page numbers. [Below decks he found to his disappointment that a gangway which made a handy short-cut had been barred for the first time in his experience, probably in connection with the disembarkation of so many passengers, and he had painfully to find his way down endlessly recurring stairs, through corridors with countless turnings, through an empty room with a deserted writing-table, until in the end, since he had taken this route no more than once or twice and always among a crowd of other people, he lost himself completely. A:12]

narrative. Both moments lead him to adopt hastily the role of the Stoker's spokesperson without critically examining the latter's story in spite of the many linguistic signs that the Stoker is engaged in what one might call "phobic discourse". Phobic discourse is a "rhetoric of fear" which is produced less by means of metaphorical signs than in the very material of drives.[7] As the chapter unfolds it becomes clear that the Stoker is actually Karl's own phobic alter ego because he — like Karl — suffers from an acute sense of abjection.

An early example of this invasion of the abject is the Stoker's tirade against his superior, Schubal. Karl prepares the ground by presenting an apparently bad case of miscarriage of justice. The captain agrees to hear the Stoker out. Karl's intervention seems to help the Stoker to voice his grievance in a rational manner: "Der Heizer begann seine Erklärungen und überwand sich gleich am Anfang, indem er den Schubal mit Herr titulierte. Wie freute sich Karl am verlassenen Schreibtisch des Oberkassierers, wo er eine Briefwage immer wieder niederdrückte." (21) [The Stoker began to state his case and controlled himself so far at the very beginning as to call Schubal 'Mr. Schubal'. Standing beside the Head Purser's vacant desk, Karl felt so pleased that in his delight he kept pressing the letter-scales down with his finger. A: 23] Karl's joy and his symbolical adoption of the role of judge turn out to be premature as the Stoker's speech soon deteriorates into an obsessional tirade devoid of argumentative rationality:

> Herr Schubal ist ungerecht. Herr Schubal bevorzugt die Ausländer. Herr Schubal verwies den Heizer aus dem Maschinenraum und ließ ihn Klosette reinigen, was doch gewiß nicht des Heizers Sache war. Einmal wurde sogar die Tüchtigkeit des Herrn Schubal angezweifelt, die eher scheinbar als wirklich vorhanden sein sollte. [...] Immerhin erfuhr man aus den vielen Reden nichts eigentliches [...]. (21)[8]

Quite clearly, the Stoker's tirade and his obsessional repetition of Schubal's name is reminiscent of a child's anguished attempt at self-defence: his fear of being abject is turned into aggression and projected away from the self onto an other. In this manner, the phobic subject attempts to maintain the fragile

---

[7] Kristeva describes the phobic person as a "subject in want of metaphoricalness." *Powers of Horror*, 37. Her analysis of the speech of adult phobic discourse reads like a running commentary on Karl's own rhetoric: "The speech of the phobic adult is also characterised by extreme nimbleness. But that vertiginous skill is as if void of meaning, traveling [sic] at top speed over an untouched and untouchable abyss, of which, on occasion, only the affect shows up, giving not a sign but a signal." (Ibid., 41).

[8] [Mr. Schubal was unfair! Mr. Schubal gave preference to foreigners! Mr Schubal ordered the Stoker out of the engine-room and made him clean water-closets, which was not a Stoker's job at all! At one point even the capability of Mr. Schubal was called into question, as being more apparent than real. [...] All the same, nothing definite emerged from the Stoker's outpourings [...]. A: 23].

boundaries between self and other. The Stoker is Kristeva's abject who produces Schubal as the object of his xenophobia which, simultaneously, condenses his fear and reveals his powerlessness. His verbal attack is the frantic attempt to keep the threatening abjection of self at bay.

While the Stoker's defence resembles the temper tantrums of a child, Karl's own manner seems strikingly rational. Thus for example Karl makes a point of explicitly noting the lack of clarity and precision in the Stoker's speech which results in a "trauriges Durcheinanderstrudeln" (23) [a sad whirlpool] of all his complaints. Analysing the Stoker's rhetorical shortcomings and registering his body language, Karl seems to continue to take the Stoker's part while at the same time distancing himself somewhat from this former (subconscious) alliance in favour of a rationality that is associated with the symbolic order. This strategy is an interesting compromise which allows him to gratify both his need for identification with the phobic Stoker as well as his desire to get the approval of the representatives of the symbolic order: whereas on the level of explicit support he hangs on to the Stoker, he engages in actual fact in a rhetorical exercise, effectively reprimanding the Stoker for his uncontrolled emotional outburst.

> Sie müssen das einfacher erzählen, klarer, der Herr Kapitän kann das nicht würdigen so wie Sie es ihm erzählen. Kennt er denn alle Maschinisten und Laufburschen beim Namen oder gar beim Taufnamen, daß er, wenn Sie nur einen solchen Namen aussprechen gleich wissen kann, um wen es sich handelt. Ordnen Sie doch ihre Beschwerden, sagen Sie das Wichtigste zuerst und absteigend die andern, vielleicht wird es dann überhaupt nicht mehr nötig sein, die meisten auch nur zu erwähnen. (23)[9]

By asking the Stoker to observe the rhetorical rules of judicial proceedings Karl makes a demand which the Stoker cannot possibly meet. For as a phobic subject he has no language other than a symptomatic gesturing. In his overt criticism, Karl seems to apply H. P. Grice's famous "co-operative principle" which states a general principle of conversation and a number of maxims which speakers should obey: "Make your conversational contribution such as is required, at the stage at which it occurs, by the accepted purpose or direction of the talk exchange in which you are engaged."[10] Clearly, Karl wants to be seen as changing sides; that is why he appeals so explicitly to the stable social code governed by collective rules and shared

---

[9] [You must put things more simply, more clearly; the Captain can't do justice to what you are telling him. How can he know all the mechanics and ship's boys by name, far less by their first names, so that when you mention so-and-so he can tell at once who is meant? Take your grievances in order, tell the most important ones first and the lesser ones afterwards; perhaps you'll find that it won't be necessary even to mention most of them. A: 25].
[10] Cited in Gilian Brown and George Yule, *Discourse Analysis*. Cambridge, London, New York etc.: Cambridge University Press, 1983: 31.

conventions which regulate the symbolic. As Elizabeth Grosz puts it, "the Symbolic is the domain of *positions* and *propositions* [...], the order in which the object is *posited*, the proposition affirmed and the statement located so that truth or falsehood can be attributed to it. [...] It functions by hierarchical subsumption, using relations of logical and grammatical convention [...]"[11] However, Karl's overt advocacy of the symbolic order turns out to be feigned since his speech act is based on a lie, as he admits to himself: "Wenn man in Amerika Koffer stehlen kann, kann man auch hie und da lügen, dachte er zur Entschuldigung." (23) [If boxes could be stolen in America, one could surely tell a lie now and then as well, he thought in self-excuse. A: 25] Evidently the lie undermines the whole purpose of the exercise from the very beginning because it destroys the propositional content of the speech act as well as the social relation between speaker and addressee which, according to the idealised model of Grice's conversational maxims, must be based on truthfulness in order to function.[12] Although Karl intentionally flouts the conversational maxims, he does not, however, erode or destabilise the rules of the symbolic order. The lie allows him to feign mastery of a social code which, as the ensuing story unfolds, he does not really control.

Kafka on the Couch?

Against this background one could be easily lead to the assumption that Karl is truly subversive, that he is an artist who reintroduces the silenced other to the social sphere as Kristeva's "flow of *jouissance* into language":

> Art — this semiotization of the symbolic — [...] represents the flow of *jouissance* into language. Whereas sacrifice assigns *jouissance* its productive limit in the social and symbolic order, art specifies the means — the only means — that *jouissance* harbors for infiltrating that order. In cracking the socio-symbolic order, splitting it open, changing vocabulary, syntax, the word itself and releasing from beneath them the drives borne by vocalic or kinetic differences, *jouissance* works its way into the social.[13]

---

[11] Elizabeth Grosz, *Sexual Subversions. Three French Feminists*. Sydney, Wellington etc.: Allen & Unwin, 1989: 48.
[12] The maxim of quality states: "do not say what· you believe to be false." The maxim of relation: "be relevant", and, finally, the maxim of manner: "be perspicuous". Cf. Brown and Yule, *Discourse Analysis*, 32. These idealised maxims make it possible to describe what types of meaning speakers convey when they flout the maxims. By flouting a maxim, the speaker adds a "conversational implicature" to the literal meaning of his utterance. Ibid., 31ff.
[13] Julia Kristeva, *Revolution in Poetic Language*. Translated by M. Waller with an introduction by L. S. Roudiez, New York: Columbia University Press, 1984: 80.

Although this passage certainly characterises Kafka's relationship with language, the same does not hold for his character Karl Roßmann. Unlike the artist or the work of art which, as a catalyst, restores the other to the social order by, for example, inducing crises of representation, Karl suffers from a splitting that he cannot name but only express on the symptomatic level. This is an important point which I cannot stress enough since it quite clearly demarcates the crucial difference between those early psychoanalytic readings of Kafka which analyse the aesthetic universe in terms of the author's biography, treating the work of art simply in terms of a manifest dream behind which a latent truth lies waiting,[14] and, on the other hand, a reading practice which is concerned with the very function of the transgressions of art in the social order. Whereas Karl is permeated by abjection on the symptomatic level, the narrative as a whole engages in the sublimation of abjection through its very articulation. "Sublimation", writes Kristeva, "is nothing else than the possibility of naming the pre-nominal, the pre-objectal [...]. In the symptom, the abject permeates me, I become abject. Through sublimation, I keep it under control. The abject is edged with the sublime."[15]

Sublimation through the very narration of abjection — such is the project of Kafka's narratives. By writing abjection into his narrative universe, Kafka implicitly diagnoses abjection as the stigma of the modern subject which suffers from it on a variety of levels, from family constellations, socio-cultural processes (examples of which are the experience of emigration or anti-Semitism), the prohibitions and taboos of society engendered by the "Law of the Father", to man's ontological insecurity and metaphysical anguish in a world in which Nietzsche's "God is dead!" has become a commonplace. In other words, my analysis refuses to prolong the psychoanalytic trend of the Sixties and Seventies which reduced Kafka's œuvre to the level of individual pathography, interpreting — or rather diagnosing — it as a symptom of the author's pathological disturbances. In his critical assessment of competing methodological approaches to Kafka's work, Peter U. Beicken has, with reference to the large body of psychoanalytic interpretations, rightly warned against the tendency to view his art merely in terms of an expression of unconscious conflicts.[16] Beicken agrees

---

[14] A critical overview of this psychoanalytic reading practice can be found in Peter U. Beicken, *Franz Kafka. Eine kritische Einführung in die Forschung*. Frankfurt am Main: Athenaion,1974: 193-213, and, more recently, in Franz R. Kempf, *Everyone's Darling: Kafka and the Critics of His Short Fiction*. Drawer, Columbia: Camden House, 1994: 12-14. For a thorough analysis and critique of Freud's own interpretive methods along such lines see Jean Starobinski, *Psychoanalyse und Literatur*. Translated from the French by Eckhart Rohloff, Frankfurt am Main: Suhrkamp, 1990: 104-109.
[15] Kristeva, *Powers of Horror*, 11.
[16] Beicken, *Franz Kafka*, 198.

with Peter Foulkes' view according to which the equation of Kafka's writing with a dream has to be rejected since it is a consciously induced process and not a dream recollection.

Although I am critical of those early psychoanalytic readings which treat the literary text as a pathological symptom that requires clinical diagnosis, I do not join the camp of those critics who, on the basis of Kafka's aphorism of 1917 "Zum letztenmal Psychologie!" [for the last time psychology!], discard all psychoanalytic or psychological interest in his work. Hartmut Binder pointed out that this aphorism has been misread as Kafka's rejection of Freud.[17] Kafka's interest in the psychoanalytic movement can be easily traced. In his Kafka handbook Binder documents that from 1912 onwards Kafka encountered psychoanalytic ideas through a variety of publications, ranging from *Neue Rundschau, Aktion, Pan* to Theodor Reiks *Flaubert und seine Versuchung des heiligen Antonius*.[18] According to Binder, this reception of a body of literature which was informed by psychoanalysis helped Kafka to *refine* his own analysis of his family constellation. Thus for example, in a famous diary entry, dated 23 September 1912, describing the genesis of his narrative *Das Urteil,* Kafka reflects on the physical as well as psychological aspects of the act of writing: "Nur so kann geschrieben werden, nur in einem solchen Zusammenhang, mit solcher vollständigen Öffnung des Leibes und der Seele. Vormittag im Bett. Die immer klaren Augen."[19] [One can write only like this, only in such a context, with such complete openness of body and soul. Morning in bed. Eyes always clear.] Interpreting the story as the product of an all-engaging exercise in complete openness of body and soul, he then jots down: "Gedanken an Freud natürlich" (ibid.) [thoughts of Freud of course]. This suggests that Kafka was aware of Freud's ideas while writing a story of oedipal conflict as well as of the connection between the process of writing and the therapeutic project of bringing repressed material to the surface.

In Kafka's own analysis, writing becomes first and foremost a physically and psychologically engaging activity in the course of which subjectivity gives birth to itself. This is far from the simple exercise of sublimating a neurotic subjectivity into art but is rather a radical process which engenders subjectivity and, at the same time, attests to its crisis. In a famous letter to Felice Kafka explains: "Mein Leben besteht und bestand im Grunde von jeher aus Versuchen zu schreiben und meist aus mißlungenen. Schrieb ich aber nicht, dann lag ich auch schon auf dem Boden, wert hinausgekehrt zu

---

[17] Hartmut Binder, *Kafka Handbuch*, vol. 1, *Der Mensch und seine Zeit*. Stuttgart: Kröner, 1979: 411.
[18] Ibid., 410.
[19] Franz Kafka, *Tagebücher. Band 2: 1912-1914*. Frankfurt am Main: Fischer, 1994: 101. Henceforth cited as TB 2.

werden."[20] [My life consists, and basically always has consisted, of attempts at writing, most unsuccessful. But when I didn't write, I was at once flat on the floor, fit for the dustbin. LF: 20]. This is certainly a strong image, conjuring up Kafka's *Metamorphosis* in which the life of the salesman Gregor Samsa is narrated from his transformation into a huge bug until his death and final disposal as waste.

In our context, Kafka's reference to waste also points to the connection between abjection and sublimation which relate to each other like two sides of the same coin. For Kafka's drastic metaphor spells out that, when the process of writing fails, the writer turns into mere waste, a cadaver which has to be disposed of. Why? — It is the very nature of waste to upset the order of meaning, to be abject. Without his writing, the writer is waste — we see that in Kafka's radical thinking, the notion of a subjectivity anterior and posterior to the act of writing is rejected. In addition, the passage also suggests that writing always voices the very instability of subjectivity and thus its crisis. In this process, the concept of representation becomes destabilised since, according to Kafka, the writer never succeeds in representing his subjectivity through the work of art, but rather engenders it only momentarily through the bodily act of writing. As a result of this, writing becomes an exercise in survival: "Aber schreiben werde ich trotz alledem, unbedingt, es ist mein Kampf um die Selbsterhaltung." [But I will write in spite of everything, by all means, this is my battle for survival. TB 2: 165] We have moved a long way from early psychoanalytic interpretations according to which Kafka's writing ultimately resembles a neurotic activity, to a view which emphasises Kafka's departure from the concept of a stable subjectivity in favour of a radical exploration of the price of the symbolic function. By naming the abject, Kafka reintroduces the repressed of the social order, and yet at the same time ensures his — admittedly precarious — distance from it, a distance that is completely dependent on the act of writing.

But it is time to return to Karl who is still delivering his speech in the Captain's cabin: I have argued that Karl's acceptance of the norms and codes of the symbolic order is feigned because it is based on a lie. But on closer analysis one finds that this is not the first time that Karl lies because he has already uttered the same lie in his initial speech when he attested to the Stoker's integrity, deliberately concealing the important fact that he only made the latter's acquaintance a few minutes before:

---

[20] Franz Kafka, *Briefe an Felice und andere Korrespondenz aus der Verlobungszeit*. Ed. by Erich Heller and Jürgen Born, Frankfurt am Main: Fischer, 1983: 65. Henceforth cited as F in brackets with page number. The translations of Kafka's letters are from the following edition cited as LF: Franz Kafka, *Letters to Felice*. Ed. by Erich Heller and Jürgen Born, translated by James Stern and Elisabeth Duckworth, London: Secker & Warburg, 1974.

Ich erlaube mir zu sagen [...], daß meiner Meinung nach dem Herrn Heizer Unrecht geschehen ist. Es ist hier ein gewisser Schubal, der ihm aufsitzt. Er selbst hat schon auf vielen Schiffen, die er ihnen alle nennen kann, zur vollständigen Zufriedenheit gedient, ist fleißig, meint es mit seiner Arbeit gut und es ist wirklich nicht einzusehen, warum er gerade auf diesem Schiff, wo doch der Dienst nicht so übermäßig schwer ist, wie z. B. auf Handelsseglern, schlecht entsprechen sollte. Es kann daher nur Verläumdung sein, die ihn in seinem Vorwärtskommen hindert und ihn um die Anerkennung bringt, die ihm sonst ganz bestimmt nicht fehlen würde. (19)[21]

Whereas the Stoker's affect-ridden linguistic whirlpool is reminiscent of a child's phobia, revealing an original anguish, Karl seems to be the master of his language.[22] But the structure of his sentences, which increasingly include qualifying subclauses, his usage of modal verbs and the subjunctive suggest a rationality that, on closer inspection, is devoid of meaning since Karl has really nothing to say about the Stoker's behaviour or performance on board the ship. This strategy to rely on a rhetoric of rationality which is cut off from reality characterises Karl's verbal behaviour throughout the narrative even in the most distressing of circumstances, for example when he receives his uncle's letter of expulsion or when he loses his job in the Hotel Occidental. In all these distressing episodes Karl barricades himself behind a discourse through which, as Kristeva comments in *Powers of Horror*, "no current flows — it is a pure and simple splitting, an abyss without any possible means of conveyance between its two edges. No subject, no object: petrification on one side, falsehood on the other."[23]

---

[21] [May I be allowed to say [...] that in my opinion an injustice has been done to my friend the stoker? There's a certain man Schubal aboard who bullies him. He has a long record of satisfactory service on many ships, whose names he can give you, he is diligent, takes an interest in his work, and it's really hard to see why on this particular ship, where the work isn't so heavy as on cargo boats, for instance, he should get so little credit. It must be sheer slander that keeps him back and robs him of the recognition that should certainly be his. A: 21f.]
[22] For an analysis of the Stoker's language see p. 52 of this chapter.
[23] Kristeva, *Powers of Horror*, 47.

Uncle Jacob's "Matter of Discipline"

At the end of chapter one the episode is resolved through a recognition scene: his uncle Jacob, the embodiment of both the American myth of the self-made man as well as of the "Law of the Father", identifies Karl as his nephew and adopts him. Although Karl makes one more attempt to defend the Stoker's case as "eine Sache der Gerechtigkeit" [a matter of justice] in the end he accepts his uncle's contention that the Stoker's case is first and foremost a matter of discipline and thus the captain's sole responsibility. Uncle Jacob reinstates a clear hierarchical order and its penal system, thus demonstrating his strong allegiance to the symbolic order on which both his entrepreneurial success as well as his private views are based.

When he expels Karl from his parental care only two chapters later his decision is not based on an act of irrational vindictiveness. Rather it reflects his stern adherence to precisely those principles which govern the symbolic order and which are first articulated in his assessment of the episode with the Stoker. His rejection of Karl later on in the novel thus ensures that the boundaries and hierarchies of the symbolic order are not violated. And this is exactly how the Law of the Father operates in Kafka's stories: as a relentless adherence to rules which silence and repress the other of the symbolic order.

Chapter one finishes with Karl's doubt "ob dieser Mann ihm jemals den Heizer werde ersetzen können" (42) [whether this man would ever be able to take the stoker's place, A: 41]. This doubt is reinforced when his uncle avoids eye-contact with Karl: "Auch wich der Onkel seinem Blicke aus und sah auf die Wellen hin, von denen ihr Boot umschwankt wurde." (ibid.) [And his uncle evaded his eyes and stared at the waves on which their boat was tossing. A: 41] From the very beginning, Karl's adoption by his uncle is rather precarious. The narrative prepares the reader for Karl's fall from grace when only one chapter later he fails to notice his uncle's hostile reaction to his excursion with Herr Pollunder to the latter's country house. When Karl and Pollunder leave New York for this trip, the traffic assumes a chaotic, labyrinthine quality which, as in the scene on board the ship, is a symbol of Karl's status as a maze-walker who is unable to read his environment. Karl is oblivious to the rejection and displacement awaiting him: leaning on Pollunder's arm he is only concerned with "Herrn Pollunders dunkle Weste, über die quer eine goldene Kette ruhig hieng." (58) [with Herr Pollunder's dark waistcoat which was peacefully spanned by a gold chain. A: 54] This is a very telling moment in that Pollunder's soft physical appearance and his protective cradling of Karl show that he adopts a maternal role towards Karl who responds with an infant's facination with the gold chain.

This rare moment of intimacy suggests an unresolved pre-oedipal attachment to the maternal, or in Kristeva's terminology, to the semiotic sphere.[24]

This brings me to the central point of this chapter: Kafka's narrative is exemplary of a body of German-Jewish travel writing in which reality is conceived of as a labyrinth highlighting not only the dislocating experience of rapid technological change, industrialisation and the expansion of the metropolis but also the self's abjection within the harsh symbolic order. I am arguing that the experience of reality as labyrinth always points to the physical, epistemological and psychological disorientation suffered by a subject that has gone astray, or a maze-walker who cannot assimilate an environment which only mirrors the subject's disorientation. Although the socio-economic changes associated with these processes of urbanisation certainly reinforce the experience of dislocation and disorientation, they are not the ultimate cause of the loss of identity in Kafka's *Der Verschollene*.[25]

The latter stance was taken by Wilhelm Emrich who in his influential Kafka study declares that Kafka's novel renders an acute analysis of modern industrialised society and its "satanical consequences" for the individual,[26] a reading which was dismissed a few years later by Heinz Politzer who emphasises the psychological conflict of the novel arguing that "the reality in *Der Verschollene* is only secondhand material" based on Kafka's knowledge of secondary sources.[27] I agree with Ritchie Robertson's view that:

---

[24] Elizabeth Grosz gives the following concise definition of the semiotic sphere: "The semiotic is composed of non-signifying raw materials. It is an anarchic, formless circulation of sexual impulses and energies traversing the child's body before sexuality is ordered and hierarchically subsumed under the primacy of genitality and the body becomes a coherent entity. [...] It is the symbiotic shared by the mother's and child's indistinguishable bodies." Grosz, *Sexual Subversions*, 43.

[25] What we find in Kafka's *Der Verschollene* and other German-Jewish narratives such as Joseph Roth's *Hiob*, Elias Canetti's *Die Stimmen von Marrakesch* Albert Drach's *Unsentimentale Reise* and Wolfgang Hildesheimer's *Tynset*, is a modern version of the myth of the Wandering Jew which — as Edward Timms argues— has, over the centuries, been treated in a variety of different ways, from being seen as a symbol of piety and repentance to being used in a highly defamatory, anti-Semitic manner. Cf. Edward Timms, 'The Wandering Jew — A Leitmotif in German Literature and Politics'. Professorial Lecture given at the University of Sussex on Tuesday 26 April 1994. In clear contrast to the latter interpretation, the modern German-Jewish travelling narrative adds to the leitmotif of the Wandering Jew the maze-walker who has lost his bearings due to the abjection of self/other.

[26] Cf. Wilhem Emrich, *Franz Kafka*. Bonn and Frankfurt am Main: Athenäum, 1957: 227. Emrich's view was echoed by marxist critics such as Klaus Hermsdorf who also read the novel as a "representation of society in its totality". Cf. Klaus Hermsdorf, 'Kafka's *America*.' In: Kenneth Hughes (Ed.), *Franz Kafka. An Anthology of Marxist Criticism*. Hanover and London: University Press of New England, 1981: 22.

[27] Heinz Politzer, *Franz Kafka. Der Künstler*. Frankfurt am Main: Suhrkamp, 1978: 120.

> the opposition between America and Karl, between Emrich's and Politzer's interpretations, is [...] a false one. The critical problem here is not to decide whether America is theme or setting, but to discover how Kafka has interrelated the novel's two main themes: on the one hand, the human implications of industrial and technological society, and, on the other, the moral and psychological significance of Karl's adventures.[28]

Taking up Robertson's point I shall argue that Kafka skilfully engages with contemporary America and reality through the only form that is available to him: its various representations in stereotypes, images, myths, popular and literary narratives. We will see that Kafka draws upon these materials in order to deconstruct the great American myth of boundless opportunities and Liberty by creating a "space of anxiety" that externalises and maps out Karl's sense of abjection.

It is important to emphasise that my reading does not address abjection merely in terms of character analysis, that is on the level of the individual's pathology, but first and foremost as a major theme of modern literature. If modernity questions the stability of representations, it does so by voicing the silenced other of rationality, one example of which is the narration of abjection in *Der Verschollene*. In order to analyse the various manifestations of the symbolic order and abjection as well as the precarious relationship between self and other my reading necessarily moves away from the common focus on the question of Karl's innocence or guilt. Although one can certainly share Ritchie Robertson's conclusion that "the widely held view of him as an innocent and ingenious character seems to be broadly correct", it seems to me that this discussion misses out on the question what motivates Karl's continued displacement in *Der Verschollene*.[29] If one suspends one's judgement on the issue of Karl's innocence or guilt and follows his labyrinthine movement through a space of anxiety, the connection between his repetitive experience of dislocation and the theme of abjection becomes obvious. Karl challenges the rules and boundaries of the symbolic sphere to such an extent that — from the viewpoint of its representatives — he has to be expelled from its working order and signifying practices.

When the representatives of this order judge Karl to be guilty of a series of transgressions, their judgements are always motivated by the relentless logic of this order; they are not just "obscure and unfathomable" decisions as was suggested by the Marxist critic Klaus Hermsdorf.[30] Hermsdorf's conclusion that uncle Jacob's rejection of Karl, for instance, "is not motivated as

---

[28] Ritchie Robertson, *Kafka: Judaism, Politics, and Literature*. Oxford: Clarendon Press, 1985: 46.
[29] Robertson, *Kafka*, 69.
[30] Hermsdorf, 'Kafka's *America*', 23.

an expression of his social being"³¹ overlooks the crucial function of such acts within the narrative universe: they always serve to reinstate the authority and functioning of the symbolic order which Karl unwittingly challenges by ignoring the rules and boundaries that are its very substance. This is, however, not to suggest by any means that Kafka's narrative actually endorses the judgements that are made by Karl's opponents — on the contrary, on the level of narration, the novel foregrounds both the fictionality of such clear boundaries and divisions between the proper and improper as well as the price to be paid for erecting the symbolic, namely the repression of otherness through acts of abjection. That repression is inherent in the symbolic order is already hinted at in the first chapter when Karl's uncle refers to the episode with the Stoker as a "matter of discipline" rather than a "matter of justice". However, by embodying abjection, Karl attests to the presence of the silenced other of reason and consciousness as well as to the constant threat that the silenced other poses to rationality. From this angle, the question of his innocence or guilt is beside the point.

A Suitcase, a Passport and a Photograph

In *Der Verschollene* Kafka employs one striking leitmotif to express Karl's sense of abjection: remember that at the beginning of the narrative Karl left his suitcase in the care of a fellow passenger in order to search for his umbrella in the lower deck.³² In the series of events, leading to the recognition scene between Karl and his uncle, the suitcase seems to be forgotten. At the end of the chapter we see him leave with his rich uncle, who — in the words of the captain — has the means to offer Karl a "glänzende Laufbahn" (30) [a brilliant career]. Uncle Jacob himself has no doubts about his role as a saviour: he explains that, had it not been for his intervention, Karl would probably have died miserably in some backstreet of New York, having been dispatched by his parents to America "mit unverantwortlich ungenügender Ausrüstung" (33) [with irresponsibly insufficient equipment].³³ At this point of the narrative, it seems that the word "equipment" quite literally refers to Karl's few European belongings. These are declared to be insufficient in the American environment. We hear nothing more of them until the end of chapter three, when he receives his

---

³¹ Ibid., 24.
³² An earlier version of the following sub-chapter was previously published under the same title in Jeff Morrrison and Florian Krobb (Eds.), Text into Image/Image into Text. Amsterdam, Atlanta: Rodopi, 1997: 193-201.
³³ The Muir edition translates this as "shamefully unprovided for" (A: 33). However, a more literal translation of the expression is better suited for my interpretative puposes.

uncle's letter of expulsion and — to the surprise of Karl and the reader who may well have forgotten them — his cap and suitcase.

From now on the suitcase acquires strong symbolic overtones. First and foremost, it is a symbol of Karl's European baggage, of his individual history and the family background which he carries around as an ultimately non-disposable burden. This burden stops him from setting up a home anywhere. With an ironic twist, Kafka alludes to the literal and metaphorical meaning of "belonging(s)". Whenever Karl's European belongings resurface in the story, he is always homeless and does not belong anywhere. His baggage becomes thus a powerful symbol of abjection. If we trace this a little further with reference to Karl's baggage we will see how the narrative carefully builds up a network of associations between the hero's sense of existential non-belonging and his ownership of a burdening past.

At this point it is worthwhile having a look at the content of Karl's suitcase: after his fall from his uncle's grace, Karl stays the night in a cheap hotel on the margins of New York, where he finds himself sharing a room with two migrant workers, Delamarche and Robinson. Upon his arrival, Karl decides to examine the contents of his suitcase because he is afraid that "das Wertvollste schon verlorengegangen sein dürfte." (101) [The most precious (items) [...] might well have disappeared. A: 92]. Initially he is shocked at the great disorder of his belongings, but finds on closer inspection that none of his things has gone missing: all his clothes are there, his money, passport and his watch, even a Veronese salami that has been added by his mother, as well as a bible, writing paper and one photograph of his parents. This sense of a caring order associated with his home is, however, not to be trusted: the reader already knows that Karl's relationship with his parents is highly disturbed; after all they dispatched him to America as punishment for having been seduced by a female servant.[34] This image of order, care and stability originally associated with the suitcase begins to fade away upon closer examination of some of its contents.

Let us first consider the passport since it is *the* official document endorsing the immigrant's identity. It attests to his name as well as to his place and date of birth. It should also contain the visa which gives the immigrant official entry rights and entitles him to work and to settle down. The reader first comes across Karl's passport in chapter one: when asked

---

[34] The female servant, Johanna Brummer, incorporates characteristics of the engulfing seductress and the motherly figure. It is in line with this that it was Brummer who wrote to uncle Jacob explaining Karl's expulsion from his family and asking uncle Jacob to take care of Karl (33). On the other hand, Karl recalls the sexual act with her as an engulfing and threatening experience, in fact as having been raped. For an in-depth analysis of the female figures in Kafka's work see Reiner Stach, *Kafkas erotischer Mythos. Eine ästhetische Konstruktion des Weiblichen*. Frankfurt am Main: Suhrkamp, 1987.

what his name is, he answers briefly "ohne wie es seine Gewohnheit war, durch Vorlage des Passes sich vorzustellen, den er erst hätte suchen müssen: Karl Roßmann." (29) [Without, as was his custom, introducing himself by means of his passport which he would have had to tug out of his pocket: Karl Roßmann. A: 30] There is a notable incongruity in this episode: Karl introduces himself here in a straightforward manner by giving his first and second name, but a typically kafkaesque subclause reveals that he normally prefers to produce his passport on such occasions. In other words, he normally delegates the act of introducing himself to an official document.

Karl's reluctance to utter his own name is a first trace of his lack of a proper self with well-defined boundaries: it appears that he must have missed out on that vital phase in a child's development when the child learns to name parts of the world and to make them separate from each other, thus learning to distinguish between self and other. The fact that Karl normally delegates this task to an official document is indicative of his lack of a sense of identity. The second, more indirect reference to Karl's passport occurs at the beginning of chapter two where Karl imagines what his fate would have been, had he not met his uncle who had no doubt that the American immigration officials would have sent him straight back to Europe, "ohne sich weiter darum zu kümmern, daß er keine Heimat mehr hatte." (43) [without regard to the fact that he no longer had a home. A: 42] Karl's parents dispatched him to the United States without a proper visa, from the outset imposing the status of illegality on him. A close inspection of Karl's passport thus reveals that from the very beginning of the narrative he is an illegal subject with neither a proper identity nor proper rights. It is clear that things do not look too good for him.

This sense of alienation and estrangement from his parents is fully brought to the fore when Karl examines the photograph of his parents.[35] Family photographs are an indispensable item in the immigrant's suitcase since — in the words of Susan Sontag — "through photographs, each family constructs a portrait-chronicle of itself, a portable kit of images that bear witness to its connectedness."[36] But this "kit of images" documents a connectedness that in the case of the immigrant is historical and highly elusive, a relic that incites the onlooker to sentimental reverie. Susan Sontag has rightly pointed to the fact that photographs have the power to

---

[35] Anthony Northey traces Kafka's narrative back to real life sources such as his cousin Robert Kafka who was seduced by a family cook at the age of fourteen or Otto Kafka, his "interesting cousin from Paraguay". Cf. Anthony Northey, *Kafka's Relatives — Their Lives & His Writing*. New Haven and London: Yale University Press, 1991: 52. Northey also reproduces the photograph of Kafka's grandparents, Joseph, the butcher from Wossek, and his wife Franziska, which inspired his description in the scene analysed above.

[36] Susan Sontag, *On Photography*. New York: The Noon Day Press, Farrar, Straus and Giroux, 1989: 8.

turn the past into an object of tender regard, suspending critical judgements, precisely because of the onlooker's pathos of looking at time past.[37] While on one level the family photograph authenticates the togetherness of this particular family at that particular place and time, on a second level it is just the opposite of documentary evidence since it constructs a history which — to quote Annette Kuhn — "is also the expression of a lack and a desire to put things right."[38] In Kafka's novel all photographs serve as fetish objects fending off the characters' anxiety about not belonging anywhere.

The reader comes across such an example of this defence against anxiety in the private rooms of the head cook of the Hotel Occidental, Grete Mitzelbach from Vienna: Karl, who is staying the night in her apartment, notices a series of carefully framed and neatly arranged photographs on a little sideboard which he studies with great attention, thinking that he too would have liked to arrange the picture of his parents in such a caring manner (138ff.). But this episode occurs after he has already lost the one and only photograph he possessed on his arrival in America. The loss of the picture upsets him greatly since it was the only private document apparently authenticating his existence. The reader already knows that Karl's desire for authentication by his parents is highly problematical since the photograph does not really succeed in terms of social rite. Instead of furnishing evidence of the family's connectedness it documents Karl's abjection.

In order to demonstrate this it is important to take a closer look at the photograph in question: the picture follows the Wilhelminian convention of showing the "pater familias" standing with one arm draped on the back of an armchair and the other one on an illustrated book on a little table by his side, while his mother occupies the armchair. Again Kafka carefully includes two highly revealing iconographic details in his description: his father's hand is clenched to a fist while his mother sits in her armchair slightly sunk into herself (105). This suggests a dynamic revolving around a threatening father and a weak mother. Karl's alienation from the sphere of the paternal — or in Kristeva's words: the symbolic order — is further reinforced when he examines the picture more closely but fails to catch his father's eye: no matter how hard he tries, his father's image does not gain life. Clearly, Karl experiences here a frustration that is somehow connected to the length of the gaze: the longer we look the more the photograph turns into a veil behind which we now desire to see. In the words of Victor Burgin, "to remain long with a single image is to risk the loss of our imaginary command of the look, to relinquish (sic) it to that absent other to

---

[37] Ibid., 71.
[38] Annette Kuhn, 'Remembrance.' In: Jo Spence and Patricia Holland (Eds.), *Family Snaps — The Meaning of Domestic Photography*. London: Virago, 1991: 23.

whom it belongs by right — the camera."³⁹ Karl is the onlooker who does not have any imaginary command to bring the picture of his father to life precisely because his lingering gaze is motivated both by complete alienation from the paternal sphere as well as the desire to heal this wound on an imaginary level. But since the wound is real, the gaze cannot compensate for it.

In stark contrast to this, the iconographic representation of his mother, particularly her forced smile suggesting "Leid" [suffering], has a strong and overwhelming emotional effect on him: it unleashes some pre-oedipal attachment or rather unfulfilled want and desire in Karl. In the passage this is referred to as Karl's "unumstößliche Überzeugung eines verborgenen Gefühls des Abgebildeten" (105) [complete certainty of the secret feelings of the person shown in it] and his ensuing desire to kiss his mother's dangling hand. The dynamic between Karl as the onlooker or outsider and his parents suggests that he has not managed to enter the symbolic order as a "proper subject" capable of building up lasting object relations. And this is so, as the picture reveals, because of two factors: a negative paternal metaphor, visually translated by his inability to connect with his father whose expression remains lifeless, and his corresponding desire for his mother from whom he has been emotionally separated since his childhood. It is precisely this combination of desire and separation as well as the absence of a working paternal metaphor which is at the heart of Karl's sense of abjection of self and other.

This reading is backed up by one of Karl's very few childhood memories: when he examines the strange mechanism of his American writing desk in chapter two, he remembers the Nativity scenes which he saw as a child at the Christmas market at home. Once more Kafka carefully weaves a few iconographic details in this scene suggesting an original want that is related to his latent sense of abjection. While the child is depicted as being utterly fascinated and excited by the "stockenden Vorwärtskommen der heiligen drei Könige, dem Aufglänzen des Sternes und dem befangenen Leben im heiligen Stall" (46) [the jerky advance of the Three Holy Kings, the shining out of the Star and the humble life of the Holy Manger, A: 44], that is by the symbolic celebration of the Christian promise of the birth of the Son and Saviour, it seems to Karl that his mother does not follow the events carefully enough despite his many attempts to attract her attention. Moreover, she puts an end to her son's excitement by pressing her hand on his mouth and relapsing into "ihre frühere Unachtsamkeit" (ibid.) [her former inattention]. By negating both the symbolic promise embodied in the

---

³⁹ Victor Burgin, 'Looking at Photographs.' In: Victor Burgin (Ed.), *Thinking Photography*. Houndsmills and London: Macmillan, 1994: 152.

Nativity scene as well as the importance of her own son, Karl's mother effectively denies him access to a place in a meaningful symbolic order, leaving him with a wound that cannot heal because he is unable to establish an other as the object of his desire. This is one factor motivating his straying through America as an abject character in search of a home that he cannot find because he is caught up in re-enacting the abjection of self and other.

Food Nausea

The drama of abjection is carefully staged in the dinner scene in Pollunder's country house. After Karl's and Pollunder's arrival at the country house they learn that they have been joined by Mr. Green, a business friend of Pollunder and uncle Jacob, who wants to stay for dinner and spend the evening in their company. Pollunder immediately interprets Green's visit as an intrusion and considers sending Karl back to New York since "der heutige Abend ist schon von vornherein gestört" (61) [the evening's spoilt beforehand, A: 57]. Karl himself loses "jede Hoffnung diesem Manne den Herrn Pollunder heute abend irgendwie zu entlocken" (62) [all hope of luring Mr Pollunder away from the man that evening, A: 58]. Both Pollunder's and Karl's negative reaction to Green's arrival suggest a dynamic between the three that is characteristic of the oedipal triangle: Karl in the role of the son and Green, the towering phallocentric father-figure so typical of Kafka's world, compete for Pollunder's exclusive attention. I have already noted that, despite his gender, Pollunder acts as a mother surrogate,[40] assuming an extremely protective and caring role towards Karl, which is further reinforced by his physical appearance:

> Übrigens hatte man, wenn er so neben Herrn Green stand, den deutlichen Eindruck, daß es bei Herrn Pollunder keine gesunde Dicke war, der Rücken war in seiner ganzen Masse etwas gekrümmt, der Bauch sah weich und unhaltbar aus, eine wahre Last, und das Gesicht erschien bleich und geplagt. Dagegen stand hier Herr Green, vielleicht noch etwas dicker als Herr Pollunder, aber es war eine zusammenhängende, einander gegenseitig tragende Dicke, die Füße waren soldatisch zusammengeklappt, den Kopf

---

[40] According to Ritchie Robertson Pollunder represents the kindly, weak father type as opposed to the harsh father-figure, a typology that does not seem to me to make much sense since the father in Kafka's earlier texts is ultimately always the representative of a harsh paternal principle, of an unrelenting "Law of the Father" which tends to crush the protagonist who suffers from abjection. This is so in 'Die Verwandlung,' 'Das Urteil' and *Der Verschollene*. The car scene between Karl and Pollunder only makes sense if one reads it as an re-enactment of a pre-oedipal attachment to a maternal figure. Cf. Robertson, *Kafka*, 70.

trug er aufrecht und schaukelnd, er schien ein großer Turner, ein Vorturner zu sein. (89)[41]

Pollunder's big lips and soft, somewhat floppy features and his pale, burdened expression suggest a certain indecisiveness as well as a leaning towards the pleasure principle which, in Kafka's earlier works, is generally associated with the female figure, ranging from Johanna Brummer, who embodies both an overwhelming corporeality as well as maternal care, to the maternal head cook Grete Mitzelbach and the overtly physical Brunelda whose body is dominated by a radically externalised sexuality.[42]

After setting up an oedipal rivalry between Karl and Green, Kafka gives an extremely elaborate description of the ensuing dinner. We follow the dinner from Karl's viewpoint, who carefully observes with rising nausea how Green works his way through one course to the next, starting with the soup, moving on to a pigeon [also dove in German] which he carves with "scharfen Schnitten" (64) [incisive strokes] while engaging Pollunder in a conversation. Karl, who has been losing his appetite all along, then notes with even greater disgust how Green puts a bite in his mouth, "wo die Zunge [...] mit einem Schwunge die Speise ergriff" (65) [where the tongue, in one swing, took possession of the food].[43] Feeling nauseous, Karl gets up in order to leave but both Pollunder and his daughter Klara intervene as if it were their "natürliche Aufgabe, Karl zu beruhigen, wenn es ihm Übelkeiten verursachte" (ibid.) [natural duty to comfort Karl when it had made him sick]. Not surprisingly, Karl feels depraved at the end of the dinner scene: standing at a window by himself he observes how Klara, Pollunder and Green form a circle. The smoke of Green's cigar rises from the circle as if spreading Green's influence to the corners of the room. Karl, by contrast, feels expelled (66).

The dinner scene is a prime example of one of the most archaic forms of abjection, namely the food loathing as discussed before. If one follows the

---

[41] [One also had the definite feeling as he stood there beside Mr Green that Mr Pollunder's fatness was not a healthy fatness. His massive back was somewhat bent, his paunch looked soft and flabby, an actual burden, and his face was pallied and worried. Mr Green, on the other hand, was perhaps even fatter than Mr Pollunder, but it was a homogeneous, balanced fatness; he stood with his heels together like a soldier, he bore his head with a jaunty erectness. He looked like a great athlete, a captain of athletes. A: 79].
[42] Elizabeth Boa has rightly argued that *Das Schloß* marks a shift of perspectives from *Das Urteil* and *Die Verwandlung* where an absent or weak mother is subservient to the overwhelming father of the male protagonist. "In *Das Schloß* fathers are absent or broken, husbands are puny and women are powerful. Yet despite this shift, women's power goes to sustain an institutional male supremacy whose root lies in sexuality." Cf. Elizabeth Boa 'Letters from a Bachelor. Kafka's Letters to Felice and Milena.' In: *London German Studies V*, London: 1993: 129.
[43] I prefer a literal translation to Muir's version which reads "where his tongue, as Karl chanced to notice, took it in charge with a flourish." (A: 60).

different stages of this episode one cannot but notice that it is Karl who abjects himself from the others through his nausea. By feeling nauseous, he rejects not only his oedipal rival Green but also his mother surrogate Pollunder who, after all, provides the food. Kristeva's passage on food loathing helps to explain Karl's position in the dinner scene:

> nausea [...] separates me from the mother and father who proffer it (the food, AF). 'I' want none of that element, sign of their desire; 'I' do not want to listen, 'I' do not assimilate it, 'I' expel it. But since the food is not an 'other' for me, who am only in their desire, I expel myself, I spit myself out, I abject myself within [sic] the same motion through which 'I' claim to establish myself.[44]

After rejecting Pollunder as a feeble surrogate mother who only replicates the weakness of his own mother, Karl fantasises about his immediate return to his uncle. He imagines himself marching into his uncle's bedroom, hoping to surprise him in his nightshirt rather than meeting him dressed and buttoned up to his neck (68). This fantasy culminates in the vision of uncle and nephew regularly sharing breakfast in the uncle's bedroom in an atmosphere of undisturbed intimacy. Ultimately, his fantasy of a motherly father-figure is just another re-enactment of his search for a surrogate mother. But due to the logic of Kafka's world, Uncle Jacob remains the representative of the unrelenting "Law of the Father" which crushes the son not because he is disobedient but because of his lack of clear boundaries, a lack which implicitly challenges the rules, positions and boundaries that are the very stuff of the symbolic order.

---

[44] Kristeva, *Powers of Horror*, 3.

Of Animals and Hunger Artists

Food metaphors play an important part in Kafka's narrative universe. In 'Die Verwandlung' [Metamorphosis, 1912], for example, the metamorphosis of the traveling salesman Gregor Samsa into a type of cockroach goes hand in hand with his disgust at the food that he used to like as a human. Gregor's food nausea is characterised by a splitting between conscious thought and somatic reaction: when his sister brings him some milk and white bread he is almost overjoyed but discovers soon that he does not like the milk any more although it used to be his favourite drink:

> so schmeckte ihm überdies die Milch, die sonst sein Lieblingsgetränk war, und die ihm ja gewiß die Schwester deshalb hereingestellt hatte, gar nicht, ja er wandte sich fast mit Widerwillen von dem Napf ab und kroch in die Zimmermitte zurück. (70)[45]

And when Grete finally brings him some kitchen garbage unfit for human consumption, Gregor eats it with considerable relish:

> Rasch hintereinander und mit vor Befriedigung tränenden Augen verzehrte er den Käse, das Gemüse und die Sauce; die frischen Speisen dagegen schmeckten ihm nicht, er konnte nicht einmal ihren Geruch vertragen und schleppte sogar die Sachen, die er essen wollte, ein Stückchen weiter weg. (73)[46]

While on the somatic level Gregor separates himself here from the family by rejecting the food that is fit for human consumption, on the level of consciousness he still regards himself as a family member who seeks to alleviate the "Unannehmlichkeiten" [inconveniences] caused to the family "durch Geduld und größte Rücksichtnahme" (71) [by being patient and utterly considerate, M: 144]. However, the food scene in 'Die Verwandlung' demonstrates the unconscious logic of abjection according to which the "I" claims to establish itself through the very rejection of that which is deemed to be edible.

---

[45] Franz Kafka, *Sämtliche Erzählungen*. Ed. by Paul Raabe, Frankfurt am Main: Fischer, 1984: 56-99. Page numbers are henceforth cited in brackets. I cite the following English translation of 'Die Verwandlung' as M with page numbers: Franz Kafka, *The Metamorphosis, In the Penal Colony and Other Stories*. Translated by Joachim Neugroschel, New York etc.: Scribner Paperback, 1995. [But he did not care for the milk, even though it had always been his favourite beverage, which was no doubt why his sister had placed it in his room. As a matter of fact, he turned away from the bowl almost with loathing and crawled back to the middle of the room. M: 142]

[46] [His eyes watered with contentment as he gulped down the cheese, the vegetables, and the sauce in rapid succession. By contrast he did not relish the fresh foods, he could not even stand their smell, and he actually dragged the things he wanted to eat a short distance away. M: 145]

Kafka further reinforces the impact of abjection by adding to Gregor's preference for garbage his loss of human language as a means of communication. When Gregor tries to communicate with his family and the Prokurist (the executive secretary of the company) through the door of his bedroom, the Prokurist hears "eine Tierstimme" (64), an animal's voice. Gregor's loss of language is reinforced at the end of chapter one, when, on the level of conscious intention, he is eager to explain his failure to turn up for work on time, but is unaware of his physical appearance as a cockroach as well as his lack of a comprehensible language (68). This loss has far-reaching consequences: it amounts to an unconscious renunciation of his participation in the symbolic order, powerfully enacting Gregor's abandoning of the subjective and social identities that are dependent on its phallic economy.[47] By repudiating a commonly shared code, Gregor revolts against a phallic order that, in his experience, is omnipresent and stifling, but it is a revolt that has lost the vital nexus with the signifier and therefore turns into a prelinguistic unleashing of drive on the somatic level.[48] In Gregor's case the price to be paid for his attempt to separate himself from the symbolic order is very high: the price for becoming an other through abjection is ultimately his own death. At the end of the story, the maid announces proudly to the relieved family that she will dispose of "das Zeug von nebenan" (99) [that stuff in the next room, M: 187]. The representatives of the symbolic order view Gregor's dead body as refuse that has to be thrust aside in order to make room for life.

Food nausea is at the very heart of Kafka's 'Ein Hungerkünstler' [A Hunger Artist] which he published in *Die Neue Rundschau* in 1922 and which, like 'Die Verwandlung', has attracted considerable interpretive attention since.[49] In order to highlight the importance of abjection in 'Ein Hungerkünstler' I want to briefly run through the structure of the narrative: at the beginning of the story an omniscient narrator sets the scene by declaring that public interest in the hunger artist has considerably decreased over the past decades. And he continues: "Während es sich früher gut lohnte, große derartige Vorführungen in eigener Regie zu veranstalten, ist

---

[47] Kristeva accepts Freud's and Lacan's privileging of the phallus as the condition of sexual difference and the symbolic order: according to this view "the paternal agency alone, to the extent that it introduces the symbolic dimension between 'subject' (child) and 'object' (mother), can generate such a strict object relation. Otherwise, what is called 'narcissism', [...], becomes the unleashing of drive as such, without object, threatening all identity [...]." Kristeva, *Powers of Horror*, 44. And, with reference to signification, she writes: "the speaking subject enjoys the possibility of condensation because it is inscribed in the oedipal triangle. By means of that inscription [...] it finds itself subjected to paternal function." Ibid., 52.
[48] An example of this would be Gregor's newly discovered enjoyment of crawling up and down the walls of his room.
[49] Of the many interpretations I found Ingeborg Henel's reading most informative. Cf. Ingeborg Henel, *'Ein Hungerkünstler.'* In: *Deutsche Vierteljahresschrift* 38 (1964): 230-247.

dies heute völlig unmöglich. Es waren andere Zeiten." [Whereas in former times it was worth one's while to manage such big performances on one's own, today this is absolutely impossible. Times were different then. H: 163].[50] The narrator introduces here an almost absolute opposition between the present and a quasi-mythic past, thus structuring his ensuing narrative and, moreover, bracketing the events set in the past off as a time of otherness.

The first section revolves around the past: the reader is told of the immense popularity which the starvation artist enjoyed, his relations with the public, his guardians, his manager and the chosen ladies who support him at the end of his forty day long fast. Despite his great popularity, the hunger artist is frustrated because his achievement is not properly appreciated. It turns out that members of the public suspect him of trickery, and, to make things worse, some of his guardians want to give him a chance to eat during their watch. This depresses him since such suspicions are completely unfounded. Despite his obvious preference for a second group of guardians who watch him incessantly, thus allowing him to demonstrate that there was nothing edible in his cage and "daß er hungerte, wie keiner von ihnen es könnte" [that he was fasting like none of them could, H: 165], neither the public nor his manager believe in his assertion that he could fast on and on. "Er allein nämlich wußte, auch kein Eingeweihter sonst wußte das, wie leicht das Hungern war. Es war die leichteste Sache von der Welt. Er verschwieg es auch nicht, aber man glaubte ihm nicht [....]." [He alone knew, and not even an insider knew how easy it was to fast. It was the easiest thing in the world. He did not conceal it either, but people did not believe him. H: 165] In spite of the ease with which the hunger artist fasts, his manager imposes a forty day limit to the fasting period for business reasons. At the end of this period there is a public celebration of the hunger artist's achievement which he hates. During this ceremony he has to endure being picked up by the manager and being led by a few chosen ladies to a table with food, the mere thought of which makes him feel nauseated (H: 166).

This mythical period of public celebration of the hunger artist comes to an end when the public's interest in his performance diminishes to such an extent that he has to find new employment in a circus where his cage is placed in a far less central position, somewhere on the way to the stables. Hardly noticed by the public, who rush past his cage, he can now fast as long as he wants since nobody cares any longer, until one day, a guardian wonders why the cage with rotten straw is not in use, as a result of which the now dying hunger artist is found.

---

[50] The translations of quotations from 'Ein Hungerkünstler' are mine. Page references are henceforth cited as H in brackets and refer to Franz Kafka, *Sämtliche Erzählungen*. Ed. by Paul Raabe, Frankfurt am Main: Fischer, 1984: 155-185.

In a last conversation the hunger artist reveals his real motivation for fasting. When asked why he could not stop fasting, he replies: "weil ich nicht die Speise finden konnte, die mir schmeckt. Hätte ich sie gefunden, glaube mir, ich hätte kein Aufsehen gemacht und mich vollgegessen wie du und alle" [because I could not find the food which I relished. Had I found it, believe me, I would not have made a fuss but would have eaten my fill, like you and everybody else, H: 171].

A summary of the hunger artist's relationship with the general public helps to highlight his attitude to the symbolic order. In the first part of the narrative, set in a mythical past, the hunger artist seems to enjoy great popularity since he attracts large crowds. However, this popularity turns out to be rather ambivalent since it arises from the titillation and horror engendered by all that which is placed outside the boundaries of the symbolic order. Food taboos, corporeal alteration and death, as well as the feminine body are four culturally active categories of abomination.[51] One could argue that, by not eating at all, the hunger artist carries food taboos to the extreme, thus flouting the very logic of prohibitive laws which are erected to keep abjection at bay. Instead of pushing abjection back, the hunger artist is the very embodiment of abjection which puts him on the other side of the social order. The general public guards its identity through the public exhibition of an otherness which is kept in a cage and is therefore exterior to its order. This shows that his fame is not really founded on his art but on his otherness. This otherness is at stake in the second part of the narrative, where the public loses all interest in the hunger artist in favour of the physical beauty and strength of animals whose wildness is attractive. "Man gewöhnte sich an die Sonderbarkeit, in den heutigen Zeiten Aufmerksamkeit für einen Hungerkünstler beanspruchen zu wollen, und mit dieser Gewöhnung war das Urteil über ihn gesprochen." [People got used to the strange notion that in these times attention was called to a hunger artist, and their getting used to this sealed his fate, H: 170]. Clearly, the hunger artist is doomed once the public gets used to him as a "Sonderbarkeit" [an oddity] which signifies a fundamental change of position: although he is now free to perfect his art of fasting, as a mere oddity he is not on the other side of the social order any more.

The public's manifest disinterest in the hunger artist shows that the boundary between society and his art as its other has been effectively eroded. Since he is not publicly "other" any longer the hunger artist tries, in a final move, to reinstate abjection by confessing that his fasting was never an art but always nothing but a necessity since he could not find the food he liked. By disclaiming his art, the hunger artist ultimately internalises and rein-

---

[51] Kristeva, *Powers of Horror*, 93.

states the very abjection which society has denied him. It is not surprising that this internalisation of abjection results in his death.

Ultimately, 'Ein Hungerkünstler' is a story about what happens when the sublimation of abjection fails. The hunger artist acts out abjection on the literal level disguising it as an art, whereas his author, Kafka, is Kristeva's phobic writer "who succeeds in metaphorizing in order to keep from being frightened to death; instead he comes to life again in signs."[52]

Encroaching Women and a "Mother in the Distance"

At this point it is useful to say a few words about Karl's relationships with women. Detlef Kremer suggested in his interpretation of *Der Verschollene* that Kafka varies one narrative pattern throughout the novel which starts with the hero's seduction, resulting in his misdemeanour, trial and, finally, condemnation.[53] According to Kremer, the novel is structured around a dominant father figure and seducing females, ranging from Johanna Brummer, Klara, the head cook to Brunelda. He argues that in Kafka's work the offence of the male protagonist always consists in his inability to resist female seductiveness and temptation.[54] It seems to me that Kremer's analysis fails to examine the precise characterisation of the female figures in the novel or to elaborate on their function which is more complex than Kremer's simplified narrative pattern suggests.

In a study of Kafka's "erotic myth", Rainer Stach has convincingly demonstrated that, while on the level of characterisation, Kafka's female figures reflect a male fantasy according to which womanhood is deficient, on the level of narrative function they increasingly represent a particular type of female power.[55] Stach argues that there is a deep affinity between Kafka's tendency to characterise women as "egoless non-persons" and Otto Weininger's *Geschlecht und Charakter* [Sex and Character, 1903] which I already discussed in chapter one. In this male handbook of misogynist fantasies Weininger essentially claimed that woman is nothing, but a nothingness that is coloured by sexuality. Introducing the notion of "womanhood" as opposed to women, in other words, a typological concept which is immune to empirical observation or refutation, Weininger set out to prove that egoless woman encroaches upon the male ego to destroy and

---

[52] Ibid., 38.
[53] Detlef Kremer, 'Verschollen. Gegenwärtig. Franz Kafkas Roman *Der Verschollene*.' In: *Text & Kritik*, special issue. Franz Kafka VII (1994): 243.
[54] Ibid.
[55] Rainer Stach, *Kafka's erotischer Mythos*, 191.

deindividualise it.[56] With respect to female desire Weininger claimed that all female desire is directed towards mixing and merging, irrespective of women's innate roles as mothers or whores.[57]

Stach has rightly pointed out that, in *Der Verschollene*, Brunelda appears like a grotesque embodiment of Weininger's egoless woman:[58] she is described as monstrously big; her formless massive body makes animal-like noises and is hardly capable of moving:

> sie hatte beim Sitzen die Beine weit auseinandergestellt, um ihrem übermäßig dicken Körper mehr Raum zu verschaffen, nur mit größter Anstrengung, unter vielem Schnaufen und häufigem Ausruhn, konnte sie sich so weit bücken um ihre Strümpfe am obersten Ende zu fassen und ein wenig herunterzuziehn, gänzlich ausziehn konnte sie sie nicht, das mußte Delamarche besorgen. (231)[59]

Consciousness is alien to this regressive being which is entirely driven by bodily needs and somatic impulses that require instant gratification. To emphasise the impact of this drive-controlled being, Kafka heavily draws upon the iconography of the brothel, such as the red lights in her room (261), her red dress (228), heavy breathing (231) and the way in which she moves "mit der dicken roten Zunge zwischen den Lippen hin und her" (288) [her thick red tongue between her lips]. This iconography equips her with a sexuality that within the system of cultural signification represents shameless womanhood and complete otherness to male consciousness. As a massive body entirely subjected to drives, Brunelda resembles a grotesque caricature of Weininger's egoless woman. Clearly, Kafka exaggerates this culturally encoded iconography of female sexuality to such an extent that its origin in the male fantasy factory becomes overt. However, with regard to Karl's response, it is striking that, despite Brunelda's radically externalised sexuality, he is far from being attracted to her or, as Kremer suggests, seduced by her. On the contrary, he registers Brunelda's sexualised body from a position of complete immunity. In clear contrast to Delamarche, who adores Brunelda, Karl remains indifferent to her sexuality. And this is so, as I have argued before, because as an abject character he has no desire for an other, unless it is a mother substitute.

We come across such a substitute in the character of the head cook of Hotel Occidental. Critics ranging from Emrich and Politzer to Robertson,

---

[56] Ibid., 59ff.
[57] For a critique of Weininger see Stach, *Kafkas erotischer Mythos*, 61-66.
[58] Ibid., 68.
[59] [She had spread her legs wide where she sat so as to get more room for her disproportionately fat body; only with the greatest effort gasping and frequently pausing to recover her breath, could she bend far enough forward to catch hold of her stockings at the top and pull them down a little; she could not possibly take off her own clothes; Delamarche would have to do that. A: 197]

have made much of the fact that her name, Grete Mitzelbach, alludes to the protagonist of a pornographic novel by Felix Salten, Josephine Mutzenbacher.[60] This allusion creates an erotic undercurrent which is further reinforced by her addressing Karl as "Kleiner" [little boy] and her gesture of taking Karl by the hand. Despite this subtle colouring her overall function seems to me to be diametrically opposed to Brunelda's: whereas the latter represents nothing but an amorphous physicality and drive energies, the head cook is physically strikingly different. For although she is also "sehr dick" [very big] her face has a "fast zarte Bildung" [an almost tender form][61] and, unlike Brunelda, she moves "mit einer bei ihrer Dicke bewundernswerten Beweglichkeit" (122) [with an agility wonderful in one so fat, A: 109], traits which are further reinforced by the calm and thoughtful manner she displays throughout the chapter. And when Karl notices her for the first time in the overcrowded restaurant, he intuitively decides to place his modest order with her because, as the only woman, she seemed to be "eine Ausnahme vom allgemeinen Lärm und Jagen" (121) [she stood out as an exception in the general hubbub. A: 108].

Within the narrative universe of *Der Verschollene* the head cook is a maternal figure, fulfilling the cultural role of mothering: she feeds Karl, puts him up for the night, and, finally, finds him a job as a lift boy. She is the very embodiment of Kafka's own fantasy of the ideal mother, a fantasy which he projected onto his sister Ottla in a letter to Felice:

> Ottla scheint mir zuzeiten so, wie ich eine Mutter in der Ferne wollte: rein, wahrhaftig, ehrlich, folgerichtig, Demütigkeit und Stolz, Empfänglichkeit und Abgrenzung, Hingabe und Selbständigkeit, Scheu und Mut in untrüglichem Gleichgewicht. (F: 730)[62]

It is precisely this maternal authority which the head cook emanates when Karl is dismissed by the head waiter. Much has been made of the fact that there seems to be an erotic relationship between the head cook and the head waiter which is alluded to twice: first when the head waiter smoothes the head cook's collar standing close to her (190) and at the end of the scene: "Während er sich zum Abschied verbeugte, sah er flüchtig, wie der Oberkellner die Hand der Oberköchin wie im Geheimen umfaßte und mit ihr spielte." (198) [As he bowed himself out, he saw the Head Waiter surreptitiously seizing her hand and fondling it. A: 170] Stach reads this episode in terms of an oedipal catastrophe for Karl, and Robertson sees it as an act of

---

[60] Cf. Emrich, *Franz Kafka*, 242; Politzer, *Franz Kafka*, 227; Robertson, *Kafka*, 71.
[61] Muir's translation reads here: "her face was almost delicately modelled" (A: 109).
[62] [Now and again I think that Ottla would be the kind of mother I should like in the background: pure, truthful, honest, consistent — with humility and pride, receptiveness and reticence, devotion and self-reliance, timidity and courage, in unerring equilibrium. LF: 525].

"implied betrayal".[63] However, I want to suggest that the implied narrator ensures the integrity of the head cook's role as a maternal authority: when she leaves the room she is described as a "große stattliche Frau, die sich in ruhigem Schritt und freier Haltung von ihm entfernte" (196) [the tall stately woman who walked away from him with her light step and easy bearing, A: 169], thus embodying the very characteristics that Kafka invoked in his letter to Felice.

These maternal traits become even more pronounced in direct comparison with the stern paternal attitude as embodied by the Head Waiter: throughout the scene, the head waiter acts as a sophisticated prosecutor who clings to the letter and not the spirit of the law, exposing each and every contradiction in Karl's defence in order to gather evidence against him. In clear contrast to his attitude, the head cook represents a completely different sense of justice, one which is based on intuition and common sense. When she arrives at a conclusion — "Gerechte Dinge haben auch ein besonderes Aussehn und das hat, ich muß es gestehn, deine Sache nicht. Ich darf das sagen und muß es auch sagen, denn ich bin es, die mit dem besten Vorurteil für Dich hergekommen ist" (194)[64] — her judgement is less based on an abstract notion of justice or the letter of the Law than on her personal integrity and good intentions. Moreover, the simplicity of her statement contrasts with the Head Waiter's verbose condemnation of Karl and the brutality of the main porter who has no other interest in the matter than to gratify his own sadistic impulses.

Finally, the head cook sums up by saying that Karl's guilt appears to be irrefutable (194), but she qualifies her judgement once more, considering the possibility of human error: "Vielleicht hast Du bloß unüberlegt gehandelt, vielleicht aber bist Du nicht der, für den ich Dich gehalten habe." (194) [Perhaps you merely acted without thinking, but perhaps too you aren't the boy I thought you were. A: 167] It is precisely this recognition of the possibility of human error on both sides which distinguishes her from all the paternal authorities in the novel. It is this recognition which makes her ultimately rely on her intuition, maintaining her belief that Karl is a decent boy: "Und doch [...] kann ich es mir noch nicht abgewöhnen, Dich für einen im Grunde anständigen Jungen zu halten." (194) [And yet [...] I can't help still thinking of you as a fundamentally decent lad! A: 167] And in stark contrast to his parents as well as uncle Jacob, she does not withdraw her protection from Karl: writing a recommendation on his behalf to Pension Brenner, she advises Therese to pack his suitcase, promises to take care of

---

[63] Cf. Stach, *Kafkas erotischer Mythos*, 109; Robertson, *Kafka*, 71.
[64] [When things are right they look right, and I must confess that your actions don't. I am entitled to say so and I am bound to say so; I am bound to admit it, for it was I who came here with every prepossession in your favour. A: 167].

Karl's money and, finally, announces that she would visit him the following day in order to discuss his future. In addition to her practical caretaking she also promises not to abandon Karl emotionally: "Verlassen werde ich Dich nicht, das sollst Du jedenfalls schon heute wissen." (196) [I won't forsake you, you should know this right now], thus explicitly appealing to an emotional bond between him and her. But Karl is unable to hear and respond to the head cook's maternal care and engagement on his behalf. Whereas Therese, the head cook's quasi-adopted daughter expresses her joy at this positive turn of events, Karl feels abject: he "wußte aber nicht, warum er darüber froh sein sollte, daß man ihn als einen Dieb wegschickte." (196) [Yet could not see why he should be glad because he had been dismissed as a thief. A: 169] Barricading himself behind his feeling of abjection, he cannot accept the care that is offered to him. In the economy of his being, abjection has taken the place of the (m)other.

To summarise briefly: Karl travels through an essentially catastrophic universe which turns into an increasingly threatening space of anxiety where, step by step, he is stripped of the last relics of a past which could equip him with a localisable, albeit fictitious sense of identity: for instance, when Karl goes to Hotel Occidental to buy some food, Delamarche and Robinson break into his suitcase and throw his things around as a result of which his one and only photograph gets lost. To make things worse, Karl loses his jacket and his passport after his dismissal from the Hotel when he has to slip out of his sleeves in order to escape from the terrible grip of the porter who wants to beat him up. This process of eroding Karl's sense of belonging by robbing him of all belongings that are icons of a meaningful past and a home, finally culminates in the fragmentary Oclahama (sic) Theatre episode where Karl enrols as "Negro": stripped of a proper name and a proper self, Karl finally seems to embrace the role of outsider and abject in relation to society.

Kafka's *Der Verschollene* stages a drama of abjection in which the protagonist Karl Roßmann embarks on a labyrinthine journey for which he is truly ill-equipped. His uncle's initial assessment that he has been dispatched to America with irresponsibly insufficient equipment turns out to be correct not only in the material but also in the existential sense of the word. Although Karl arrives like the immigrants in Lewis Hine's photograph with a suitcase, a passport and a photograph, a more detailed inspection of these icons of parental care reveals a structure of feeling based on the abjection of self and other. Karl's universe is made up of pseudo-objects which can never compensate for his want of boundaries between self and other. But this would be the very pre-condition for real object relations. Arising from this lack Karl always ends up rejecting the care that is offered to him simply in order to be. And this is why he has to move on, a blind maze-walker who, at each narrative turn, encounters his own minotaur: this is the abjection of self and other which devours the subject's being and thus stops him from founding a home anywhere. Kafka as an author comes to life through signs; and, paradoxically, that life is an effective exploration of the abject through art.

Roth's Ambivalence: The Logic of Separation in His Writings on Eastern Jewry

Abjection and the Denial of Kinship

> The one by whom the abject exists is [...] a *deject* who places (himself), *separates* (himself), situates (himself), and therefore *strays* instead of getting his bearings, desiring, belonging, or refusing. Situationist in a sense, and not without laughter — since laughing is a way of placing or displacing abjection. Necessarily dichotomous, somewhat Manichaen, he divides, excludes, and without, properly speaking, wishing to know his abjections is not at all unaware of them.[1]

Kristeva's analysis of the role separation plays in the life of an abject character provides an astute commentary on Joseph Roth and his passion for reinventing himself according to changing needs and circumstances. David Bronsen relates, for instance, that when Roth, who was born in the mainly Jewish town of Brody in Eastern Galician, arrived in Vienna in 1914 he dropped his name "Moses" and "went about effacing the Galician Jew in himself and substituting a polished Viennese in his stead".[2] Apparently, he adopted the Viennese accent to perfection and took on the demeanour of an Austrian aristocrat. Hand in hand with this masquerade went the obliteration of his real place of birth: writing to Blanche Gidon, his French translator, Roth claims that he was born "à Svaby, colonie allemande" and then reinvents his genealogy by describing his father as "un père autrichien (employé d'etat, peintre alcoolique [...]".[3] In reality, Nachum Roth was a Galician Jew of Hasidic background and a failed businessman whom Roth had never known.[4] These are just a few examples of Roth's "mythomania"

---

[1] Kristeva, *Powers of Horror*, 8.
[2] David Bronsen, 'The Jew in Search of a Fatherland: The Relationship of Joseph Roth to the Habsburg Monarchy.' In: *Germanic Review* (1979): 56. However, the registration books of the University of Vienna mention Roth's full name, i.e. Joseph Moses Roth. Cf. David Bronsen, *Joseph Roth. Eine Biographie*. Cologne: Kiepenheuer & Witsch, 1974: 128.
[3] Joseph Roth, *Briefe 1911—1939*. Ed. by Hermann Kesten. Cologne and Berlin: Kiepenheuer & Witsch, 1970: 313. Henceforth cited in brackets as (B) with the page number. [An Austrian father, a state employee and alcoholic painter.]
[4] Bronsen, *Joseph Roth*, 40.

— the central concern of Bronsen's impressive biography of Roth — and of much of the ensuing literature on the question of Roth's "true" religious and political allegiance.[5] In the context in which I will place them, these episodes are interesting not so much as "real" biographical data but because they point to the key role which this "narrative of separation" played in the construction of Roth's changing identities. The following chapter argues that the choreography of the various roles Roth adopted throughout his life reflects an ambivalence he felt towards his Eastern European background. Roth's various reinventions of his family background and his need to separate himself from his Jewishness are the starting point for this chapter. I will then go on to examine the ways in which Roth tried to "master" this ambivalence through a celebration of the *shtetl* in *Juden auf Wanderschaft* [Jews on Their Wanderings, 1927] and, to some extent, in his novel *Hiob* [Job, 1930] A detailed analysis of *Hiob* in the final section of this chapter shows, however, that Roth's celebration of the Eastern European Jew ultimately mirrors the crisis of abjection to which it responds. Roth attempted to resolve this crisis through an apotheosis of male identity which is based on the abjection of women. We will also see that this "resolution" is not least influenced by the position a woman occupies within the symbolic order of orthodox Judaism. All the texts discussed are examples of what I have previously referred to as "narratives of separation".

A characteristic example of Roth's auto-narration and the way in which he carefully choreographed his whole being for an audience is a letter he wrote to one of his publishers, Gustav Kiepenheuer, on the occasion of Kiepenheuer's fiftieth birthday. Dated 20 June 1930, this "birthday letter" is quite extraordinary in that it does not highlight Kiepenheuer's achievements, as one might expect, but instead elaborates upon and celebrates Roth's own movements and development. The jubilatory tone of this letter suggests that Roth derived considerable *jouissance* out of fictionalising his origins: this time he claims that he was born in a small village in Wolhynia and that his father was "ein Österreicher vom Schlag der Schlawiner" [an Austrian of the breed of rascals, B: 165]. Such fantasies prepare the ground for the ensuing scripting of a picaresque existence:

> In der Nacht stand ich auf, kleidete mich an und ging aus dem Haus. Ich wanderte drei, vier Tage, schlief in Häusern, deren Lage ich nicht kannte, und mit Frauen, deren Angesicht ich nicht sah und zu sehen neugierig war. Ich briet Kartoffeln auf sommerlichen Wiesen und auf harten herbstlichen Äckern. Ich pflückte Erdbeeren in

---

[5] A recent example of this debate concerning Roth's oscillating attitude to both Catholicism and his Jewishness is Hans Otto Horch's essay: '"Im Grunde ist er sehr jüdisch geblieben": Zum Verhältnis von 'Katholizismus' und Judentum bei Joseph Roth.' In: Hans Otto Horch and Itta Shedlytzky (Eds.), *Deutsch-jüdische Exil- und Emigrationsliteratur im 20. Jahrhundert*. Tübingen: Niemeyer, 1993: 205-235.

Wäldern, trieb mich mit viel halbwüchsigem Gesindel herum und wurde manchmal verprügelt, gewissermaßen irrtümlich. (B: 166)[6]

Roth's many auto-narratives never add up to a consistent story of his origin. Instead they indicate a pattern of exclusion whose precariousness hints at something unassimilable and unsaid. This structure threatens to undermine Roth's jubilatory rebirth through auto-narration. This is why Roth can never really afford to stop inventing himself: his many disguises suggest that he had to reaffirm his boundaries precisely because they were constantly being invaded by something intolerable that had to be excluded from his order of meaning. A clear manifestation of this structure is the omission of his real birthplace as well as his dropping of the name "Moses", two significant gaps, which, like the dropped stitches from a knitting needle, are ironically more conspicuous than the overt chain of signifiers. "Ejected beyond the scope of the possible, the tolerable, the thinkable"[7] these dropped signifiers suggest that he was caught up in a crisis of abjection that has — as we have seen in the previous chapter — its origin in our personal archaeology[8] as well as the precariousness of the symbolic order. Or perhaps it would be more appropriate to say that Roth, the Austrian-Jewish writer from Galicia, circumvented abjection by constantly reinventing himself through his writing. This would explain why in his auto-narratives a lot of

---

[6] [In the night I got up, dressed and left the house. I wandered about for three or four days, slept in houses whose location I did not know, and with women whose faces I did not see nor wanted to see. I fried potatoes on summery meadows and on autumnal fields. I picked strawberries in woods, hung about with adolescent riffraff and sometimes I was beaten up, sort of by mistake.] Only towards the very end of his letter does Roth address Kiepenheuer as his subject. Pointing out their overt temperamental differences Roth appeals to a secret sense of kinship, which, in his view, is founded upon a shared belief in his writing: "Er verliert an meinen Büchern. Ich auch. Er glaubt an mich. Ich auch. Er wartet auf meinen Erfolg. Ich auch. Ihm ist die Nachwelt sicher. Mir auch." [He loses money on my books. Me too. He believes in me. So do I. He is waiting for my success. So am I. He can rely on posthumous fame. So can I. B: 168]. This final, witty twist allows him once more to turn his life into a piece of writing.
[7] Kristeva, *Powers of Horror*, 1.
[8] It should be clear that I do not wish to prioritise Roth's life over his work, thus falling into the trap of all biographical readings which falsely suggest an authenticity and identity of the self outside the realm of language. It is easy to show that such readings always fail to reflect on the fundamental linguistic nature of both the symbolic order and the identities that are constructed therein as well as on the methodological difficulty of how to access a non-linguistic authentic self other than through language. These objections have become a commonplace in contemporary literary discourse. However, it seems to me to be equally naive to dismiss all autobiography in the light of Barthes's 'Death of the Author' as irrelevant or authoritarian in nature. Since the late eighteenth century and the publication of Rousseau's *Confessiones* and Goethe's *Dichtung und Wahrheit* it has been part of the autobiographical tradition to reflect on the linguistic and the fictitious nature of identity. Goethe's title *Dichtung und Wahrheit* bears witness to the inseparable interdependence of identity and fiction.

jouissance seems to directly stem from the very instability of his existence. Roth expressed this himself in a letter to Stefan Zweig on 27 February 1929:

> Mich zu fixieren, ist unmöglich. Ich habe keinen stabilen litterarischen [sic] 'Charakter'. Aber ich bin auch sonst nicht stabil. Seit meinem achtzehnten Lebensjahr habe ich in keiner Privatwohnung gelebt, höchstens eine Woche als Gast bei Freunden. Alles was ich besitze sind 3 Koffer. Und das erscheint mir gar nicht merkwürdig. Sondern merkwürdig und sogar 'romantisch' kommt mir ein Haus vor, mit Bildern und so weiter. (B: 145)[9]

This is, of course, only one metaphor that accompanies Roth's life — but as an image it points to Roth's sense of exclusion. The poetic correlative of this are the three suitcases symbolising the absence of any more permanent property in Roth's life. And, as with Kafka, the suitcase is also evocative of the complex cultural baggage which Roth, the Galician Jew, carried around with him from hotel to hotel. It is a well-known aspect of Roth's mythmaking biography that he abandoned the idea of a permanent and stable home long before his emigration years and, from the end of the First World War onwards, chose instead to live in hotels,[10] mainly in Paris, Nice and Marseille, going on hectic trips to Frankfurt, Vienna, Salzburg, Berlin, Odessa and Moscow (to name only a few of his European destinations of the 1920s). It seems as if Roth deliberately made himself into a migrant writer who drew considerable *jouissance* out of his straying. This is reflected in the opening lines of his afore-mentioned letter to Gustav Kiepenheuer in which Roth portrays himself as fundamentally exiled from any sense of belonging:

> Ich habe viele Meilen zurücklegen müssen. Zwischen dem Ort, in dem ich geboren bin und den Städten, Dörfern, durch die ich in den letzten zehn Jahren komme, um in ihnen zu verweilen, und in denen ich nur verweile, um sie wieder zu verlassen, liegt mein Leben, eher nach räumlichen Maßen meßbar als nach zeitlichen. Die zurückgelegten Straßen sind meine zurückgelegten Jahre. Nirgends, in keinem Kirchenbuch und in keinem Gemeindekataster wurde der Tag meiner Geburt eingetragen, mein Name

---

[9] [It is impossible to pin me down. I have no stable literary 'character'. But I am not stable in any other sense either. Since my eighteenth birthday I have not lived in a private apartment, unless as a guest for a week with friends. All I own is three suitcases. And I do not find that strange at all. But what I do find strange and even 'romantic' is a house, with pictures on the wall and so on.]

[10] The only exception to this was a brief period that he spent with his wife Friedl in an apartment in Berlin-Schöneberg in 1922. Gustav Kiepenheuer later described Roth's only attempt to establish something like a home in the following way: "Für kurze Zeit hatte er einmal eine Wohnung gemietet, und ich sah ihn in dem düstern, riesigen Berliner Zimmer, die Hände in den Manteltaschen, wie in einem Wartesaal auf- und abgehen, als lauere er auf die Abfahrtszeiten seines Zuges." Quoted in Bronsen, *Joseph Roth*, 222. [For a short time he had rented an apartment, and I saw him in this huge, dark room in Berlin, his hands buried in the pockets of his coat, as if he was walking up and down a waiting room, as if waiting for the departure times of his train.]

vermerkt. Ich habe keine Heimat, wenn ich von der Tatsache absehe, daß ich in mir selbst zu Hause bin und mich bei mir heimisch fühle. (B: 165)[11]

This passage severs the traditional link between a sense of belonging to a (birth)place or a home and identity. Villages, cities and places in general are not seen as stable localities which help ground the self in an identifiable environment. On the contrary, they are empty topographical markers which are only significant in terms of the distance they indicate. A birthplace and a home usually demarcate origin and identity. For Roth they are only structurally relevant as the precondition of a separation that defines him and his male protagonists as straying. Examples are Gabriel Dan in *Hotel Savoy*, Franz Tunda in *Die Flucht ohne Ende* [Flight without End] or Leutnant Trotta in *Radetzkymarsch*. In his own words he lived "als eine phantastische Erfindung" [as a fantastic invention, B: 136]. We can see why Roth may have stage-managed and orchestrated the many reinventions of his origins: it seems to have allowed him to repeat the original act of separation between self and (m)other and shift his sense of identity from the unanswerable "who am I?" to the "where am I?", thus redefining his identity in a situationist manner. Kristeva's analysis of the space the abject occupies is extremely helpful in this context:

> For the space that engrosses the deject, the excluded, is never *one*, nor *homogeneous*, nor *totalizable*, but essentially divisible, foldable and catastrophic. A deviser of territories, languages, works, the *deject* never stops demarcating his universe whose fluid confines — for they are constituted of a non-object, the abject — constantly questions his solidity and impel him to start afresh. A tireless builder, the deject is in short a *stray*.[12]

---

[11] [I have had to cover a lot of mileage. Between my birthplace and those towns and villages through which I have passed over the past ten years and briefly stayed there, and in which I only stayed to leave again, lies my entire life, more easily measurable in terms of space rather than time. Nowhere, in no church or local register was my birthday noted or my name jotted down. I have no home, apart from the fact that I am at home within myself and that I feel at home with myself.]

[12] Kristeva, *Powers of Horror*, 8. And this is also one of the reasons why for many of Roth's protagonists "Heimat" is a metaphor of the ultimate loss, death: Henry Bloomfield, a successful businessman in *Hotel Savoy* explains, for instance, that he returns specifically every year from America to visit his father's grave in Galicia: "'Ich komme jedes Jahr hierher [...] meinen Vater besuchen. Und auch die Stadt kann ich nicht vergessen. Ich bin ein Ostjude, und wir haben überall dort unsere Heimat, wo wir unsere Toten haben. Wenn mein Vater in Amerika gestorben wäre, ich könnte ganz in Amerika zu Hause sein. Mein Sohn wird ein ganzer Amerikaner sein, denn ich werde dort begraben werden." Joseph Roth (1924), *Hotel Savoy*. In: Fritz Hackert (Ed.), *Joseph Roth*, 6 vols., Cologne: Kiepenheuer & Witsch, 1989, vol. 4: 209. [I come here every year [...] visiting my father. And I cannot forget the town either. I am an Eastern Jew, and our home is where our dead are. If my father had died in America I could be completely at home in America. My son will be a perfect American, for I will be buried there.]

Roth is a deviser of languages and territories who never stops demarcating the fluid confines of his identity. Writing from Odessa to Bernard von Brentano in 1927, he declares, "daß ich ein Europäer bin, ein Mittelmeer-Mensch, wenn Sie wollen, ein Römer und ein Katholik" [that I am a European, a Mediterranean man, if you wish, a Roman and a Catholic, B: 95], apparently anchoring his sense of being in the South and, ideologically, in a principle which is akin to Heinrich Heine's sensual "Hellenentum" [Hellenic principle]. However, with Roth any identification has at best temporary validity: only five days later, Roth was to describe himself in a letter to Benno Reifenberg as "ein Franzose aus dem Osten, ein Humanist, ein Rationalist mit Religion, ein Katholik mit jüdischem Gehirn, ein wirklicher Revolutionär" [a Frenchman from the East, a humanist, a rationalist with religion, a Catholic with a Jewish brain, a real revolutionary, B: 98)]. Significantly, Roth presents himself here not as a Galician Jew living in France but as a *Frenchman* from the *East*: His strong identification with his new French identity shows that, although Roth acknowledged his Eastern Jewish origins, he did so only in terms of a peripheral ideological marker which he considered secondary to the Western cultural environment. In other words the formula "Franzose aus dem Osten" does not simply reflect a geographical position in the real world but, more importantly, it reproduces a system of representation and an ideological vision which marks the West as culturally and politically superior to the East.[13] By inscribing himself into an ideologically charged and hierarchically structured division between West and East,[14] the centre and the periphery, Roth implicitly participates in the Eurocentric discourse which stigmatised both Orientals and Eastern Jews as inferior.[15]

---

[13] This system of representation is the subject of Edward Said's widely discussed study *Orientalism*. Said defines orientalism as "a form of thought for dealing with the foreign" and "a *distribution* of geopolitical awareness into aesthetic, scholarly, economic, sociological, historical, and philological texts; it is an *elaboration* not only of a basic geographical distinction (the world is made up of two unequal halves, Orient and Occident) but also of a whole series of 'interests' which [...] it not only creates but also maintains." Edward Said, *Orientalism*, 46 and 12.

[14] For a discussion of East and West as signifiers of difference see Itta Shedletzky, 'Ost und West in der deutsch-jüdischen Literatur von Heinrich Heine bis Joseph Roth.' In: Mark H. Gelber, Hans Otto Horch et. al. (Eds.) *Von Franzos bis Canetti. Jüdische Autoren aus Österreich. Neue Studien*. Tübingen: Niemeyer, 1996: 189-200.

[15] In a recent article Ritchie Robertson has shown how in the struggle to define Jewish identity the term "Oriental" became a contested marker of difference. While anti-Semites used it to denounce Jews of Eastern Europe as unassimilable and alien, the expression gained positive connotations in the Zionist discourse. Martin Buber, for instance, redefined the term "Oriental" with reference to the Old Testament and described the Jews as a society of settled farmers. Cf. Robertson, '"Urheimat Asien" — The Reorientation of German and Austrian Jews.' In: *German Life and Letters* 49 (1996): 182-192.

The World of the *Shtetl*

At first sight this analysis seems to clash with Roth's eloquent praise of the Eastern *shtetl* in *Juden auf Wanderschaft,* a book which is an example of ghetto writing. This genre goes back to the nineteenth century when German-Jewish writers in the realist tradition — most prominent are Leopold Kompert and Karl Emil Franzos — began to publish stories from the ghetto. In collections such as Kompert's *Aus dem Ghetto* [From the Ghetto, 1848] and *Neue Geschichten aus dem Ghetto* [New Stories from the Ghetto, 1860] or Franzos's *Die Juden von Barnow* [The Jews of Barnow, 1877] and *Aus Halb-Asien* [From Half-Asia, 1876ff.] the Eastern European ghetto was portrayed as both backward and idyllic, unenlightened and loveable. The "typical" ghetto story revolved around stock characters such as the "Wunderrabbi", the "Schnorrer", "Fehlermacher" and "Schadchen" and thus reinforced stereotypes of the ghetto as a closed system based on rituals of difference.[16] These stories also tried to communicate the ordinariness of daily concerns and life in the ghetto, often in a humorous tone. Humour was favoured as an appealing code of communication because it helped to popularise Jewish themes for both the acculturated Jewish and the gentile readership.[17] While the portrayal of ghetto life in terms of quaintness and a loveable naiveté may have trivialised the social problems and pressures that traditional Jewry was faced with both from within and without, the ghetto story continued to articulate respect for the age-old Jewish ability to survive against all odds. The ghetto story thus aimed at communicating a Jewish identity to both a gentile and an acculturated Jewish readership.

A second type of ghetto story was inspired by the ambitions of Haskala, the Jewish Enlightenment movement. Writers such as Leo Herzberg-Fränkel, Nathan Samuely and Karl Emil Franzos targeted messianic Hasidism and old orthodoxy in their stories as unenlightened and backward. One better-known example of this is Karl Emil Franzos novel *Der Pojaz. Eine Geschichte aus dem Osten* [The Pojaz. A Story from the East, 1905] in which

---

[16] The "Wunderrabbi" is a rabbi who can work miracles, the "Schnorrer" is the beggar of the *shtetl*, the "Fehlermacher" is a quack who is paid for breaking a limb or causing a medical problem that allows Jewish males to escape from conscription into the army. The "Schadchen" is the Jewish match-maker.

[17] Cf. Florian Krobb's analysis of the "Sippurim"-collection, a nineteenth century collection of Jewish stories, legends and myths, published in Prague by the leading Jewish publisher Wolf Pascheles. Florian Krobb, '"Dina, was sagst du zu dem zuckrigen Gott?" Salomon Kohn und die Prager deutsch-jüdische Literatur des 19. Jahrhunderts.' In: Mark H. Gelber, Hans Otto Horch et al. (Eds.), *Von Franzos zu Canetti,* 19. On the tradition of humour in ghetto writing see Anne Fuchs, 'Edgar Hilsenrath's Poetics of Insignificance and the Tradition of Humour in German-Jewish Ghetto Writing'. In: Anne Fuchs and Florian Krobb (Eds.), *Ghetto Writing. Traditional and Eastern Jewry in German-Jewish Literature from Heine to Hilsenrath.* Columbia: Camden House, 1999: 195-209.

the protagonist, Sender Glatteis, cannot develop fully because of the repressive institutions of the *shtetl*. Although Franzos overtly criticises the backwardness of unenlightened Hasidism, there is a strong element of "Verklärung" [idealisation] in terms of style and characterisation which is in line with the nostalgic tradition of ghetto writing.[18]

In a sense *Juden auf Wanderschaft* represents the concluding chapter of this tradition: Roth attacks here Western assimilation and migration. The book opens on an extremely polemical note:

> Dieses Buch verzichtet auf den Beifall und die Zustimmung, aber auch auf den Widerspruch und sogar die Kritik derjenigen, welche die Ostjuden mißachten, verachten, hassen und verfolgen. Es wendet sich nicht an jene Westeuropäer, die aus der Tatsache, daß sie bei Lift und Wasserklosett aufgewachsen sind, das Recht ableiten, über rumänische Läuse, galizische Wanzen, russische Flöhe schlechte Witze vorzubringen. Dieses Buch verzichtet auch auf die 'objektiven' Leser, die mit einem billigen und sauren Wohlwollen von den schwanken Türmen westlicher Zivilisation auf den nahen Osten hinabschielen und auf seine Bewohner; aus purer Humanität die mangelhafte Kanalisation bedauern und aus Furcht vor Ansteckung arme Emigranten in Baracken einsperren, wo die Lösung eines sozialen Problems dem Massentod überlassen bleibt. Dieses Buch will nicht von jenen gelesen werden, die ihre eigenen, durch einen Zufall der Baracke entronnenen Väter oder Urväter verleugnen. (W2: 827)[19]

Roth's eloquent diatribe against assimilation and the evils of Western migration now seems to reject the Eurocentric hierarchy of values according to which the West is enlightened, clean and morally superior to the Eastern ghetto, which represents closure, darkness, illness and moral inferiority. Roth explicitly targets this biased system of representation in the opening

---

[18] While nineteenth century ghetto writers wrote about the ghetto in German, a new generation of ghetto writers emerged who wanted to represent the authentic character of ghetto life through Yiddish. Arthur Landsberger's *Das Volk des Ghetto* [The People of the Ghetto, 1916] was a collection of Yiddish, Russian and Polish stories from the ghetto translated into German. On the German ghetto story cf. Gabriele von Glasenapp, *Aus der Judengasse*. Tübingen: Niemeyer, 1996; Anne Fuchs and Florian Krobb (Eds.), *Ghetto Writing*. A general introduction to the ghetto story is provided by Jost Hermand (Ed.) in *Geschichten aus dem Ghetto*. Munich: Athenäum, 1987: 7-21.

[19] Joseph Roth (1927), *Juden auf Wanderschaft*. In: Joseph Roth, *Werke*. Ed. by Fritz Hackert, 6 vols. Cologne: Kiepenheuer & Witsch, 1990, vol 2: 827. Henceforth cited from this edition with volume and page number in brackets. [This book dispenses with the applause and approval but also with the opposition and criticism of those who ignore, despise, hate and persecute the Eastern Jews. It is not addressed to those Western Europeans who derive from the fact that they grew up with lifts and flushing toilets a right to make bad jokes about Romanian lice, Galician bugs, Russian fleas. This book dispenses also with the 'objective' readers, who, with their cheap and sour benevolence, look down from their swaying towers of Western civilisation on the East nearby and on its inhabitants; who, out of pure humanity, regret the lack of drains and who, out of their fear of infectious diseases, incarcerate poor emigrants in barracks where a social problem is solved by death in vast numbers. This book does not want to be read by those who deny their own fathers and forefathers who, by mere chance, escaped the barracks.]

essay of *Juden auf Wanderschaft*, 'Ostjuden im Westen'. Here he attacks the binary contrast of West and East by accentuating the precariousness of such boundaries with reference to the geopolitical changes experienced by Poland and Prussia:

> Wer ist 'Westjude'? [...] Ist ein Jude aus Breslau, das lange Zeit Wroclaw hieß und eine polnische Stadt war, mehr Westjude als einer aus Krakau, das heute noch polnisch ist? Ist derjenige schon Westjude, dessen Vater sich nicht mehr erinnern kann, wie es in Posen oder in Lemberg aussieht? Fast alle Juden waren einmal Westjuden, ehe sie nach Polen und Rußland kamen. Und alle Juden waren einmal 'Ostjuden', ehe ein Teil von ihnen westjüdisch wurde. (W2: 837)[20]

Roth's analysis erodes the notion of a fixed and permanent border separating sameness and difference, a notion which structures our social order. As persuasive as Roth's critique may be, he still remained caught up in the very form of thought and in the system of representation which he so eloquently set out to discredit in his essays.[21] In my view *Juden auf Wanderschaft* did not really resolve Roth's ambivalence about his own Eastern European background. The essay 'Das jüdische Städtchen' does celebrate the *shtetl* as a space of moral and human integrity, but as this space is essentially epic in character, this resolution seems to me to operate mainly on the level of fantasy. For this reason I disagree with Stefan H. Kaszynski's recent assessment according to which Roth analysed Eastern European Jewry along a historical, political, geographical and societal axis.[22] It is certainly correct that Roth describes sociopolitical changes such as emigration, the position of Eastern Jews in Western ghettos and the genesis of Zionism as a reaction to Western nationalism. But these developments are never seen to constitute part of a living and changing culture but are exclusively presented in terms of a threat or an evil which erodes the true spirit of Eastern European Jewry. This can be demonstrated with reference to Roth's analysis of the migration movements from East to West in the first essay 'Ostjuden im Westen'. At

---

[20] [Who is a 'Western Jew?' [...] Is a Jew from Breslau, which, for a long time, was called Wroclaw and Polish, more a Western Jew than one from Krakau which is still Polish today? Is he already a Western Jew whose father cannot remember what Posen and Lemberg look like? Nearly all Jews were at one time Western Jews before they came to Poland and Russia. And all Jews were at one time 'Eastern Jews' before some of them became Western Jewish.]

[21] In a letter to Paula Grübel, written during the First World War, Roth denounced the *shtetl* precisely along the lines of the above-mentioned axis: "Ich befinde mich gegenwärtig in einem ostgalizischen Augiasstall, einem ganz kleinen Städtchen. Im grauen Dreck sieht man bloß ein paar Judengeschäfte. Alles schwimmt, wenn es regnet, alles stinkt, wenn die Sonne scheint." (B 35) [At the moment I am in an Eastern Galician Augias-stable, a small town. All you can see in the grey dirt is a few Jewish shops. Everything is drowned in water when it rains, everything stinks when the sun shines.]

[22] Stefan H. Kaszynski, 'Der jüdische Anteil an der Literatur in und über Galizien.' In: Mark H. Gelber, Hans Otto Horch et al. (Eds.), *Von Franzos bis Canetti*. Niemeyer, 1996: 136f.

the beginning of his essay, Roth focuses on a variety of factors which motivate emigration, namely pogroms and the absence of legal protection both of which have had a formative influence on the collective psyche of Galician Jewry:

> Der Ostjude fürchtet sich in fremden Dörfern und Wäldern. Er ist teils freiwillig, teils gezwungen ein Abgesonderter. Er hat nur Pflichten und keine Rechte, außer denen auf dem bekannten Papier, das nichts verbürgt. Aus Zeitungen, Büchern und von optimistischen Emigranten hört er, daß der Westen ein Paradies sei. In Westeuropa gibt es einen gesetzlichen Schutz vor Pogromen. Juden werden in Westeuropa Minister und sogar Vizekönige. [...] Der große Reichtum der Rothschilds wird im Osten märchenhaft übertrieben. (W2: 829)[23]

This highly empathetic analysis evokes how, as a result of pogroms and exclusion from legal protection, a collective psyche is formed which associates the East with the experience of fear and abjection and projects all hope on a utopian and fictionalised West. However, in Roth's view real migration to the West results in a loss of "true" Jewish identity because of gradual assimilation:

> Sie gaben sich auf, indem sie Händler im Westen wurden.
> Sie gaben sich auf. Sie verloren sich. Ihre traurige Schönheit fiel von ihnen ab, und eine staubgraue Schicht von Gram ohne Sinn und niedrigem Kummer ohne Tragik blieb auf ihren gekrümmten Rücken. Die Verachtung blieb an ihnen kleben — früher hatten sie nur Steinwürfe erreicht. Sie schlossen Kompromisse. Sie veränderten ihre Tracht, ihre Bärte, ihr Kopfhaar, ihren Gottesdienst, ihren Sabbat, ihren Haushalt. (W2: 833-34)[24]

This passage is an interesting one not so much because Roth identifies assimilation as the major threat to the identity of traditional and Eastern Jewry, but because of his idealisation of poverty in the *shtetl*: while the poor Galician Jew's life in the East is for Roth still meaningful in terms of "tragedy", a "sad beauty" and stoic heroism, the emigrant's poverty turns into drab mundaneness in the West. These equations reflect a system of meaning in which East and West do not designate geographical and socio-

---

[23] [The Eastern Jew feels afraid in unknown villages and forests. He lives partly by choice, partly perforce the life of an outsider. He has no rights, only plights, with the exception of the well-known piece of paper which does not guarantee anything. He learns from newspapers, books and optimistic emigrants that the West is a paradise. In Western Europe he is legally protected from pogroms. Jews become ministers and even vice-kings in Western Europe. The enormous wealth of the Rothschilds' is fabulously exaggerated in the East.]

[24] [They gave themselves up by becoming businessmen in the West. They gave themselves up. They lost themselves. Their sad beauty fell from them, and a dusty and grey layer of pain without sense and sorrow without tragedy stuck to their bent backs. The experience of contempt stuck onto them — before only a few stones had reached them. They changed their outfits, their beards, hair, their worship, their Sabbath, their housekeeping.]

political areas but moral territories. The passage contrasts the integrity of the Eastern Jew with the loss of identity and integrity in the West. Ultimately, Roth poses a moral choice between East and West in aesthetic categories: the East as the space of integrity is also a space of poetry while the West as the space of assimilation is presented as a prosaic space without any symbolic or metaphorical potential. And this explains why the passage glosses over the anti-Semitic pogroms that, from the mid-nineteenth century, took place ever more frequently in Eastern Europe. Here they are reduced to "ein paar Steinwürfe" [a few stones thrown].

Roth's *shtetl* is a poetic metaphor at a remove from reality. His system of meaning catapults the "true spirit" of Eastern European Jewry outside the realm of history into a purified epic land. This is emphatic in the central essay 'Das Jüdische Städtchen' where Roth evokes the *shtetl* in epic terms: he depicts a world whose meaningfulness is based upon its imperviousness to history and social change; furthermore he portrays the community of the *shtetl* as a closed system in which the function, position and value of one member (character/type) is premised upon the function, position and value of all remaining members. And finally Roth's *shtetl* shares with the epic world its orientation towards God as the source of all meaning, his *shtetl* is an essentially timeless system in which all acts are assessed with reference to messianic hope:

> Die Händler und die andern im Leben stehenden Juden beten sehr schnell und haben noch hie und da Zeit, Neuigkeiten zu besprechen und die Politik der großen Welt und die Politik der kleinen. Sie rauchen Zigaretten und schlechten Pfeifentabak im Bethaus. Sie benehmen sich wie in einem Kasino. Sie sind bei Gott nicht seltene Gäste, sondern zu Hause. Sie statten ihm nicht einen Staatsbesuch ab, sondern versammeln sich täglich dreimal an seinen reichen, armen, heiligen Tischen. Im Gebet empören sie sich gegen ihn, schreien zum Himmel, klagen über seine Strenge und führen bei Gott Prozeß gegen Gott, um dann einzugestehen, daß sie gesündigt haben, daß alle Strafen gerecht waren und daß sie besser sein wollen. (W2: 840-41)[25]

Ultimately, the narrator in *Juden auf Wanderschaft* speaks from a position of sentimental reverie, a position of exteriority[26] which allows him to look

---

[25] [The traders and the other worldly Jews pray very quickly, occasionally they have a little time to exchange news and to discuss the politics of the big and the small worlds. They smoke cigarettes and bad tobacco in the prayer-house. They behave as if they were in a casino. They are not God's rare guests but are at home with him. They do not pay him an official visit, but assemble three times per day at his rich, poor, holy tables. In their prayers, they are angry with him, they shout at heaven, complain about his severity and, with God, they are engaged in proceedings against God, until, finally, they admit that they have sinned, that all his punishments are justified and that they want to be better people.]

[26] Edward Said's observation that "Orientalism is premised upon exteriority, that is, on the fact that the Orientalist, poet or scholar, makes the Orient speak, describes the Orient, renders its mysteries plain for and to the West" is applicable to the binary division between

back on the *shtetl* as a mysterious world saturated with meaning. By ignoring the socio-historical reality in 'Das jüdische Städtchen' and idealising the many hardships that went with life in the ghetto, Roth also masked the ambivalence that he continued to feel towards his own Eastern Jewish background.[27]

While Roth's epic idealisation is a rather late example of German ghetto writing, others engaged in a social discourse and addressed the poor social conditions of Eastern European Jewry. A prominent example of a more socio-critical approach is the work of Bertha Pappenheim (generally known as Freud's Anna O.) who dedicated her life to fighting the poor social conditions in the *shtetl* and, in particular, of Jewish girls and women. Pappenheim attacks the narrow-mindedness of Hasidim and of the Jewish elementary school, the 'cheder' in the following terms:

> In engen, nie gelüfteten Räumen, zusammengedrängt wie die Schafe in einem Pferch, sitzen, stehen oder kauern die Kinder, 60, 80, 100 an der Zahl, auf, oder zwischen Tischen und Bänken. Ein Mann, der zu sonst nichts taugt ist entweder als Unternehmer oder als Beamter der Gemeinden der Lehrer 'Melamed'. Da er mit seinen Schülern bei einer Methode, nach der er mit jedem einzelnen Kinde besonders pauken oder 'knellen' muß, unmöglich fertig werden kann, so hat er junge Unterlehrer 'Belfer — Behelfer', Bürschchen von 17 bis 19 Jahren, die mit ihm in der Anwendung des Stockes oder des Kantuk, einer Peitsche mit Lederriemen, wetteifern [...].[28]

Her critique of Hasidism as the dominant religious movement in Galicia is equally scathing:

> Von morgens bis abends, von Beginn des keimenden Lebens bis zum erlischenden Atemzuge ist das menschliche Leben von Vorschriften begleitet. Was einst deren Zweck war, in allen Lebensäußerungen Gott zu suchen und zu finden, der Seele Aufschwung zu geben vom Alltäglichen ins Unendliche, — hängt heute wie ein Bleigewicht an dem Alltäglichen und verflacht und versumpft und erdrückt die Menschen. Nur daraus ist es erklärlich, daß in und neben dieser orthodoxen

---

East and West in Roth's *Juden auf Wanderschaft*. Cf. Edward Said, *Orientalism*. Harmondsworth: Penguin, 1991: 21.

[27] A good analysis of the social conditions of Galician Jewry and the impact of the migration movements from Galicia to Vienna can be found in Robert Wistrich, *The Jews of Vienna in the Age of Franz Joseph*, 40ff. By 1914 Galician Jewry constituted one quarter of Viennese Jewry, a rise which was due to "a combination of factors — the economic backwardness of the region, endemic poverty, malnutrition, population pressures, Polish nationalism, and anti-Semitism." Ibid., 49.

[28] Cf. Bertha Pappenheim, *Die Anna O. Sisyphus: Gegen den Mädchenhandel — Galizien*. Ed. by Helga Heubach. Freiburg: Kore, 1992: 50. [In narrow, airless rooms, crammed together like sheep in a pen, some 60, 80, 100 children sit, stand or cower on or between the tables and benches. A man who is good for nothing else is the community's teacher, the 'melamed'. Since he cannot possibly control his pupils with a method, according to which he has to cram with each individual child, he employs young sub-teachers, 'Belfer — helpers', boys aged between 17 and 19 years, who compete in the application of the cane or the 'Kantuk', a whip with a leather strap.]

Lebensweise Zustände tiefster sittlicher Verkommenheit unter den galizischen Juden herrschen können.²⁹

While this still seems to be an example of critical ghetto writing in the tradition of Karl Emil Franzos, Pappenheim radicalised her critique considerably by focusing on the poor educational and social conditions of Jewish girls and women who — according to her analysis — were not only left without any worthy education but who suffered from social marginalisation. Her essay *Zur Lage der jüdischen Bevölkerung in Galizien. Reiseeindrücke und Vorschläge zur Verbesserung der Verhältnisse* [On the Condition of the Jewish Population in Galicia. Impressions of a Journey and Suggestions how to Improve the Conditions, 1904] was groundbreaking in that it addressed prostitution and the establishment of Jewish girls as commodities in the prostitution trade as issues that demanded social intervention.³⁰ Pappenheim explained, for instance, the occurrence of "secret" prostitution not only among the impoverished classes but also among orthodox girls and women from so-called better families, with reference to the religious, social and intellectual marginalisation of women within Judaism:

> Da seit Jahrtausenden unter den Juden die Frau nur als Geschlechtswesen bewertet, auf gegenseitige Zuneigung aber und geistige Anteilnahme am Leben des Mannes kein Gewicht gelegt worden ist, so war für die Hingabe der Frau weder ein ehrlich sinnlicher noch ein feingeistiger Reiz vorhanden. Eine gewisse Abstumpfung der jüdischen Frauen in geschlechtlichen Dingen hat infolgedessen Platz gegriffen.
> Hierzu tritt, daß durch die Unbildung der Frauen ihrem Geiste und ihren oft

---

²⁹ Bertha Pappenheim, *Die Anna O. Sisyphus*, 79. [From morning till night time, from the beginning of developing life to one's dying breath human life is accompanied by laws. While it used to be their aim to help one search and find God in all life, to lift one's soul from everyday life into eternity, they now hang heavy as leaden weights upon everyday life, making people shallow, pulling them down and engulfing them. Only this explains that in the midst and next to the orthodox way of life, conditions of utter moral deprivation can exist amongst Galician Jews.]

³⁰ Pappenheim, the founder of the 'Jüdischer Frauenbund', circulated information leaflets at railway stations warning travelling Jewish girls of the danger of trusting strangers. Many of Pappenheim's observations have been supported by recent studies. Cf. John Cooper's article on 'Jewish Sexual Attitudes in Eastern Europe 1850-1920'. In: Jonathan Magonet (Ed.), *Jewish Explorations of Sexuality*. Oxford: Berghahn, 1995: 181-189. Cooper also mentions the vulnerability of orthodox girls: "In 1913 a Jewish gang which specialised in procuring girls, mostly servants and women from dressmaking establishments, for brothels at Vilna, Minsk and Riga were arrested, and from this we can surmise the background of the girls who were recruited for these houses. At the same time, orthodox girls were vulnerable to the wiles of pimps, partly because Jewish education for girls was often sketchy, and partly because their elementary sexual knowledge was so deficient. As we have seen, many of these girls remained religious or at least traditional, even when they went overseas to the bawdy houses of Argentina and Brazil." John Cooper, 'Jewish Sexual Attitudes', 187.

lebhaften Empfindungen jede gesunde Nahrung abgeschnitten ist, so daß diesen außerhalb des körperlichen Ich kein Spielraum gegeben wird.[31]

Her scathing socio-historical critique of the living conditions of Jewish women in the *shtetl* thus offers a stark contrast to Roth's celebration of the *shtetl* as a space of moral integrity. This is not to say that Pappenheim's social critique should be the yardstick for Roth's *Juden auf Wanderschaft* — however, the comparison does accentuate Roth's distance from the ghetto as a lived reality. His essay 'Das jüdische Städtchen' gives — in the words of Claudio Magris — expression to his longing for a "Gemeinschaft ganz außerhalb der Geschichte"[32] [community completely outside history].

Roth's celebration of *shtetl* culture seems to remain strangely at odds with his otherwise many attempts to disguise his place of birth and to reinvent his parental line. From a psychological viewpoint, this apparent contradiction accentuates once more the ambivalence which characterises the crisis of abjection which is the central concern of this study. One should remember that abjection always entails both the breaking away from and the violent mourning for the lost *chora*, which in Kristeva's own words is "receptacle, unnameable, improbable, hybrid, anterior to naming, to the one, to the father, and consequently maternally connoted."[33] The *chora* as the locus in which mother and child enjoy an unmediated relationship is, of course, the space of the *semiotic*, where pre-oedipal drives circulate freely prior to being organised into oppositional binary structures such as gender. In the archaeology of the subject, the *chora* as the locus of the mother's and child's indistinguishable bodies is eventually replaced by the symbolic order and its dichotomous structures, such as ego versus non-ego, inside versus outside. This step is critical for the constitution of the subject. "But from that moment on, while I recognise my image as sign and change in order to signify, another economy is instituted. The sign represses the *chora* and its eternal return. Desire alone will henceforth be witness to that 'primal

---

[31] Heubach, *Bertha Pappenheim*, 86. [Since for thousands of years the Jews have defined woman only as a sexual being, without any emphasis on mutual affection and spiritual participation in the husband's life, there was neither any sensual nor spiritual incentive for the wife's dedication. As a result of this a certain moral degradation in sexual matters amongst Jewish women has become widespread. In addition, the lack of women's education has cut off their minds and imagination from any healthy nourishment as a result of which these have no other sphere of realisation than the physical self.]

[32] Claudio Magris, *Weit von wo*, 188. Magris argues that Roth idealised the *shtetl* retrospectively in response to the destruction of its world as a "hypothetische und utopische Alternative zum Unbehagen in der westlichen Gesellschaft" [hypothetical and utopian alternative to the unease experienced in western society] thus turning it into a "Mythos des Nicht-mehr-Möglichen" [myth of the no-longer possible]. Ibid.,19.

[33] Julia Kristeva, *Desire in Language*. Transl. by Leon S. Roudiez. Oxford: Basil Blackwell, 1980: 133.

pulsation'."[34] Although the *chora* is given up on the road to becoming a subject, inscriptions of these infantile impulses return "in the form of rhythms, intonations, melody, accompanying all representation".[35] This return to the maternal is to be found less in the form of an explicit signifier than in terms of a resonance that gives voice to desire.

Roth's central chapter in *Juden auf Wanderschaft*, 'Das jüdische Städtchen', omits any overt reference to the sphere of the maternal. Nevertheless, the rhythm of his prose seems to me to connote the lost *chora*.[36] Note for instance the following dance scene in which religious devotion and sensuality merge:

> Die Chassidim faßten sich bei den Händen, tanzten in der Runde, lösten den Ring und klatschten in die Hände, warfen die Köpfe im Takt nach links und rechts, ergriffen die Thorarollen und schwenkten sie im Kreis wie Mädchen und drückten sie an die Brust, küßten sie und weinten vor Freude. Es war im Tanz eine erotische Lust. Es rührte mich tief, daß ein ganzes Volk seine Sinnenfreude seinem Gott opferte und das Buch der strengsten Gesetze zu seiner Geliebten machte und nicht mehr trennen konnte zwischen körperlichem Verlangen und geistigem Genuß, sondern beides vereinte. Es war Brunst und Inbrunst, der Tanz ein Gottesdienst und das Gebet ein sinnlicher Exzeß. (W2: 848)[37]

Juden auf Wanderschaft can thus be read as the invocation of the *shtetl* as the locus of the lost maternal *chora*. Ultimately it is a eulogy which, because of the narrator's exteriority, both mourns and re-enacts the breaking with a maternally connoted space, a space which is both self-contained and stifling.

---

[34] Kristeva, *Powers of Horror*, 14.
[35] Elizabeth Grosz, *Sexual Subversions. Three French Feminists*. Sydney etc.: Allen & Unwin, 1989: 44.
[36] Helen Chambers has identified three categories of female characters in Roth's work: mysterious and exotic women, dangerous and destructive women and, finally, natural women who "have their origins in the Eastern outposts of European civilization." Helen Chambers, 'Predators or Victims? — Women in Joseph Roth's Works.' In: Helen Chambers (Ed.), *Co-Existent Contradictions. Joseph Roth in Retrospect. Papers of the 1989 Joseph Roth Symposium at Leeds University*. Riverside, California: Ariadne Press, 1991: 120. Chambers points out that, although the relationships between mothers and sons are dysfunctional in Roth's work and, although Roth's portraits of mothers tend to concentrate on "negatively tinged behaviour patterns", "there is nonetheless an underlying assumption that women have maternal instincts and that it is their allotted role to care for their offspring." Ibid., 116. This analysis adds support to my reading according to which Roth's writing re-enacts the violent breaking with and the mourning for a maternally connoted space which is represented as both stifling and protective.
[37] [The Hasidim took each other by their hands, danced in a round, opened the circle up and clapped their hands, threw their heads left and right, keeping time, grasped the Thora rolls and swung them around in a circle like girls, pressing them to their chests, kissing them and crying for joy. There was erotic desire in their dancing. I was deeply touched that a whole people sacrificed its sensuality to their God and turned the book of the strictest laws into their lover, until they could not distinguish between physical desire and spiritual enjoyment any longer, but united both. There was ardour and fervour, the dancing was a service and the prayer sensual excess.]

"Ich bin mit Wonne ein Abtrünniger": The Pleasure of Being Abject

The ambivalence that characterises Roth's attitude to his Eastern Jewish origins acquired an almost desperate urgency after the victory of National Socialism in Germany and the resulting uncertainty concerning Austria's position. Although the question of his Jewish allegiance becomes now a regular, if not prominent theme in his correspondence with Stefan Zweig, Roth, the writer of *Juden auf Wanderschaft*, still refuses to recognise his Jewish origins as the foundation of his being. Roth explained his position before the Nazis' rise to power in June 1932 when he wrote to Zweig:

> Die Juden sind sehr dumm. Nur die noch dümmeren Anti-Semiten können glauben, die Juden seien gefährlich klug. Nach 2000 Jahren gelingt es ihnen nicht, sympathisch zu werden — und ihre Köpfe sind so töricht, sich und das Judentum für den Mittelpunkt der Welt zu halten. Ähnlich wie die Neue Freie Presse. Wie klein und dumm ist das Alles — und wie gelöst ist man plötzlich von jeder Bindung, *jeder*: ich bin, zu meinem Bedauern, nicht mehr in der Lage, mich zu diesem, sich selbst fortwährend desavouierendem Judentum zu bekennen. (B: 243)[38]

While this diatribe smacks of the internalised Jewish self-hatred of Otto Weininger, a letter written on 24 August 1933 to Max von Hohenlohe-Langenburg suggests, however, that Roth utterly refused to accept the treacherous Aryan-Jew dichotomy which structured fascist discourse:

> Weder Landauer, noch ich, noch auch Herr Ludwig Bauer haben das Gefühl, wir seien 'Juden' in dem Sinne, in dem die Nazis 'Arier' sind. Mir persönlich, der ich ein gläubiger Katholik bin, ist mein Judentum etwa Das, was einem chassidischen Wunderrabbi: eine metaphysische Angelegenheit, weit, hoch über allem, was mit 'Juden' auf dieser Erde passiert. [...] Ich weiß natürlich wie Sie, daß die Juden überall gehaßt werden. Gott will es, also kann es nicht anders sein. Nicht die Juden werden Hitler besiegen, Gott selbst wird es. (B: 275)[39]

In this passage Roth turns his Jewishness into a sublime signifier which bears no reference to the concrete socio-historical experience of European

---

[38] [The Jews are stupid. Only the even thicker anti-Semites can believe that the Jews are dangerously clever. After 2000 years they do not manage to become likeable — and in their heads they are so daft as to take themselves and Judaism as the centre of the world. How small and silly all this is — and how free one suddenly is from all bonds, *all of them*, I am, sadly, not able any more to declare myself part of a Jewishness which constantly disavows itself.]

[39] [Neither Landauer nor I nor even Herr Ludwig Bauer feel that we are 'Jews' in the sense in which the Nazis are 'Aryans'. To me, a believing Catholic, my Jewishness is similar to that which, for a Hasidic rabbi, would be a metaphysical matter, far and high above everything that is happening to 'Jews' in this world. [...] Of course I know as you do that the Jews are hated everywhere. God wants it, for this reason it cannot be different. It is not the Jews who will overcome Hitler but God.]

Jewry in the 1930s. By transporting his Jewishness into such a metaphysical realm, Roth may have kept the terrible experience of abjection under control. And this is hardly surprising for "the abject is edged with the sublime. It is not the same moment on the journey, but the same subject and speech bring them into being."[40] But the price for Roth's sublimation of abjection is his implicit denial of any cognisance of the collective historical experience that shaped Eastern European Jewry for centuries. Roth's letters from the 1930s vehemently deny that his Jewishness is a relevant signifier either of his identity or alterity. Writing to Stefan Zweig on 26 March 1933, for example, Roth attacks the fascist dichotomy of an absolute difference between the familiar and the strange, the Aryan and the Jew. He does this by on the one hand pointing out ideological differences between Zweig and himself, and, on the other hand, invoking a shared humanness which — in Roth's eyes — transcends any such ideological signification:

> Sie sind als Jude gegen den Krieg gegangen und ich als Jude in den Krieg. Wir haben viele Kameraden, beide. Wir sind nicht in der Etappe geblieben.
> Es gibt auf dem Schlachtfeld der Humanität, könnte man sagen, ebenfalls Etappen-Juden.
> Solch einer darf man nicht werden.
> Ich habe niemals die Tragik des Jüdischen überschätzt, besonders nicht jetzt, wo es schon tragisch ist, ein anständiger Mensch schlechthin zu sein.
> Es ist die Gemeinheit der Andern: Juden zu sehn. Es schickt sich nicht, daß wir durch Zurückhaltung allzusehr das Argument der törichten Tiere bestätigen.
> Als ein Soldat und Offizier war ich kein Jude. Als ein deutscher Schriftsteller bin ich auch kein Jude. (In dem Sinn, in dem wir jetzt sprechen). (B: 260)[41]

Roth emphasised this point more than once in his letters to Zweig:

> Man konnte das 6000jährige jüdische Erbe nicht verleugnen; aber ebensowenig kann man das 2000jährige *nicht jüdische* verleugnen. Wir kommen eher aus der 'Emanzipation', aus der Humanität, aus dem 'Humanen' überhaupt als aus Ägypten. Unsere Ahnen sind Goethe Lessing Herder nicht minder als Abraham Isaac und Jacob. (B: 257)[42]

---

[40] Kristeva, *Powers of Horror*, 11.
[41] [As a Jew you opposed the war and as a Jew I fought in the war. We have many comrades, both of us. We did not get stuck behind the lines. On the battle-field of humanity there are, as one might say, also Jews of the baseline. One must not become one of them. I have never overrated the tragedy of Jewishness, particularly not now, when it is tragic enough to be a decent person. The others are mean to see Jews. It is not right for us to remain reserved about the issue and thus confirm the argument of those stupid animals. As a soldier and officer I was not a Jew. As a German writer I am not a Jew either (in the sense that we are discussing now).]
[42] [One could not deny the 6000 years of Jewish heritage; but neither can one deny 2000 years of an non-Jewish one. We come more from the age of 'emancipation', humanity, 'humanism' in general rather than from Egypt. Our forefathers are just as much Goethe, Lessing, Herder as Abraham, Isaac and Jacob.]

Both passages clearly champion the humanism of the Enlightenment period, which had brought the German Jews "emancipation" albeit at the price of assimilation. In their *Dialektik der Aufklärung*, Adorno and Horkheimer were to show retrospectively that the Enlightenment supposition of a set of universally shared ideals already carried the seeds of totalitarian destruction.[43] While such a humanism became contested after the Shoah, in Roth's eyes it allowed him to escape the sinister Aryan-Jew dichotomy. This is exemplified in his extraordinarily vehement attack on Chaim Weizmann as the major contemporary exponent of Zionism, a movement which Roth rejected for its nationalist orientation.[44] In a letter, dated 14 August 1935, Roth went so far as to equate Zionism and National Socialism:

> Ein Zionist ist ein Nationalsozialist, ein Nazi ist ein Zionist. Ich glaube gerne, ich bin dessen sogar gewiß, daß Herr Weizmann weit mehr ist, als nur ein 'Jude'. Aber seine Funktion sperrt ihn im Judentum ein, gar im nationalen. [...] Ich bin mit Wonne ein Abtrünniger, von Deutschen und Juden und ich bin stolz darauf. (B: 420)[45]

Clearly, this equation of Zionist and Nazi is extremely scandalous in the context of the 1930s and the Nazis' known policies of oppression which led from the "Gleichschaltungsgesetze" [co-ordination laws] in 1933 to Auschwitz. Roth's deeply ingrained antagonism to any form of nationalism[46] blinded him here to the fundamental difference between the totalitarianism of German fascism on the one hand and the Jewish demand for national self-determination on the other. This, after all, was a direct response to the substantial growth in anti-Semitism from the late 1880s onwards and the failure to protect the civil and human rights of the Jewish population.

---

[43] This is supported by Chris Thornhill's recent article, "Grenzfälle': Galician Jews and Austrian Enlightenment' which traces the fusion of the liberal tradition of Austrian Enlightenment with anti-Semitism in early ethnographic works on Galicia. He finds that these works "propagate a latently totalitarian Enlightenment, paying lip-service to the requirements of learned tolerance but condemning all which does not participate in this." Chris Thornhill, "Grenzfälle': Galician Jews and Austrian Enlightenment.' In: *German Life and Letters* 49 (1996): 172.

[44] Mark H. Gelber has recently argued that Roth's attitude to Zionism was more complex than is generally recognised in critical literature. He rightly points to *Juden auf Wanderschaft* where Roth came to the conclusion that it was more desirable to form a nation than to be abused by other nations. However, Gelber also concludes that Roth's attitude towards Zionism was generally negative. Mark H. Gelber, 'Zur deutsch-zionistischen Rezeptionsgeschichte. Joseph Roth und die *Jüdische Rundschau*.' In: Mark H. Gelber, Hans Otto Horch et al. (Eds.), *Von Franzos bis Canetti*, 207.

[45] [A Zionist is a National Socialist, a Nazi is a Zionist. I am willing to believe, actually I am certain of it, that Herr Weizmann is more than just a 'Jew'. But his function imprisons him in his Jewishness, even in the national. I take great pleasure in being an apostate, both from the Germans and the Jews, and I am proud of it.]

[46] For a discussion of Roth's resentment of any form of nationalism see Hartmut Scheible's essay, 'Joseph Roth's Flucht aus der Geschichte'. In: *Text & Kritik: Joseph Roth* (1982): 56-66.

While Roth's equation of Zionism and National Socialism is, of course, ideologically motivated by his well-known hatred of any form of nationalism and his continued belief in a restitution of the supra-national Austro-Hungarian monarchy, from a psychological viewpoint, the vehemence of his attack seems to suggest a more troubled and unconscious origin of his hatred of Zionism. Roth's phrase "Ich bin mit Wonne ein Abtrünniger" [I take great pleasure in being an apostate] is revealing: it alludes to a structure of feeling which helps Roth to defend the precarious boundaries of his subjectivity by refusing to recognise his Jewish kinship. This non-recognition of kinship is crucial in the drama of abjection. Remember that the abject self occupies a catastrophic territory "whose fluid confines [...] constantly question his solidity and impel him to start afresh."[47] Clearly, such a phobic configuration does not allow for any sense of familiarity, since the notion of the familiar presupposes a subject which has the ability to identify with a true object. But since "the phobic has no other object than the abject"[48] this identification cannot take place. And this in turn means that such a life is not driven by desire but, essentially, by exclusion.[49] Against this background, the emotional force that characterises Roth's various attacks in particular on liberal European Jewry can be read in a new light: they now appear as acts of expulsion based on fear, for example when he writes to Blanche Gidon on 27 February in 1935: "Les Juifs — [...] — ont amenées le socialisme et la catastrophe de la culture européenne. [...] Ils sont les vrai berceau de Hitler et du règne des concierges." [The Jews have caused socialism and the collapse of European culture. They are the real cradle of Hitler and of the janitors' rule, B: 406]

On the other hand, Roth continues to maintain his admiration for what — in his eyes — represents genuine Jewishness. Thus, for instance, he pays tribute to Schalom Asch, the Yiddish writer of the *shtetl*, as "den Homerischen Juden" [the Homeric Jew, B: 285] or praises a novella by Isaac Grün in the following words: "Ich bin selbst überrascht: *die Novelle ist gut.* Und der Mann heißt Isaac. In der Emigration scheint mir das noch richtiger." [I am myself surprised: the novella is good. And the man's name is Isaac. In emigration this seems to me to be even more appropriate. B: 300] However, these moments do not so much reflect lasting identification as the type of sentimental reverie which already characterised the narrative viewpoint of *Juden auf Wanderschaft.*

Roth's letters bear witness to his great art of inventing himself through a linguistic role play which shows language up for what it is: a fetish which

---

[47] Kristeva, *Powers of Horror*, 8.
[48] Ibid., 6.
[49] Ibid., 6.

keeps abjection at bay. In Kristeva's words, language and the signifying chain erect a fetishist screen which protects us from "the void upon which rests the play with the signifier and primary processes. Such a void and the arbitrariness of that play are the truest equivalents of fear."[50] Language can act as the ultimate fetish precisely because it denies the void upon which it is erected. "Because of its founding status, the fetishism of 'language' is perhaps the only one that is unanalyzable."[51] And this indispensable fetishism of language also helps to explain how contemporary literature achieves the sublimation of abjection: it has become a substitute for the role formerly played by the sacred, but a substitute that does not erect boundaries containing morality, law and religion.[52] For while the moral, legal and religious rules that regulate social interaction function on the basis of prohibition, contemporary literature "like perversion, [...] takes advantage of them, gets round them, and makes sport of them. Nevertheless, it maintains a distance where the abject is concerned. The writer fascinated by the abject, imagines its logic, projects himself into it, introjects it, and as a consequence perverts language — style and content."[53] According to Kristeva writing implies the ability to "imagine the abject, that is, to see oneself in its place and to thrust it aside only by means of the displacements of verbal play."[54] The following sub-chapters focus on the way in which the abject is imagined and mastered in Roth's novel *Hiob*.

---

[50] Ibid., 37.
[51] Ibid., 37.
[52] Ibid., 27.
[53] Ibid., 16.
[54] Ibid., 16.

Roth's *Hiob*: A Jewish Story of a Simple Man, a Simple Story of a Jewish Man?

Roth's *Hiob. Roman eines einfachen Mannes* [Job. The Story of a Simple Man] was published on 12 October 1930. Desperately in need of money, Roth was greatly relieved when it became a major success with a first edition of 30,000 copies and the publication of the American translation in 1931 where it became "Book-of-the-Month" in November and was soon a best-seller.[55] Some six years later, a Hollywood production company used Roth's novel as the basis for a film, entitled *Sins of Man*, the script of which, however, was radically altered to suit white Christian middle class taste: Roth's pious orthodox Jew, Mendel Singer, who in the novel comes from the fictional Eastern European *shtetl* Zuchnow, reappeared on the screen as a pious Catholic from South Tyrol. It is hardly surprising that this alteration caused considerable dismay among critics and the public when it was screened in Jerusalem in 1938.[56] While the crudeness of this adaptation shows up Hollywood's indifference to issues of ethnic and religious diversity, this episode also points to one question that has shaped much of the critics' debate about the novel: the question of its Jewishness. Is Roth's *Hiob* simply the story of a little man (as the Hollywood film suggests) or is it rather the Jewish story of a simple man or perhaps the simple story of a Jewish man?

For the Roth-biographer, David Bronsen, the Jewishness of the story is so obvious that he contrasts the "erzösterreichischen *Radetzkymarsch*" [the arch-Austrian *Radetzky March*] with the "erzjüdischen *Hiob*" [the arch-Jewish *Job*].[57] However, while his discussion of both novels under the chapter heading 'Der künstlerische Höhepunkt' [the artistic pinnacle] is evidence of Bronsen's lasting admiration of both books, the chapter does not really elaborate upon the above-cited label "erzjüdisch". Mentioning the similarities between the biblical Job-story and Roth's novel in terms of plot structure and style, Bronsen then emphasises the difference between the biblical and modern version of Job in terms of social status: whereas the biblical Job is a devout wealthy man chosen and tested by God, his modern counterpart is — in the words of Bronsen — "auserwählt [...] nur als Heimgesuchter, als der leidende Mensch, der scheinbar unverschuldete Schläge so lange ertragen muß, bis er an Gott irre wird und sich gegen ihn auflehnt"[58] [chosen only as the afflicted, as the suffering man, who — so it seems — has to bear blow after blow through no fault of his own, until he loses his faith in God and rebels against him]. With this reading Bronsen has

---

[55] David Bronsen, *Joseph Roth. Eine* Biographie, 389ff.
[56] Ibid., 391.
[57] Ibid., 12.
[58] Ibid., 382.

effectively bypassed the question as to what makes the novel Jewish — now its appears to be a universal parable, the story of a simple (albeit Jewish) man.[59]

The question of the novel's Jewishness is implicitly addressed by Claudio Magris for whom the setting of the first part of the novel in a fictional Eastern European *shtetl* is essential to the novel's symbolism which contrasts Mendel's Eastern European Jewishness favourably with the alienation experienced in Western society. For Magris it is only logical that Roth's Mendel does not develop, that he hangs on to his Eastern European background which in Roth's system of meaning always symbolises a moral space. When Singer undergoes his religious crisis it does not affect the core of his very being which is firmly rooted in the lost *shtetl* culture of Eastern Europe.[60] In Magris's reading the whole symbolism of the novel is premised upon Roth's idealisation of the *shtetl* as a "Seelenlandschaft" [spiritual landscape], that is a psychological space of moral integrity rather than a real location on the map. Magris focuses on Mendel as the main symbol, calling the novel "ein Roman des Vaters"[61] [the novel of the father] and criticises Roth for his tendency to reduce complex social questions to moral ones.[62] His reading therefore suggests that Roth's *Hiob* is the all too simple story of a Jewish man.

In contrast, Geoffrey P. Butler argues in a more recent article that the label "Jewish" for Roth's novel has tended to "obscure the profane components at its core which may in fact account for much of its durability."[63] Contesting the importance of the Jewishness of the protagonists, Butler concludes that *Hiob* is "for the most part a credible story of human distress — with a fairy-tale happyish ending which, by the time it is reached, even sophisticated readers would be glad to believe."[64] Butler's formula "not a Jew but a sufferer" points to the implicit assumption upon which his reconsideration of Roth's novel is premised: that an essentially Jewish story could not have had such a wide appeal. His claim that the "durable core" of the novel is not essentially Jewish is based on the observation that, unlike the biblical Job, Mendel Singer is a rather "indistinct personification of poverty

---

[59] However, it has to be said at this point that Bronsen does not set out to analyse the Jewishness which for him seems to be self-evident. Instead, his interpretation focuses on an equally contested question, namely as to whether ·the fairy-tale ending of the novel is poetically justifiable. Cf. Bronsen, 387.
[60] Magris, *Weit von wo*, 120f.
[61] Ibid., 122.
[62] Ibid., 154.
[63] Geoffrey P. Butler, 'It's the Bitterness that Counts: Joseph Roth's 'Most Jewish' Novel Reconsidered.' In: *German Life and Letters* 41 (1988): 227.
[64] Ibid., 231.

and of patience"[65] and secondly, that Roth's portrayal of the Russian world is insulated from the gross realities of anti-Semitism. The argument first cited, namely that Mendel's poor and indistinct background makes him less a Jew (in biblical terms) than a sufferer with a universal appeal, only demonstrates the critic's Eurocentric bias. When one compares Mendel's status in the novel with the socio-economic position of the real "melamed" (teacher) in the *shtetl* one finds that Mendel's lack of status and economic power would make him more rather than less Jewish. While Roth's descriptions of Mendel Singer emphasise his commonness (which Butler links to the "durable core"), it is a commonness which is specific to a unique culture, that of the Eastern European Jewish *shtetl*. Moreover, the opening lines and pages of Roth's *Hiob* do not just evoke "universal" poverty but the poverty of the Jewish *melamed* in the *shtetl*:

> Zwölf sechsjährige Schüler unterrichtete er im Lesen und Memorieren der Bibel. Jeder von den zwölf brachte ihm an jedem Freitag zwanzig Kopeken. Sie waren Mendel Singers einzige Einnahmen. Dreißig Jahre war er erst alt. Aber seine Aussichten, mehr zu verdienen, waren gering, vielleicht überhaupt nicht vorhanden. Wurden die Schüler älter, kamen sie zu andern, weiseren Lehrern.[66]

This is in line with Mark Zborowski's and Elizabeth Herzog's anthropological study of the Eastern European *shtetl* which shows that the *melamed* is despised by the entire *shtetl* community:

> He barely manages to live on the meager tuition fees he receives from their parents, so that he and his family are chronically underfed. There are tales of how the melamed's wife or daughters manage to spirit away the bread and butter given to the child by his mother from the noon-day meal and then explain, 'the cat stole it.'
> To add to the melamed's trouble, he is looked down upon by the whole community. To share a wealth of knowledge is among the most 'beautiful' deeds; to sell a meagre stock of it is unworthy.[67]

---

[65] Ibid., 231.
[66] Joseph Roth, *Hiob. Roman eines einfachen Mannes*. In: Joseph Roth, *Werke*, V: 4. Henceforth cited from this edition as W with volume and page number. Translations into English cite the following edition as J with page numbers in square brackets: Joseph Roth, *Job. The Story of a Simple Man*. Translated by Dorothy Thompson. London: Chatto & Windus, 1983. [He instructed twelve six-year-old scholars in the reading and memorizing of the Bible. Each of the twelve brought him twenty kopeks every Friday. This was Mendel Singer's only income. He was just thirty years old but his chances of earning more were small, perhaps non-existent. When the students grew older they would go to other, wiser teachers. J: 5]
[67] Mark Zborowski and Elizabeth Herzog, *Life is with People. The Culture of the Shtetl*. New York: Schocken, 1970: 89. Although Butler admits towards the end of his article that Mendel's story "cannot be dissociated entirely from its hero's particular circumstances", he continues in the same breath that the readers' tears "seem explicable without reference to any particularised 'Leidensfähigkeit'". Geoffrey Butler, 'It's the Bitterness that Counts', 231. At the best of times, this is poor logic which once more begs the question as to why the readers'

This description captures Mendel Singer's poor social and economic position in the *shtetl*.

In a more recent article Ritchie Robertson examined the Jewishness of Roth's *Hiob* from a fresh angle by reading the novel as an example of German-Jewish ghetto fiction.[68] Robertson places the narrative in the "nostalgic camp"[69] of ghetto fiction and shows that the main characters of the novel are identifiable types with a long tradition in ghetto fiction: Roth's Mendel is a typical *melamed*, an example of which can be found in Franzos's *Der Pojaz*, his son Jonas typifies the physically strong Jew, a figure which, in the nostalgic tradition of ghetto fiction, served to counteract the stereotype of the feeble Jew, and Mendel's daughter Mirjam stands in the tradition of the "schöne Jüdin"[70] [beautiful Jewess]. Robertson rightly emphasises the importance of the "Wunderrabbi", another well-known figure in ghetto fiction, "whose prophesy is fulfilled at the end, and who thus gives the novel its artistic unity."[71] By reading Roth's novel as an example of ghetto fiction, Robertson points to a specific literary system of meaning which originates in the German-Jewish culture of the nineteenth century. And while it is important to say that this system of meaning operates at a remove from reality, it is equally important to note that it tackles specifically Jewish problems of identity. With reference to *Hiob* this means that, at a remove from reality, Roth's novel engages with the pressures traditional Jewry were faced with both from within and without. This makes the novel a German-Jewish story of a simple Russian-Jewish man.

In what follows I shall read Roth's *Hiob* as as an essentially Jewish family story in which the psychodynamic between the family members of an orthodox Eastern European family is articulated or scripted on the basis of ritual and abjection. My reading is informed by the systems theory model of family life (as developed by Gregory Bateson and Paul Watzlawick) which seems to me to offer a good framework for the analysis of the stress factors which have an impact on Mendel Singer and his family.

---

tears should at all be explained without reference to the hero's particular circumstances in the novel — clearly, Butler's argument effectively silences the articulation of cultural difference in order to arrive at the aforementioned humanist core.
[68] Ritchie Robertson, 'Roth's *Hiob* and the Traditions of Ghetto Fiction.' In: Helen Chambers (Ed.), *Co-Existent Contradictions*, 185-200, here 187ff.
[69] Ibid., 191.
[70] For a discussion of "die schöne Jüdin" cf. Florian Krobb, *Die schöne Jüdin. Jüdische Frauengestalten in der deutschsprachigen Erzählliteratur vom 17. Jahrhundert bis zum ersten Weltkrieg*. Tübingen: Niemeyer, 1993.
[71] Ritchie Robertson, 'Roth's *Hiob*', 200.

A Systemic View of the Family

Systems theory views the family as an organic eco-system which is faced with the task of maintaining some form of identity and structure while at the same time adapting to change. From a cybernetic viewpoint the family is not just the sum of its individual members but a self-regulating system in which the members' thoughts and feelings are mutually interdependent. While this may seem to be self-evident, this view departs from psychological explanations of the family which tend to emphasise the importance of families in nurturing and raising children. In contrast to traditional views, systems theory offers a different level of analysis by studying patterns of interaction that, over a period of time, display regularity. The systems view thus entails a fundamental shift away from explaining problems in terms of personality traits or in terms of linear causality (A causes B) towards a circular view according to which the agents in patterned interactions feed each other's behaviour.[72] According to Rudi Dallos "the model proposes that the family members act together in a concerted way so that over a period of time they display regularity. Over time a system functions so as to maintain a dynamic equilibrium; deviations from equilibrium are continually corrected. This whole process is called homeostasis [...]."[73] Research in this area has, for example, shown that, over a period of time, a family's interdependencies become patterned and organised in so-called "family scripts":

> The ways that families steer their way through the various stages of the life cycle are not simply capricious. One important source of direction comes from the family traditions going back several generations and in some cases hundreds of years. We can start to see this in episodes of storytelling in the family [...]. These anecdotes provide a store of experience generated by the traditions of family experimentation. These traditions have been conceptualized in terms of family scripts [...] which serve to guide how successive generations of children come to regulate their family lives.[74]

Elizabeth A. Carter and Monica McGoldrick have proposed a two-dimensional model for the analysis of the various stressors that influence a family life cycle: they distinguish between a vertical flow into the system which includes all patterns of behaviour, taboos, attitudes and expectations that are passed down the generations, and, secondly, a horizontal flow which includes both the predictable stresses (which tend to occur at points of

---

[72] Paul Watzlawick, Janet Helmick Beavin, Don D. Jackson, *Pragmatics of Human Communication. A Study of Interactional Patterns, Pathologies and Paradoxes*. London: Faber & Faber, 1968.
[73] Rudi Dallos, *Family Belief Systems, Therapy and Change. A Constructional Approach*. Milton Keynes etc.: Open University Press, 1991: 15.
[74] Ibid., 10.

transition from one life cycle stage to the next) and unpredictable events such as sudden illness, untimely death or war.[75]

The concept of the family life cycle has since been criticised as an exclusively normative view that does not represent alternative contemporary families.[76] However, and this brings us back to Joseph Roth's *Hiob*, the model offers an extremely useful tool for the analysis of the family dynamics in an orthodox or traditional Jewish family such as Mendel Singer's. In comparison with, for instance, an assimilated Western European Jewish family, an orthodox family from Eastern Europe can be described as a relatively closed system whose life cycle is entirely regulated by the laws and prohibitions of Judaism. This is equally true of the *shtetl* as a whole, where every aspect of life and the position of every member is defined by and assessed with reference to Judaism as the core of the *shtetl's* culture, a belief system which has been vertically passed down for centuries. Mark Zborowski and Elizabeth Herzog describe the position of the individual in such a cohesive system in the following words:

> In the closely knit community, where each is responsible for all and all are responsible for each, privacy is neither known nor desired. Everyone is subject to inspection and criticism, everyone is free to inspect and criticize. The strongest sanction is public opinion, the highest reward is public approval. As a last resort one 'calls to people,' even against the ostensible authority. And it is the will of the people that implements the ruling of the rabbi in his court. [...] The only absolute authority is the spirit of the Torah.[77]

Historical factors such as the shared experience of discrimination, pogroms and anti-Semitism reinforce the cohesiveness of the system; however, the *shtetl's* cohesion ultimately depends on Judaism which controls membership of the system on the basis of kinship (rather than on fellowship as in Christianity). As a result of the kinship-principle one fundamental boundary that regulates the *shtetl's* and the family's entire relations with the world is the Jew-Goj distinction and the prohibition on sexual relations or marriage with a non-Jewish person,[78] a rule which helps to erect the pure-impure distinction upon which Judaism and the orthodox family's belief

---

[75] Elizabeth A. Carter, Monica McGoldrick (Eds.), *The Family Life-Cycle. A Framework for Family Therapy*. New York: Gardner, 1980: 10.
[76] Rudi Dallos, *Family Belief Systems*, 8ff.
[77] Mark Zborowski and Elizabeth Herzog, *Life is With People*, 421f.
[78] For a brief discussion of sexual relations in orthodox Judaism cf. Hannah Rockman's, 'Sexual behaviour among Ultra-Orthodox Jews. A Review of Laws and Guidelines'. In: Jonathan Magonet (Ed.), *Jewish Explorations of Sexuality*. Oxford: Berghahn, 1995: 191-204. See also John Cooper's 'Jewish Sexual Attitudes in Eastern Europe 1850-1920'. A detailed analysis of the Halakhic sources regulating sexual and marital relations in Judaism can be found in Rachel Biale's book *Women and Jewish Law. An Exploration of Women's Issues in Halakhic Sources*. New York: Schocken, 1984.

system rests. I would like to exemplify the importance of this with reference to one episode in Roth's *Hiob* before moving on to a more systematic examination of ritual and abjection in the narrative.

In the novel it is Mirjam who first breaks a ground rule when she is caught having a sexual relationship with a Russian Cossack. Mirjam trespasses here against two of the many prohibitions which define sexual relations in orthodox life: firstly the prohibition on relationships with a Goj, and secondly, on relationships outside marriage. Only if one is aware of the significance of these and other prohibitions for an orthodox family does the full weight of Mendel's discovery that Mirjam is seeing a Russian Goj become apparent. First and foremost, Mirjam's affair is an offence against the Covenant with God. Her intimacy with a non-Jew thus allows the impure and the abject to invade and threaten the family at the very core of its belief system. After his terrible discovery, Mendel, who is visibly shaken, goes to the prayer-house where he opens his prayer book:

> Er klappte es auf und langte nach seinem alten, schwarzen und schweren Buch, das in seinen Händen heimisch war und das er unter tausend gleichartigen Büchern ohne Zögern erkannt hätte. So vertraut war ihm die lederne Glätte des Einbands mit den erhabenen runden Inselchen aus Stearin, den verkrusteten Überresten unzähliger längst verbrannter Kerzen, und die unteren Ecken der Seiten, porös, gelblich fett, dreimal gewellt durch das jahrzehntelange Umblättern mit angefeuchteten Fingern. Jedes Gebet, dessen er im Augenblick bedurfte, konnte er im Nu aufschlagen. Eingegraben war es in sein Gedächtnis mit den kleinsten Zügen der Physiognomie, die es in diesem Gebetbuch trug, der Zahl seiner Zeilen, der Art und Größe des Drucks und der genauen Farbtönung der Seiten. (W5: 46)[79]

Roth's description emphasises Mendel's intimate familiarity with the prayer book which is formed by and, in turn, sustains the meaningfulness of the Covenant with God. But here it is not so much the word of God but more the signs of daily usage that Mendel experiences as reassuring. This recognition prepares him for the following prayer:

> Allmählich glitt sein Oberkörper in das altgewohnte regelmäßige Schwanken, der ganze Körper betete mit, die Füße scharrten die Dielen, die Hände schlossen sich zu Fäusten und schlugen wie Hämmer auf das Pult, an die Brust, auf das Buch und in die Luft. Auf der Ofenbank schlief ein obdachloser Jude. Seine Atemzüge begleiteten und

---

[79] [He lifted the lid and reached for his old black, heavy book, which felt so at home in his hands, that he could have recognised it instantly, without hesitation, among a thousand similar books. So familiar to him was the leather smoothness of the binding, with the round, raised island of tallow, the encrusted remains of innumerable candles burned long ago; so familiar the lower corners of the pages, yellowish, porous, greasy, thrice curled by a decade of turning them with moistened fingers. Any prayer that he needed at the moment he could turn to immediately. It was buried in his memory with the smallest feature of that physiognomy which it carried in this book, the number of the line, the character and size of the print, and the exact colour tone of the page. J: 80]

unterstützten Mendel Singers monotonen Gesang, der wie ein heißer Gesang in der gelben Wüste war, verloren und vertraut mit dem Tode. Die eigene Stimme und der Atem des Schlafenden betäubten Mendel, vertrieben jeden Gedanken aus seinem Herzen, nichts mehr war er als ein Beter, die Worte gingen durch ihn den Weg zum Himmel, ein hohles Gefäß war er, ein Trichter. So betete er dem Morgen entgegen. (W5: 46-47)[80]

It is neither the words nor the meaning of the prayer which help Mendel counteract the invasion of the impure and abject but the internalised ritual of praying which erects a protective boundary and keeps abjection at bay. The next morning, after regaining his equilibrium, Mendel tells his wife Deborah that the family will accept Schemarjah's invitation and emigrate to America because of Mirjam's affair: "'Sie geht mit einem Kosaken.' Das Glas fiel klirrend aus den Händen Deborahs." (W5: 47) ["She is going with a Cossack." The glass fell ringing from Deborah's hand. J: 82]. Deborah's shock reinforces the sense of crisis that is associated with Mendel's discovery. From a systemic viewpoint, the Singers' emigration is their way of resolving the imminent threat to the family's homeostasis. Emigration as a response to threats (mainly pogroms or poverty, here the threat to Judaic laws) is, of course, part of the ethnic script that informed most Eastern European Jewish families' perception of the world.

Crises and the drama of abjection had jeopardised the stability of the Singer family long before Mirjam's affairs. The following sub-chapter examines the interplay between ritual and abjection that shapes the Singers' experience of life. I hope to show that the Jewishness of the novel does not only reside in the Biblical Job-story and the tradition of ghetto fiction but, to a significant degree, in the scripting of the family system, its inter-dependencies, and the way in which the family members attempt to resolve perceived threats and crises.

---

[80] [Gradually his torso slipped into the old, customary swaying, his whole body prayed with him, the feet scraped the floor, the hands closed to fists, and pounded like hammers on the desk, on his breast, on the book, and in the air. On the stove bench slept a homeless Jew. His breathing accompanied and supported Mendel Singer's monotonous song, which was like a hot chant in the yellow desert, lost, and familiar with death. His own voice and the breathing of the sleeper numbed Mendel, drove every thought out of his heart; he was nothing more than a man praying; the words passed through him to heaven; he was a hollow vessel, a funnel for prayer. So his prayers went out to meet the morning. J: 81]

Ritual and Abjection in Roth's *Hiob*

Ritual is the keynote of the opening paragraphs of the novel in which Mendel Singer is introduced as a common orthodox Jew, "ein ganz alltäglicher Jude" (W5: 3) [an entirely commonplace Jew] and *melamed*, who teaches Torah and Talmud in his kitchen with the same enthusiasm and as little sensational success as hundreds of thousands before him. Here and in the following paragraphs the narrator's language is characterised by a biblical rhythm which communicates both the long tradition in which Mendel Singer's life stands and Mendel's own sense of his place in an unshakeable God-given order. This is particularly obvious in the third paragraph where the narrator adopts Mendel's perspective on life:

> Singer schien wenig Zeit zu haben und lauter dringende Ziele. Gewiß war sein Leben ständig schwer und zuweilen sogar eine Plage. Eine Frau und drei Kinder mußte er kleiden und nähren. (Mit einem vierten ging sie schwanger.) Gott hatte seinen Lenden Fruchtbarkeit verliehen, seinem Herzen Gleichmut und seinen Händen Armut. Sie hatten kein Gold zu wägen und keine Banknoten zu zählen. Dennoch rann sein Leben stetig dahin, wie ein kleiner armer Bach zwischen kärglichen Ufern. Jeden Morgen dankte Mendel Gott für das Schlaf, für das Erwachen und den anbrechenden Tag. Wenn die Sonne unterging, betete er noch einmal. Wenn die ersten Sterne aufsprühten, betete er zum dritten Mal. Und bevor er sich schlafen legte, flüsterte er ein eiliges Gebet mit müden, aber eifrigen Lippen. Sein Schlaf war traumlos. Sein Gewissen war rein. Seine Seele war keusch. Er brauchte nichts zu bereuen, und nichts gab es, was er begehrt hätte. Er liebte sein Weib und ergötzte sich an ihrem Fleische. Mit gesundem Hunger verzehrte er schnell seine Mahlzeiten. Seine zwei kleinen Söhne, Jonas und Schemarjah, prügelte er wegen Ungehorsams. Aber das Jüngste, die Tochter Mirjam, liebkoste er häufig. (W5: 3)[81]

Both the rhythm and the maxim-like brevity of the sentences communicate the sense of ritual that patterns Mendel's life, the validity of which does not reside in any worldly achievements but rests entirely on the observance of the Jewish laws. And although Deborah is introduced as the stereotypical nagging Jewish wife who despises her husband for his lack of status and who envies other people's wealth, she too is part of the same ritualised world

---

[81] [Singer seemed to have little time and a lot of pressing engagements. True, his life was always hard and at times even a torment to him. A wife and three children had to be clothed and fed. (She was carrying a fourth.) God had given fertility to his loins, equanimity to his heart, and poverty to his hands. They had no gold to weigh and no bank-notes to count. Nevertheless his life flowed along like a poor little brook between bare banks. Every morning Mendel thanked God for his sleeping, for his awakening, and for the dawning day. When the sun went down he said his prayers once again. When the first stars began to sparkle, he prayed for the third time, and before he laid himself down to sleep he whispered a hurried prayer, with tired but zealous lips. His sleep was dreamless, his conscience was pure, his soul was chaste. He had nothing to regret, and he coveted nothing. He loved the woman, his wife, and took delight in her flesh. His two small sons, Jonas and Shemariah, he beat when they were disobedient, but the youngest Miriam, he was constantly caressing. J: 4]

consisting of a "Reigen aus Mühsal" [weary cycle] punctuated by the "bekümmerte Festlichkeit" (W5: 5) [troubled solemnity] of the Sabbath. When Deborah gives birth to Menuchim, at first nothing much seems to change: Menuchim is circumcised eight days after his birth and becomes thus part of the alliance with the God of the chosen people. However, the first signs of a crisis occur only a year later when Deborah finds that she cannot wean Menuchim who, with a contorted face, makes strange noises (W5: 11). When a non-Jewish doctor diagnoses epilepsy and offers to cure Menuchim, Mendel refuses his offer because the required hospital stay would dictate a breach of the dietary laws for Menuchim, which, in Mendel's eyes, is a greater evil than his illness:

> Soll er unter russischen Kindern aufwachsen? Kein heiliges Wort hören? Milch und Fleisch essen und Hühner auf Butter gebraten, wie man sie im Spital bekommt? Wir sind arm, aber Menuchim's Seele verkauf' ich nicht. (W5: 7)[82]

While from the outsider's perspective, Mendel's judgement may appear as ill-informed, from the insider's viewpoint of an orthodox Jew, his decision highlights the importance of the dietary laws for Jewish religious life, the basic principles of which I shall explain briefly.

In orthodox Judaism, the dietary laws, "Kashrut", are not simply ceremonies to be discarded at will, but "divine rules of life for the people of God, eternal and inviolable."[83] Since it is the purpose of the dietary laws to safeguard man against an undue strengthening of his animal nature, all food that makes the body active in a carnal direction is to be avoided. The consumption of blood and all carnivorous animals are forbidden because of the danger that the animal's cruel habits enter the body. A similar symbolical interpretation applying to the all-important law prohibiting mixing meat and milk belongs to the category of laws which "forbid a mixture of species as contrary to God's order of creation."[84] Any admixture would result in a confusion of the species and thus jeopardise the clear boundary between the pure and impure, a boundary which keeps abjection at bay.

The general principle behind the laws concerning meat consumption is summarised by Grunfeld as follows: "the nearer an animal is to the vegetable world in its habits and composition, the less likely it is to arouse the animal nature in man, and its meat becomes the more suitable for human consumption."[85] Animals which are entirely clovenfooted and chew

---

[82] [Should he grow up among Russian children? Never hear a holy word? Eat milk with meat and chickens roasted in butter, the way people get them in the hospital? We are poor but I will not sell Menuchim's soul. J: 10]
[83] I. Grunfeld, *The Jewish Dietary Laws*. London etc.: Soncino, 1972, vol. I: 3.
[84] Ibid., 22.
[85] Ibid., 9.

the cud are allowed: they are tame and passive and therefore they do not threaten to overthrow man's moral nature. "Kashrut" thus serves to uphold the pure-impure distinction upon which the chosen people's alliance with God rests.

We now see that Mendel's decision not to allow Menuchim to be treated in hospital is based on a body of inviolable Laws, the observance of which guarantees the meaningfulness of his life:[86] "Er beschloß, Gottes Hilfe für seinen Jüngsten zu erflehen und zweimal in der Woche zu fasten, Montag und Donnerstag."(W5: 7) [He decided to beseech God's help for his youngest and to fast twice in the week, Mondays and Thursdays. J: 10]

Many years after this episode Deborah decides to travel to the Rabbi in Kluczysk to seek spiritual advice. Roth describes him as a Hasidic "Wunderrabbi" who can work miracles.[87] While this constitutes in Mendel's eyes an intervention that he cannot disallow, as a traditional orthodox Jew he rejects the view of the rabbi as a visionary intermediary between man and God: "Er lächelte über den Glauben seiner Frau an den Rabbi. Seine schlichte Frömmigkeit bedurfte keiner vermittelnden Gewalt zwischen Gott und den Menschen." (W5: 11) [He smiled at his wife's simple faith in the Rabbi. His modest piety required no mediator between God and men. J: 18]. At the end of the novel the "Wunderrabbi" turns out to be the chief spiritual authority in the narrative when his prophesy is fulfilled and Menuchim returns as a cured and famous composer. According to Ritchie Robertson, the miraculous ending "confirms the wisdom of the *Wunderrabbi* but shows how thoroughly the modern world has lost contact with his wisdom. It provides perfunctory disguise for a message of despair."[88]

Prior to this resolution, competing belief systems threaten the Singer family's equilibrium from within and without. One example of this is Mendel's violent outburst when Deborah tells him of the Wunderrabbi's prophesy:

> Er fühlte nicht, wo er stand. Er wirbelte mit dem schwingenden, knallenden Gürtel umher, traf die Wände, den Tisch, die Bänke und wußte nicht, ob ihn die verfehlten Schläge mehr freuten oder die gelungenen. Endlich klang es drei von der Wanduhr, die Stunde, in der sich die Schüler am Nachmittag versammelten. Mit leerem Magen [...] begann Mendel, Wort für Wort, Satz auf Satz aus der Bibel vorzutragen. Der helle

---

[86] The same issue arises later when Schemarjah and Jonas are drafted into the army. Mendel imagines the following nightmare scenario: "Sie aßen Schweinefleisch und wurden von Offizieren mit der Reitpeitsche geschlagen. Sie trugen Gewehre und Bajonette." (W5: 19) [They ate pork and were beaten by officers with riding whips. They carried guns and bayonets. J: 33]
[87] Hasidism was a movement which became increasingly powerful in the Eastern European *shtetl* and which, unlike traditional orthodox Jewry, emphasised mystical beliefs and viewed the rabbi as an agent of miracles.
[88] Ritchie Robertson, 'Roth's *Hiob*', 200.

Chor der Kinderstimmen wiederholte Wort für Wort, Satz für Satz, es war als würde die Bibel von vielen Glocken geläutet. Wie Glocken schwangen auch die Oberkörper der Lernenden vorwärts und zurück, indes über den Köpfen der Korb Menuchims fast im gleichen Rhythmus pendelte. Heute nahmen Mendels Söhne am Unterricht teil. Des Vaters Zorn versprühte, erkaltete, erlosch, weil sie im klingenden Vorsagen den andern voran waren. (W5: 12)[89]

While on the rational level Mendel's outburst highlights his rejection of the Hasidic belief system, emotionally it points to the lack of control he experiences in relation to Menuchim's slow development. Roth's description of the way in which Mendel's anger evaporates emphasises again the power of ritual in Mendel's life: as before it is the internalised repetition of the same words and body movement which control the escalation and restores the homeostasis of the family system. In the first part of the novel, ritual erects a protective boundary around Mendel and offers him a constant fallback position at points of crisis. The same does not apply to the same degree to Deborah as we will see now.

Women and "the Place of Rot"

Deborah's position within the symbolic order of orthodox Judaism is much more vulnerable than Mendel's because women are traditionally excluded from the heart of the orthodox belief system. In her discussion of Jewish family psychodynamics, Esthelle Roith quotes some examples of the legal and moral bias against women within orthodox Judaism: A woman cannot be part of the Minyan (the quorum of ten males required for worship), she cannot testify as a witness in Jewish courts, she is excluded from the study of Hebrew, the sacred Tongue, and cannot be called up to read the Torah in the synagogue, she cannot say Kaddish (the death prayer for parents), she cannot become a rabbi, she is impure during menstruation and for the following seven days, she must be divorced if she is childless after ten years of marriage, as a widow she must marry her husband's brother unless he releases her by carrying out the ceremony of "chalitzah", and, finally, men must recite a daily prayer thanking God for not having made them a

---

[89] [He did not know where he stood. He whirled the swinging, cracking belt about, hit the walls, the table, the benches, and did not know which pleased him most, the blows which failed or those which reached their mark. Finally the clock on the wall struck three, the hour when the pupils assembled in the afternoon. With an empty stomach [...], Mendel began to recite the Bible, word for word, verse after verse. It was as though the Bible was being tolled by many bells. The torsos of the scholars swung like bells, backward and forward, while over their heads Menuchim's basket swung in almost the same rhythm. Today Mendel's sons participated in the instruction. The father's rage calmed down, cooled, died out, because in the chanting recitative his boys surpassed the others. J: 19]

woman."⁹⁰ These and many more prohibitions serve to define women as closer to nature than men and, ultimately, as impure. An extreme expression of the male hostility towards women that is inscribed in orthodox Judaism is the definition of the uterus as a "place of rot".⁹¹ This extremely negative evaluation of the female reproductive organ reflects a fear of maternal power and fertility which Judaism tries to harness and control by forcing women to partake in specific rites of purity after menstruation and childbirth. As Roith argues, such punitive measures reinforce the sense of women as "other"⁹² and assign them to the category of the "impure" that has to be abjected.

Kristeva describes the same process in the following way:

> the pure/impure mechanism testifies to the harsh combat Judaism, in order to constitute itself, must wage against paganism and its maternal cults. It carries into the private lives of everyone the brunt of the struggle each subject must wage during the entire length of his history in order to become separate, that is to say, to become a speaking subject and/or subject to Law.⁹³

From this viewpoint the circumcision of the male's foreskin cannot exclusively be interpreted in terms of the alliance with God, but must also been seen as an act which separates the male from feminine impurity and defilement: "By repeating the natural scar of the umbilical cord at the location of sex, by duplicating and thus displaying through ritual the preeminent separation, which is that from the mother, Judaism seems to insist in symbolic fashion — the very opposite of what is "natural" — that the identity of the speaking being (with his God) is based on the separation of the son from the mother."⁹⁴

The reverse side of woman's exclusion from any significant role within the synagogue community is her even greater confinement to the home and to the role of wife and mother. "She bears males, is married off by and to them and she links the generations between them. [...] She acquires merit — the route to heaven — only by sending her sons to study Torah and by facilitating her husband in doing so."⁹⁵ In Roith's view, by confining women to the reproductive function, Judaism ensures that a woman's investment in her "'symbol-saturated' males [...] is of a particularly intense and anxious

---

⁹⁰ Esthelle Roith, *The Riddle of Freud. Jewish Influences on His Theory of Female Sexuality*. London and New York: Tavistock, 1987: 95ff.
⁹¹ Ibid., 99.
⁹² Ibid., 91.
⁹³ Kristeva, *Powers of Horror*, 94.
⁹⁴ Ibid., 100.
⁹⁵ Esthelle Roith, *The Riddle of Freud*, 94.

nature," a point which brings as back to Deborah's position in the Singer family, and, in particular, to her relationship with Menuchim.[96]

There is an episode early on in the narrative which, although it has, to my knowledge, not received critical attention, is a defining moment in Deborah's and Mendel's relationship. We witness how Deborah examines her body in front of a mirror:

> Sie fuhr mit kalten strählenden Fingerspitzen durch ihren schütteren Scheitel, zog eine Strähne nach der andern vor die Stirn und suchte nach weißen Haaren. Sie glaubte, ein einziges gefunden zu haben, ergriff es mit einer harten Zange aus zwei Fingern und riß es aus. Dann öffnete sie ihr Hemd vor dem Spiegel. Sie sah ihre schlaffen Brüste, hob sie hoch, ließ sie fallen, strich mit der Hand über den hohlen und dennoch gewölbten Bauch, sah die blauen verzweigten Adern an ihren Schenkeln und beschloß, wieder ins Bett zu gehn. Sie wandte sich um, und ihr Blick stieß erschrocken auf das geöffnete Aug' ihres Mannes. 'Was schaust du?' rief sie. Er antwortete nicht. Es war, als gehörte das offene Auge nicht ihm, denn er selbst schlief noch. Unabhängig von ihm hatte es sich geöffnet. Selbständig neugierig war es geworden. Das Weiße des Auges schien weißer als gewöhnlich. Die Pupille war winzig. Das Auge erinnerte Deborah an einen vereisten See mit einem schwarzen Punkt darinnen. Es konnte kaum eine Minute offen gewesen sein, aber Deborah hielt diese Minute für ein Jahrzehnt. (W5: 14f.)[97]

While mirror scenes normally re-enact the myth of Narcissus, Deborah's examination of herself in this scene shows up the murky underground of self-love, namely abjection. Instead of investing her body with self-love she views it with a "cool heart" and a "clear eye" as a barren wasteland deprived of its reproductive function. Her gaze is extremely clinical and mimics the unconscious "icy" gaze of her sleeping husband, cutting her off from any narcissistic affect which normally protects the self from the invasion of abjection. Deborah's shocking experience of her body as waste thus reproduces a patriarchal orthodox belief system which denigrates the female body as a "place of rot". We have seen previously that it is only through the birth of a son that a woman can compensate for her biblical corruption and impurity and gain at least secondary status in the symbolic order. However, in Deborah's case the birth of Menuchim poses a serious threat to this since

---

[96] Ibid., 107.
[97] [She combed her thin hair with cold fingers, drew one strand after another over her forehead, and looked for white hairs. She thought she found a single one, grasped it with the hard tongs of two fingers, and tore it out. Then she opened the chemise before the mirror. She saw her flaccid breasts, lifted them, let them fall, stroked her hand over her empty yet swollen stomach, saw the blue branching veins on her thighs and decided to go to bed again. She turned, and her scared glance met the opened eye of her husband. 'What are you looking at?' she cried. He did not answer. It was as though the open eye did not belong to him, as though he himself still slept. It had opened independently of him. It had become independently inquisitive. The white of the eye seemed whiter than usual. The pupil was tiny. The eye reminded Deborah of a frozen lake with a black spot in it. It could hardly have been open a minute but to Deborah this minute seemed a decade. J: 24]

Menuchim's illness also puts him on the other side of the symbolic order and makes him impure, non-separate and thus non-symbolic. This is highlighted in the following scene in which Menuchim is described "as a piece of dirt" eating dirt: "Sie legten ihn in eine Ecke, in einen Sack. Dort spielte er mit Hundekot, Pferdeäpfeln, Kieselsteinen. Er fraß alles. Er kratzte den Kalk von den Wänden und stopfte sich den Mund voll, hustete dann und wurde blau im Angesicht. Ein Stück Dreck lagerte er im Winkel." (W5: 13) [They stuck him in a corner, half-covered by a sack. There he played with pebbles and with the dung of dogs and horses. He ate everything. He scratched the lime from the walls and stuffed his mouth full of it, then coughed until he was blue in his face. He lay in the corner like a scrap of rubbish. J: 21]

This description of Menuchim as abject mirrors the children's point of view who violently abuse Menuchim by trying to drown him in a barrel full of worms and dirty rain water (ibid.); it also mirrors the views of the other family members who share the children's perception of Menuchim as a symptom carrier: "In der Familie Singer aber schien es, als hätte der kleine Menuchim die ganze Anzahl menschlicher Qualen auf sich genommen, die sonst vielleicht eine gütige Natur sachte auf alle Mitglieder verteilt hätte." (W5: 19) [But it seemed as though in the family of Mendel Singer little Menuchim had taken upon himself the whole catalogue of human suffering which a kind nature might otherwise have divided among all the members. J: 31f.] This is particularly true of Deborah who interprets Menuchim as a symbol of a serious crisis that threatens the core of her family. In her view, her son's illness is linked to an episode which occurred during her pregnancy: she remembers how on a hot summer day, when she was three months pregnant, she and Mirjam happened to be in a crowd when the local countess suddenly arrived in town causing a flurry of excitement and commotion among the people which allowed Mirjam to dash off. The coach driver tells her that her daughter has run into the local church:

> Deborah überlegte einen Augenblick, dann stürzte sie sich in die Kirche, hinein in den goldenen Glanz, in den vollen Gesang, in das Brausen der Orgel. Im Eingang steht Mirjam. Deborah ergreift das Kind, schleppt es auf den Platz, rennt die heißen weißglühenden Stufen hinunter, flüchtet wie vor einem Brand. Sie will das Kind schlagen, aber sie hat Angst.
> Sie rennt, das Kind hinter sich her ziehend, in eine Gasse. Nun ist sie ruhiger. 'Du darfst dem Vater nichts davon erzählen', keucht sie. 'Hörst du, Mirjam?'
> Seit diesem Tage weiß Deborah, daß ein Unglück im Anzug ist. Ein Unglück trägt sie im Schoß. (W5: 17)[98]

---

[98] [Deborah considers a moment, then dashes into the church, into the midst of the golden shining, the full-voiced music, the organ's roar. In the entrance stands Miriam. Deborah grabs the child, drags her towards the square, rushes down the hot, white steps, flees as before a conflagration. She wants to beat the child but is afraid. She runs, dragging the child behind

The images of fire and burning with their biblical undercurrent powerfully evoke the sense of crisis that Deborah experiences when she discovers her child in a Catholic church. Deborah's dramatic reaction shows that, from within the belief system, Mirjam's attraction to the singing and the golden glamour of the interior of the church is not simply seen as an example of childish curiosity but as a major transgression, a fundamental violation of the Laws of prohibition which erect a strict boundary between orthodox Jews and non-Jews. By having to fetch her daughter from within the domain of a competing belief system, Deborah too has to violate the boundary between self and other, the pure and impure, and enter a territory that she knows is taboo. Apparently, the offence is so serious in nature that it cannot be communicated to Mendel. Not only does Deborah see the episode as an unmentionable violation which opens the floodgates to impurity and abjection, but furthermore she holds herself responsible by viewing her pregnant body as the source of future calamities. Her thinking thus reflects the orthodox belief system according to which femaleness and corruption are closely linked. By implication the episode also points to the anxious and intense nature of a woman's investment in her sons.

This becomes apparent after the discovery of Menuchim's illness and the crucial mirror scene which I discussed at the beginning of this sub-chapter. Although Menuchim is circumcised and thus part of the alliance with God, his inability to speak any other word than "Mama" (W5: 16) locks him into the *chora*, the maternally connoted space in which the child's and the mother's drives are not yet separate. This binds Deborah even more closely to the pre-linguistic, pre-signifying sphere of the semiotic. Her alienation from the Law of the Father and the symbolic order reaches the point where she neglects and rejects her older children (W5: 16).[99] We can now see that Deborah's experience of abjection in the above-quoted mirror-scene is not so much motivated by Deborah's age but more by the symbiosis with her sick child and their mutual attachment to the maternal sphere, a sphere which is associated with defilement and corruption. Orthodox Judaism puts in place elaborate prohibitions and purity laws to keep the impurity of nature at bay:

> For whatsoever man he be that hath a blemish, he shall not approach; a blind man, or a lame, or he that hath a flat nose, or any thing superfluous,

---

her, into a narrow street. Now she is quieter. 'Tell your father nothing of this,' she pants. 'Do you hear, Miriam?' From this day on, Deborah knew that a misfortune was under way. She carried a misfortune in her womb. J: 29-30]

[99] Deborah rediscovers her other sons again when they are about to be drafted into the Tsar's army, another serious threat to the family belief system. (W5: 19).

Or a man that is brokenfooted, or brokenhanded [...] he shall not come nigh to offer the bread of his God.[100]

In Menuchim's case, his inability to speak aggravates his and Deborah's impurity considerably because it means that he cannot learn the Torah or become a full member of the Synagogue. It is in this religious and cultural context that one has to place the mirror scene which is potentially psychotic in character, threatening to undermine Deborah's identity. To make things worse, this alienating experience of her body is further reinforced by Mendel's unconscious but icy gaze, a gaze that undermines all desire between husband and wife forever: "Seit diesem Tage hörte die Lust auf zwischen Mendel Singer und seiner Frau. Wie zwei Menschen gleichen Geschlechts gingen sie schlafen, durchschliefen sie die Nächte, erwachten sie des Morgens." (W5: 15) [From this day on all desire between Mendel Singer and his wife ceased. Like two people of the same sex they went to sleep, slept through the night, awoke in the morning. J: 25]

Both Mendel and Deborah wonder about their sexual estrangement later on in the narrative: Mendel's reflection on his alienation from his wife — "vertraut war ihm dieses Fleisch einmal gewesen, fremd war es ihm jetzt" (W5: 43) [once this flesh had been familiar to him; it was strange to him now. J: 74] — is echoed by Deborah's awareness that he has not touched her for a long time: "sie denkt auch an Mirjams Kosaken und wie lange sie Mendel nicht mehr berührt hat." (W5: 49) [She also thought of Miriam's Cossack and how long it had been since Mendel last touched her. J: 85] And Mendel comes back to the same issue after Deborah's death in America:

> Ich habe Kinder gezeugt, dein Schoß hat sie geboren, der Tod hat sie genommen. Voller Not und ohne Sinn war dein Leben. In jungen Jahren habe ich dein Fleisch genossen, in späteren Jahren habe ich es verschmäht. Vielleicht war das unsere Sünde. Weil nicht die Wärme der Liebe in uns war, sondern zwischen uns der Frost der Gewohnheit, starb alles rings ums uns, verkümmerte alles und wurde verdorben. (W5: 95f.)[101]

Mendel recognises here the link between the absence of affection in their relationship and the invasion of abjection which he experiences in America through Schemarjah's and Deborah's death, the uncertainty about Menuchim's and Jonas's fate in Europe, and Mirjam's madness. His insight that he has neglected his conjugal duties and that this may have been sinful

---

[100] Leviticus 21, 18-21.
[101] [I have begotten children, your womb has borne them, death has taken them. Meaningless and full of poverty was your life. In my youth I took delight in your flesh; in later years I scorned it. Perhaps that was our sin. Because the warmth of love was not in us, but only the frost of familiarity, everything around us perished, or was ruined. J: 169]

should not be overlooked since it reflects rabbinical law regulating the man's sexual obligations towards his wife. This deserves some exploration.

While all Western religions harness sexuality by confining it to marriage, Judaism tries to achieve a particular balance between restraining sexuality through the woman's status as a "Niddah" (which makes her ritually unclean during and after menstruation and following the birth of a child) and acknowledging and allowing the sexual drive. Unlike Catholicism which places value on sexual abstinence in the priesthood, Judaism actually proscribes celibacy because an unmarried man who reaches the age of twenty "spends all his days in sin [...] all his days in thoughts of sin",[102] to quote a rabbinical source. Not only is the observant male Jew obliged to marry and beget children but also to fulfil the commandment of "onah" which defines his conjugal debt to his wife: he is legally obliged to have intercourse with her, an obligation which he is forbidden to repudiate: "The sexual requirements for the male all devolve on the duties of propagation and the avoidance of sin. It is his duty, however, to provide his wife with gratification."[103] Rachel Biale explains that the man's obligations towards his wife as regulated through the Law of "onah" originate in the Curse of Eve which renders the woman unable to act or fulfil her desire:

> The point is to link the woman's curse, her desire for sex and inability to initiate it, with the man's *legal obligation* to 'pay her a visit', that is, to initiate sex at a time when he knows she desires it. It appears then that the man's duty is to compensate for the woman's curse by initiating sex: this is the duty called *onah*. The curse which brings inhibition of sexual impulse is not to be perpetuated by the husband; rather, it is his duty to counteract it by initiating sex to meet the desires of his wife.[104]

Biale offers two etymologies of "onah": while according to the first one "onah" is derived from the word for "season" or "period" and defines the frequency of sexual intercourse, according to the second etymology it is derived from the word "innui" meaning "suffering or pain".[105] This would suggest that the denial of a woman's sexual rights within marriage causes her suffering or pain which brings us back to Mendel and Deborah Singer in Roth's *Hiob:* the clinical gaze of Mendel's eye in the mirror scene is, from an orthodox rabbinical viewpoint, sinful because it causes a lasting breach of "onah" within their marriage and deprives Deborah of her sexual rights.

Mendel's lack of affection and desire is matched by Deborah's exclusive relationship with Menuchim and her anxious investment in him:

---

[102] Cited in Roith, *The Riddle of Freud,* 92.
[103] Ibid., 93.
[104] Rachel Biale, *Women and Jewish Law,* 125.
[105] Ibid., 126.

> 'Sag: Mama!' — 'Mama', wiederholte der Kleine. Ein dutzendmal wiederholte er das Wort. Hundertmal wiederholte es Deborah. Nicht vergeblich waren ihre Bitten geblieben. Menuchim sprach. Und dieses eine Wort der Mißgeburt war erhaben wie eine Offenbarung, mächtig wie ein Donner, warm wie die Liebe, gnädig wie der Himmel, weit wie die Erde, fruchtbar wie ein Acker, süß wie eine süße Frucht. Es war mehr als die Gesundheit der gesunden Kinder. Es bedeutete, daß Menuchim stark und groß, weise und gütig werden sollte, wie die Worte des Segens gelautet hatten. (W5: 16)[106]

At this point in the narrative Deborah perceives Menuchim's first word as proof of the rabbinical prophesy. She anxiously invests all affection and care in her sick son because her son's future brilliance will also shine upon her and thus allow her to gain secondary access to the ceremonies and values of the symbolic order. Ultimately, the prophesy revolves around the promise that her son's experience of abjection will be sublimated. Remember that "the abject is edged with the sublime. It is not the same moment on the journey, but the same subject and speech bring it into being."[107] In *Hiob* the first sign of this sublimation occurs only after Deborah's death when Mendel hears Menuchim's song on a record player:

> Jeden Tag hatte er hier Lieder gehört, lustige und traurige, langsame und hurtige, dunkle und helle. Aber niemals war ein Lied wie dieses hier gewesen. Es rann wie ein kleines Wässerchen murmelte sachte, wurde groß wie das Meer und rauschte. 'Die ganze Welt höre ich jetzt', dachte Mendel. 'Wie ist es möglich, daß die ganze Welt auf so einer kleinen Platte eingraviert ist?' Als sich eine kleine silberne Flöte einmischte und von nun an die samtenen Geigen nicht mehr verließ und wie ein getreuer schmaler Saum umrandete, begann Mendel zum ersten Mal seit langer Zeit zu weinen. (W5: 112)[108]

Menuchim's song affects Mendel so deeply because it translates the experience of abjection that has accompanied Mendel's and his family's life into a sublime piece of music. With Menuchim's song and, a little later, their miraculous reunion, the narrative enters the realm of the sublime and thus confirms the rabbi's wisdom.

---

[106] ['Say Mama!' 'Mama' echoed the little one. A dozen times he repeated the word. A hundred times Deborah repeated it. Not in vain had been her prayers. Menuchim spoke. And this one word of the deformed child was sublime as a revelation, mighty as thunder, warm as love, gracious as Heaven, wide as the earth, fertile as a field, sweet as sweet fruit. It was more than the health of the healthy children. It meant that Menuchim would be strong and big, as the words of the blessing had promised. J: 26]

[107] Kristeva, *Powers of Horror*, 11.

[108] [Every day he had heard songs, gay ones and sad ones, slow and fast, dark and light. But never had he heard a song like this one. It ran like a little brook and murmured softly; it was vast as the ocean and roared. Now I am hearing the whole world, thought Mendel. How is it possible that the whole world can be engraved on such a little disk. Then a silver tone melted into the violin music; it sewed itself around the velvety fabric of the violin playing like an accurate little hem. Mendel began, for the first time in long, to weep. J: 196f.]

The precondition of this sublimation of abjection is, however, the son's lasting separation from the mother which is scripted into the novel with Deborah's and Mendel's decision to leave Menuchim behind when they emigrate to the United States. For as long as Menuchim remains attached to the maternal *chora* he is under the sway of a power that is both secure and stifling. Mendel is too weak a father to help Menuchim become a proper speaking subject. Compare for instance the important passage in which Mendel tries to initiate Menuchim into the sacred symbolic order of Judaism by asking him to repeat the words of God: "Hör mich, Menuchim! Ich bin alt, du bleibst mir allein von allen Kindern, Menuchim! Hör zu und sprich mir nach: 'Am Anfang schuf Gott Himmel und Erde ...' Aber Menuchim rührte sich nicht." (W5: 29) [Hear me, Menuchim! I am old, you alone are left of all my children! Listen to me, and say after me: "In the beginning God created the heaven and the earth ..." J: 49]. Mendel's attempt is doomed to failure as long as Deborah and Menuchim are driven to take refuge in their non-separate existence by the hostility of a symbolic order, which stigmatises both of them as blemished, impure and other.

Ultimately, such is the logic of separation in Roth's narrative that it premises Menuchim's successful sublimation of abjection on Deborah's death. The son can only become a sublime artist after the mother's death. Although Roth was by no means an observant Jew, his depiction of women as other shows up a structure of feeling that is, as I have shown, particularly pertinent to Judaism. This is of course not to say that such containment of matriarchal power can only be found in Judaism — on the contrary, I agree with Esthelle Roith that "woman is invariably seen as occupying a position between culture and nature, while serving as an agency for the conversion of nature into culture, through the socialization of children."[109] Most patriarchal social orders traditionally share a fear of matriarchal power. However, it is not my concern in this chapter to discuss the universal appeal of Roth's story but to show the extent to which orthodox Judaism and the belief system of Eastern European Jewry informs the logic of his narrative. In *Hiob* the terrible experience of abjection that Deborah, Mendel, Menuchim and, to some extent, their other children are subjected to is caused both by pressures from without and within. While the pressures from without have rightly been analysed in terms of assimilation — a strong symbol of which is Schemarjah's change of name to "Sam" or Jonas's willingness to enter the Tsar's army — the pressures from within the belief system play, in my opinion, an equally important role in this drama of abjection.

It is a particularly Jewish interplay between ritual and abjection that shapes the Singers' experience of life. The Jewishness of the novel resides to

---

[109] Esthelle Roith, *The Riddle of Freud*, 90.

a significant degree in Roth's scripting of a particularly Jewish family system in a recognisable Eastern European context. Whereas Mendel attempts for a long time to resolve crises through ritual (until the sense of abjection catches up with him after he seems to have lost everything), the same path is, as we have seen, not really open to Deborah. As a woman she is excluded from primary access to the symbolic order. This exclusion from any significant role within the synagogue combined with Mendel's icy gaze heightens her experience of the abjection from which all family members suffer, albeit to a lesser extent. For, although, in the second part of the novel, Mendel himself suffers from a sense of abjection, the narrative presents abjection primarily as female in nature with the female body being its primary agent. As a corollary of this, ritual — and by implication the sublime — appears as the male domain. This explains why the happy ending is scripted around Menuchim's reunion with Mendel, of father and son. Only on the basis of the containment of the abject other, the female signifier, can such a reunion take place.

This reading is further supported by the final paragraph of the novel in which Mendel looks at Deborah's photograph, now remembering her youthful warmth and eroticism with affection. Mendel's affection is not directed at Deborah his wife, but at his memory of Deborah, his dead wife; in other words, it is a sentimental reverie which has no referent in the real world. Distance towards the female carrier of abjection seems to be a necessary precondition of Mendel's sublimated sentiment here. With Deborah dead and his daughter Mirjam, the promiscuous femme fatale, institutionalised, the sublimation of female abjection can now take place. This is the unconscious logic of this novel.

The fact that it is a photograph which motivates Mendel's rediscovery of affection is of equal importance here. In the previous chapter we have seen that "through photographs, each family constructs a portrait-chronicle of itself, a portable kit of images that bear witness to its connectedness."[110] But this kit of images displays a connectedness which is always historical and fictionalised; it is a relic that incites the onlooker to sentimental reverie. An important ingredient in this process of turning the past into an object of tender regard is, according to Susan Sontag, the onlooker's pathos of looking at time past.[111] Both Sontag's argument and Annette Kuhn's observation that a photograph "is also the expression of a lack and a desire to put things right"[112] read like a commentary on the final scene of Roth's *Hiob*.

---

[110] Susan Sontag, *On Photography*. New York: The Noon Day Press, Farrar, Straus and Giroux, 1989: 8.
[111] Ibid., 71.
[112] Annette Kuhn, 'Remembrance'. In: Jo Spence and Patricia Holland (Eds.), *Family Snaps — The Meaning of Domestic Photography*. London: Virago, 1991: 23.

In addition, the final scene also illustrates that all representation is a form of control and appropriation. For the novel ends with an apotheosis of a male identity which is predicated on the control of the female signifier though representation. This also suggests that this final act of sublimating abjection is by its very nature highly ambivalent and frail. Homi Bhabha's analysis of the ambivalence of the stereotype and fetish provides an astute comment on the hidden underside of this apotheosis of male identity in Roth's novel: "The fetish or stereotype gives access to an 'identity' which is predicated as much on mastery and pleasure as it is on defence, for it is a form of multiple and contradictory belief in its recognition of difference and disavowal of it."[113] Deborah's photograph serves as Mendel's final fetish object expressing the sublimation of anxiety, and, by implication, both pleasure and defence.

Both the gender roles in *Hiob* as well as the logic of the narrative seem to be shaped by the orthodox belief system and its construction of gender roles. This is not to say that Roth was an orthodox Jew — on the contrary, I have traced his conflicting positions towards his Jewishness as well as Judaism at the beginning of the chapter — but that his early exposure to the orthodox belief system may have exercised a considerable influence on his conception of female characters. While it is arguably true that all patriarchal societies are premised on the social containment of female fertility, orthodox Judaism turns this control into a highly complex set of prohibitions which stigmatise women as abject. Although Roth did not become an observing Jew, he shares with orthodoxy a phobic perception of women as the abject other. The novel thus elaborates a structure of feeling that fends off the fear of abjection through representation.

---

[113] Homi K. Bhabha, *The Location of Culture*. London and New York: Routledge, 1994: 75.

Files against the Self: The Case of Albert Drach

When a Jew from Brody sits under a Zwetschkenbaum

"Some accuse me of being a Jew; some excuse me for being one; some even praise me for being a Jew. But all think about it."[1] These were the words of the nineteenth century assimilated writer and journalist Ludwig Börne who could not understand why he continued to be perceived as a Jew despite the assimilatory steps that he had taken, such as conversion to Protestantism, changing his name from Baruch to Börne and rejecting a mode of expression that, from the nineteenth century onwards, identified the German Jew: "mauscheln" or "jüdeln".[2] For Börne and the following generations, the project of assimilation with its aim of complete absorption into German *Kultur* and its universalist assumptions remained the unchallenged cornerstone of their private and public identities. By the end of the century the ideal of assimilation turned sour when the chauvinistic and anti-Semitic ideology of the *Volk* became increasingly popular. A climate of extreme intolerance towards Jews was produced by the rhetoric of the "Volksgeist" [tribal spirit] which presented itself as something innate and natural. As a result of this many assimilated Jews found that, although they were no longer physically separated from the Germans by ghetto walls, they were now trapped in a new ghetto of the mind. Zygmunt Bauman summarises the failure of assimilation thus:

---

[1] Cited in Sander L. Gilman, *Jewish Self-Hatred. Anti-Semitism and the Hidden Language of the Jews*. Baltimore and London: John Hopkins University Press, 1986: 162.

[2] "Mauscheln" or "jüdeln" are derogatory terms for German spoken with a slightly altered syntax, some words of Hebrew or Yiddish and a particularly "Jewish" intonation. In the words of Sander Gilman "the language of the Jew began to serve as *pars pro toto* of the Jew. The Jews' language, which became symbolic for their perceived essence as liars, falsifiers, and merchants, was captured in *mauscheln*." Gilman, *Jewish Self-Hatred*, 139. A good example of this identification of the Jews' language with moral corruption are Börne's *Briefe aus Paris* [Letters from Paris] in which he attacked the Rothschilds for both their money-making and their heavily accented language. In Börne's view, the 'good' Jew speaks 'good' German. "In making his distinction between the 'good' and the 'bad' Jew in society, Börne created a dichotomy that reflected his own sense of self." Ibid., 164.

Much to their despair, the assimilants found that they had in effect *assimilated themselves solely to the process of assimilation*. Other assimilants were the only people around who shared their problems, anxieties and preoccupations.³

The ideology of the nation-state, its practice of legitimising its authority through reference to shared blood-ties, its phobic intolerance of all difference, and, in particular, the ubiquity of anti-Semitism are the great themes in Albert Drach's writings.

Albert Drach, born in Vienna in 1902 of Jewish parents, was forced to emigrate after the so-called *Anschluß*, [annexation of Austria] in 1938, leaving his mother behind. His experience of the four years between his father's death and emigration without his mother is reported in >>Z. Z. << *das ist die Zwischenzeit* [>>I. P.<< that is the Interim Period], subtitled *Ein Protokoll* [a statement of evidence] and published in 1968. The second part of his autobiography *Unsentimentale Reise* [Unsentimental Journey, 1966], subtitled *Ein Bericht* [a report], deals with the years of emigration from 1942 to 1945: hiding in the South of France, where he was repeatedly detained, Drach managed to escape deportation to the death camps until the arrival of the Allies in 1944. After the War, he returned to Mödling near Vienna to find the parental home occupied by the very caretaker who in 1938 had denounced Drach to the SA. It took years of legal proceedings before the caretaker could be evicted and Drach could regain occupation of his house. The immediate post-war years prior to his marriage are dealt with in *Das Beileid* [Condolence, 1993], the only work of prose referred to as a novel on the cover page, although its subtitle calls it a diary.

Drach's autobiographies, in *Unsentimentale Reise* described as "ein Mosaik aus Grauen und Entsetzen" [a mosaik of dread and horror], and his great novel *Das große Protokoll gegen Zwetschkenbaum* [the Massive File on Zwetschkenbaum, 1964] are written in a style that draws attention to itself. While the author's designation of these works as "statements of evidence" places them closer to the category of non-fiction, they are nevertheless not easy to classify. As Ernestine Schlant puts it, they belong "in a non-canonical area where autobiography, reportage, witnessing [...] struggle for literary expression".⁴ These experiences are transported into the sphere of the legalistic and judicial register which is at a remove from emotional immediacy. A prominent example of this technique is *Das große Protokoll gegen Zwetschkenbaum*, written during the Second World War but only published in 1964. The following sub-chapter examines the way in which Drach employs the language of bureaucracy in this novel in order to

---

³ Zygmunt Bauman, *Modernity and Ambivalence*. Cambridge: Polity, 1991: 143.
⁴ Ernestine Schlant, 'Albert Drach's *Unsentimentale Reise*: Literature of the Holocaust and the Dance of Death'. In: *Modern Austrian Literature* 26/2 (1993): 35.

articulate the ubiquitous stigmatisation of the Jew in Austrian society after the First World War.

The plot of the novel is set in motion when one day towards the end of the First World War, the Hasidic Jew, Schmul Leib Zwetschkenbaum, born in Brody, now itinerant, is found under a plum tree in Austria. He is subsequently arrested and charged with stealing plums. When he is brought before a judge, the question arises as to whether Zwetschkenbaum is legally competent.[5] A doctor is called in who assesses Zwetschkenbaum's sanity by asking him a set of Austro-centric questions such as "what is the capital of Austria?", "on what river is the capital?", which all "reflect the world of power which sees this milieu as universal."[6] A set of "natural" questions is then put to him which he answers with reference to his own religious background: asked what the difference between men and women is, he says that men are circumcised and women are not.[7] In his report, the doctor interprets this as an indication of Zwetschkenbaum's inability to adequately distinguish between the sexes. Finally, Schmul is asked to define a plum, which he describes as a winged animal "dessen Fittiche so schön in der Sonne glänzen" [the feathers of which glitter beautifully in the sun, GP: 21], an answer which seals Zwetschkenbaum's fate in the eyes of the physician. The reader learns a little later why Schmul defined a plum in such a strange manner: apparently, some of the doctor's front teeth are missing, as result of which he mispronounces the word "Zwetschke" [plum] as "Spätzche" [sparrow, GP: 21]. Gilman has rightly observed that "the classic mispronunciation of German words by Yiddish speakers, the *Mauscheln*, which marked the discourses about Jewish difference for centuries, is projected back onto the Austrian physician."[8]

After this first psychiatric report Zwetschkenbaum is declared unfit and consequently transferred to a mental hospital where he is subjugated to new medical assessments, institutionalised violence as well as abuse by the other patients. During a fire, he manages to escape, wanders around until he is arrested again and is this time charged with setting fire to the psychiatric hospital as well as to a farm. When the charges are dropped, he is transferred back to the hospital, where, due to the involvement of some unknown benefactor, he is now treated as a first class patient until he is handed over to two Jewish families who are paid for looking after him. Attempting to find

---

[5] For a discussion of Schmul's language ("mauscheln") with reference to the notion of competence in Austrian law see Sander Gilman, 'Zwetschkenbaum's Competence: Madness and the Discourse of the Jews'. In: *Modern Austrian Literature* 26 (1993): 1-33.
[6] Sander Gilman, 'Zwetschkenbaum's Competence', 4.
[7] Albert Drach, *Das große Protokoll gegen Zwetschkenbaum*. Munich: Carl Hanser, 1989: 21. Henceforth cited as GP in brackets.
[8] Sander Gilman, 'Zwetschkenbaum's Competence', 9.

out the identity of his benefactor, Schmul travels on several occasions to Vienna where he meets two former prison inmates who set up a small business for him which, however, turns over stolen goods. Finally, Zwetschkenbaum is rearrested and brought before the same judge who dealt with the plum incident at the beginning of the novel. No matter what Zwetschkenbaum does, he always ends up under the sphere of the cursed plum tree, and by implication, before a judge.

This cyclical structure highlights the impotence of the individual caught up in an apparatus of power, the rhetorics of which systematically turn him into the deviant other, requiring judicial, medical and social control. However, the novel does not revolve around a simple dichotomy between the men of power and the social underdog, but it explores instead the ubiquity of the category of the Eastern Jew in discourse, be it the judicial, medical or outright anti-Semitic discourse of the representatives of power, the language of the assimilated Western Jews or the talk of the 'little' people, such as the patients in the mental hospital, the wardens, ordinary policemen or the crooks in the prison. Despite their religious, ideological or class differences, they all share in the stigmatisation of Zwetschkenbaum as inherently other.

A few examples may illustrate this. When Schmul is interviewed by judge Bampanello von Kladeritsch, one of the judge's first questions is whether "alle seine Geschwister so krumm seien wie er" [all his siblings were as crooked as he, GP: 16]. "Crooked" refers both to Schmul's physical disability as well as his alleged moral corruption. Added to this are references to his "oriental" appearance and behaviour (GP: 66). This theme of the Eastern Jew's physical and implied moral crookedness is taken up by the institutionalised lawyer Schimaschek who makes puns about the Eastern Jew's body (GP: 57) and later defines the Jew as a morally corrupt twilight figure. The Jew, he says, is "ein Wesen, das sich an den Tag kralle, wenn es schon Nacht sei [...]. Er wolle den Tag stehlen, um ihn bei Nacht mit Nutzen zu verkaufen." [A being clinging to daylight when it is already night. He would want to steal the day in order to sell it at a profit by night. GP: 92]

There is, however, no fundamental distinction between Schimaschek's mad ranting against the Jew and the ostensibly sane deliberations of the representatives of a rational order. The abjection of the Jew characterises even the discourse of the Westernised, assimilated Jews: when, for instance, judge Schönbein and defence lawyer Meyer, two assimilated Jews, discuss their respective conversions to Christianity, they both denounce orthodox Judaism as obsolete, backward and oriental (GP: 72). Schönbein sums up his internalised anti-Jewishness as follows: "Jude sein sei nicht nur ein dumpfer

Zustand, sondern die Verirrung in eine nirgends einmündende Gasse" [being a Jew was not only a dull existence but, moreover, the aberration into a street leading nowhere, GP: 72] and he continues that Judaic laws and practices had no other function than prolonging the estranged outsider existence of a community of dealers and hypocrites.[9]

What Schönbein puts in intellectual terms sounds in the mouth of the lower class anti-Semite Quirrl thus: "Alle Juden täten dasselbe, nämlich stellten sich auf einen Platz, der ihnen nicht gebühre [...] und den sie nicht ausfüllen könnten, daher ihr Flaus und Betrug und falscher Nimbus." [All Jews were doing the same thing, namely assuming a position that was not theirs and which they could never fill, this explained their trickery and fraud and false nimbus. GP: 120] The Jew's alleged psychological, moral and physical corruption is further characterised by the state prosecutor Dr. Franz Schmalzl who claims that both criminals and Jews lack intellectual presence of mind which, he claims, is caused by the "Verkümmerung and Verkrümmung des seelischen Apparates" [atrophy and deformation of their psychological apparatus. GP: 143] In all these essentialising discussions of the Jew's "true nature", he appears as morally, physically, intellectually and psychologically deformed. The central concern of the novel is thus society's engagement with the stereotype of the Eastern Jew; the meaning of this stereotype can easily flip over from a demonised alien to that of the oriental prophet and back again.

---

[9] He states that Judaic laws only exist in order to "der Gemeinschaft von Händlern und Heuchlern, die an ihnen festhielten, die Fortführung eines rein äußerlichen, befremdlichen Daseins zu sichern." [To guarantee this community of dealers and hypocrites, which kept practising them, the prolongation of their superficial and estranged existence. GP: 72]

Schmul goes West

In *Modernity and Ambivalence,* Zygmunt Bauman argues that the project of Jewish assimilation is a poignant example of the universalising logic of the nation state, whose most salient trait is the crusade against ambivalence. Focusing on the dynamic of the modern state, Bauman demonstrates that the modern striving towards equality goes hand in hand with the attempt to eliminate everything that is the "other of order": incongruity, obscurity, irrationality and ambiguity.[10] With regard to the Jewish experience this meant that the project of Jewish assimilation made acceptance conditional on the shedding of Jewish cultural and religious values. Western Jews internalised the assimilatory pressure to such an extent that they largely agreed with the gentiles' negative evaluation of the Eastern Jew as a filthy, uncivilised, and backward oriental:

> Loyalty to discredited values and life-styles was tantamount to confinement to the lower rungs of the cultural ladder. When persevering in such loyalties, the individuals risked exclusion from the universe selected for missionary activity, and a life-sentence of strangerhood. If, on the other hand, individuals attempted to shed the discredited values and acquire instead the endorsed ones this was interpreted as further proof of the universal validity and desirability of the dominant values and the superiority of their social carriers.[11]

The ideal of equality before the law, so desired by the German Jews, necessarily led to the state's monopoly of law-making and coercion and to a sapping of communal autonomy and authority. While the German Jews overwhelmingly subscribed to the project of assimilation, their "host" nation kept sitting in judgement as to whether the individual attempt had been genuine and successful.[12] This dynamic, according to which the motives of the assimilatory individual were always suspect, is firmly rooted

---

[10] Zygmunt Bauman, *Modernity and Ambivalence,* 7f. Although complex taxonomies, catalogues and inventories evolved as a modern practice which tried to classify the world in neat categories, ambivalence remained "the main affliction of modernity"(Ibid., 15). This is so, writes Bauman, because "both order and ambivalence are alike products of modern practice; and neither has anything except modern practice [...] to sustain it." (Ibid., 15).
[11] Ibid., 112.
[12] A good example of an intellectualised Anti-Jewishness is given in Jakob Wassermann's *Mein Weg als Deutscher und Jude.* Munich: Deutscher Taschenbuch Verlag, 1994. Wassermann is citing a conversation he had with a German friend who turns out to be anti-Jewish. Summarising the Jews' assimilation in the nineteenth century, the German comes to the conclusion: "aber in ihrem Grund blieben sie Juden" [but ultimatley they remained Jews]. And he continues: "Judentum ist wie ein Färbemittel; die geringste Quantität reicht hin, um einer unvergleichlich größeren Masse seinen Charakter zu geben oder wenigstens Spuren davon." (Ibid., 52) [Jewishness is like a coloring agent; a small quantity is enough to change the character of a great mass or, at least, to leave traces of it.]

in the ideology of the nation state which taps into a 'natural' allegiance modelled on kinship.

Nationhood and nationalism are even today uncomfortable phenomena because they are sustained by the emotional lure of kinship. This is a point made by Benedict Anderson in *Imagined Communities*, an inspiring study of the emotional attractiveness of the nation. He defines the nation as "an imagined political community — and imagined as both inherently limited and sovereign" and raises the question as to what makes it generate such colossal sacrifices as have been witnessed, for instance, in two world wars.[13] Tracing the process by which the nation came to be imagined, such as the contribution of the printing press and the distribution of vernacular administrative languages, Anderson notes a certain gap in his analysis of the social processes he describes on the one hand and the emotional attachment that people feel for the nation on the other.[14] He then tries to address this by explaining the enormous emotional attraction of nationalism with reference to the idioms of kinship (motherland, *Vaterland, patria*) and home (*Heimat*) both of which "denote something to which one is naturally tied" and he adds that:

> in everything 'natural' there is always something unchosen. In this way, nationness is assimilated to skin-colour, gender, parentage and birth era — all those things one cannot help. And in these 'natural ties' one senses what one might call 'the beauty of *Gemeinschaft*'. To put it another way, precisely because such ties are not chosen, they have about them the halo of disinterestedness.[15]

With regard to Jewish assimilation, this "halo of disinterestedness", as analysed by Anderson, is the salient point: since the ties of the assimilated Jews were obviously chosen, their cultural affiliation with Germanness could, from the viewpoint of nationalists, never share in this aura of disinterestedness. As a mere option or choice, assimilation was considered to be inherently inauthentic and therefore incompatible with the imagined community of the nation. The rhetoric of nationalism in no way reflected on the notion underlying it. Equally it overlooked the artificiality of a communion which ignored the huge economic inequality in the nation body in favour of a superior and innate comradeship. Since the nation was imagined in terms of natural ties, assimilation was, from the viewpoint of the host nation, always ultimately unnatural, a type of camouflage only capable of disguising the true nature of the Jew. As a result of this effective projection of familial ties onto the nation's body, both the cultures of

---

[13] Benedict Anderson, *Imagined Communities. Reflections on the Origin and Spread of Nationalism*. London and New York: Verso, revised ed. 1991: 6.
[14] Ibid., 141.
[15] Ibid., 143.

assimilated and unassimilated Jewry ended up being the other of the "natural" order of things.

Albert Drach's *Das große Protokoll gegen Zwetschkenbaum* can be described as a novel about the failure of assimilation. We have already seen how Schönbein and Meyer, two assimilated Jews, go out of their way to dissociate themselves from any affiliation with Jewishness. The two characters are typical of the process of embourgeoisement which is intricately linked to assimilation. Steven Aschheim has observed that "Jews did not integrate into some abstract *Volk* but into the middle class, and they spent much of the nineteenth century internalising the economic, ethical, and aesthetic standards of that class."[16] In this process the German Jews' affiliation with gentile middle class aspirations were normalised to such an extent that unassimilated, traditional Jewry now appeared to be abnormal. In Drach's novel this view is put forward by Meyer, who attacks the backwardness of orthodox Jewry and their obstinate adherence to outlived rites, dogmatism and arrogance, all of which, in his opinion, must be left behind "durch die sichtbare und sinnfällige Scheidung aus solcher Gemeinschaft vermittels Annahme der Taufe" [by means of the visible and meaningful separation from such a community by acceptance of baptism, GP: 72]. Schönbein replies that the act of conversion has to be matched by a "Willensakt zur völligen seelischen Umwandlung" [will power to achieve a complete change of one's psychological makeup, GP: 72], which, in his view, requires divine grace. What appears to be a sophisticated theological debate in favour of conversion, is, however, underpinned by the very essentialising rhetoric of nationalism and its concept of "natural ties". Although Schönbein and Meyer have adopted this rhetoric to perfection, they are ultimately trapped in their Jewishness because they can at best only imitate the naturalness of belonging to the "national family". But because an imitation is never the real thing, their very attempts to be non-Jewish mark them, in the eyes of the gentiles, as particularly Jewish. The butt of Drach's satire is, however, not so much assimilated Jewry as the national imagining which uses the category of Jewishness as a huge refuse bin for the waste of its own abjection.

We come across a second type of assimilated Jew later on in the novel, namely the philanthropic Western Jew who takes pity on his Eastern counterpart. When Schmul runs away from Meier Druckmann he bumps into two Viennese Jews who buy him a few drinks, offer him a little money and finally suggest that they would like to grant him a wish because their son returned safely from the First World War. The way in which this

---

[16] Steven E. Aschheim, *Brothers and Strangers. The East European Jew in German and German Jewish Consciousness, 1800-1923.* Madison, Wisconsin: University of Wisconsin Press, 1982: 7.

encounter is recorded ensures that the couple's philanthropy appears as an act of patronising welfare barely masking their shame. When the woman reveals "daß sowohl sie als auch ihr sie begleitender Gatte Juden, freilich Wiener Juden, wären" [that both she as well as her accompanying husband were Jews, though Viennese Jews, GP: 192], the qualification "though Viennese Jews" immediately takes away from the shared commonality that is at first evoked. A little later the reader learns, however, that the couple is not really from Vienna because their names are Wladimir and Rosa Pollack (GP: 193) which clearly suggests their own Eastern European origins. As assimilated Jews, they try to "naturalise" their membership of bourgeois, enlightened Western Jewry by dissociating themselves from their all too conspicuous Eastern brothers and sisters, who, from the 1880s on, were migrating West on a massive scale. Ultimately, the money and material help which they offer Schmul act out the shame they feel for their rejection of the anti-modern Jew. The Pollacks' response to Schmul thus exemplifies the ambivalence of the liberal Jew towards Eastern Jewry as described by Aschheim:

> Protective and dissociative modes operated side by side in uneasy alliance. German Jews undertook massive charitable work on behalf of their persecuted East European Jews at the same time that they sought the most efficacious means to prevent their mass settlement in Germany. This dialectical tension between responsibility and dissociation was built into the German Jewish liberal approach to the Ostjuden.[17]

In the novel Schmul manages for a long time to defend his identity as a Hasidic Jew. Not only does he try to adhere to the complex rituals of orthodoxy in the face of adversity by, for instance, wearing a caftan, tallit and tefillin, and praying with the ecstatic joy of the Hasidic Jew in the psychiatric hospital until his ritual objects are destroyed by a patient (GP: 39). Moreover, he adopts the role of cultural mediator or go-between. Thus, for instance, he tells Dr. Vorderauer a highly symbolic dream, which delineates three Jewish paths:

> nämlich der Weg seines Bruders Ezechiel [...] — der Weg dieses neu hinzugekommen Bruders wäre, das Heilige Land noch einmal zu heiligen —, oder der Weg des Bruders Salomon, sich in der Haut der Wölfe zu verstecken, um die Wölfe zu fressen, oder sein Weg, der Schmuls, mit allen Fingern zu finden Unglück und mit jeder Zehe zu treten in Unglück [...], aber den Kopf aufgerichtet zu haben von Gott zu Wonne und Frohlocken. (GP: 42)[18]

---

[17] Steven Aschheim, *Brothers and Strangers*, 33.
[18] [Namely the path of his brother Ezechiel [...] — the path of this newly mentioned brother was to sanctify the Holy Land for a second time — or the path of his brother Salomon which was to hide in a wolf's coat in order to eat the wolves, or Schmul's own path, which was to

Zionism, assimilation and adherence to a traditional life in the Diaspora were indeed three options debated amongst Jewry at Schmul's time. Schmul's interpretation of Jewish history is later challenged in the prison by the anti-Semite Quirrl who tells the other prison-inmates two anti-Semitic anecdotes revolving around the stereotype of the cowardly and selfish Jew who has no regard for human life. Schmul refutes Quirrl's accusation of the Jew's alleged indifference towards human life and relates the following parable:

> er bitte die Herren, wenn sie sähen einen Menschen, der trage einen Buckel und nichts darauf, zu denken, vielleicht sei es darinnen, daß dieser Mensch es trage. Aber auch, wenn es darinnen nicht sei, so bitt er sie, ihm (nämlich dem Mann) nicht übelzunehmen seinen Buckel. Er bitte sie nicht für den Mann, er bitte für die Herren. Sie würden sein weniger schlecht gelaunt, wenn sie dem Mann nicht übelnehmen seinen Buckel (GP: 129)[19]

While the first part of this parable and the metaphor of the hunchback addresses the Jewish internalisation of persecution, the second part gives Schmul's parable an interesting twist. What Schmul is really saying, it now transpires, is that this fixation with the hunchback is the problem of the gentile who projects the chip on his own shoulder onto the image of the Jew. In his own way, Schmul addresses here the dynamics of anti-Semitism that he is constantly subjected to.

Apart from such highly symbolic passages it is above all the dreams which lend Schmul the aura of the archetypal Jew who does not suffer from the disease of the Western Jew, namely self-rejection. When, for example, Schmul talks in his sleep in the hospital, another inmate, the journalist Wolf Stengel, admires the beauty of his archetypal language and calls him an ancient prophet (GP: 114), a view shared by the other prisoners of Jewish origin. The projections of the anti-Semites are here matched by the assimilated Jews' new glorification of the Eastern Jew as the embodiment of prophetic wisdom, ancient authenticity and wholeness. What we witness in these scenes is a parody of the "cult of the Ostjude" which gathered momentum after 1914 when the disillusionment generated by the First World War began to materialise.[20] Steven Aschheim rightly points out that "the cult of the Ostjude always proceeded from a comparative East-West

---

touch misfortune with all his fingers and to walk into misfortune with all his toes [...] but to keep his head high in order to rejoice and exult in God.]

[19] [He would beg the dear sirs, if they saw a man with a hump but nothing on it, to think that the man carried the load inside. But even if it was not inside, he would ask them not to hold the hump against the man. He did not ask for the man but for the dear sirs themselves. They would not be in such a bad mood if they did not bear ill will towards the man with his hump.]

[20] For a detailed analysis of this new cult see Steven Aschheim, *Brothers and Strangers*, 185-214.

Jewish analysis. The Ostjude was a foil for the presentation of the Western Jew as shallow, imitative, and assimilating."[21] Drach deflates this cult considerably by highlighting the ease with which positive stereotypes can flip back into negative images. Schmul's inflated image takes quite a fall when he finally wakes up with a big fart, as a result of which the "mystische Glorie" [the mystical halo, GP: 121] around him disappears and the real and extremely embarrassed Schmul reappears in his earthy humanness.

Drach, however, has to ensure that the reader does not fall into the same trap of essentialising Schmul as the living embodiment of authentic and archetypal Jewry. He achieves this by, firstly, distancing Schmul from the reader through the *Protokoll*, a point to which I will return later, and secondly by weakening Schmul's affiliation with Hasidism. Towards the end of the novel Schmul goes literally and metaphorically West. Before he sets up a shop in Vienna (trying to avoid dependency on his unknown benefactor) he falls prey to the path of assimilation which he dismissed earlier on. However, it is important to note that Schmul does not assimilate — instead, he is assimilated by the forceful attempts of Hermine, an ugly and desperate Jewess, who adopts the role of his educator in order to mould him into a potentially suitable husband. Hermine's package of assimilation includes all the ingredients of the traditional nineteenth-century *Bildungsprozeß* which turned the ghetto Jew of old into the urbanised modern German Jew: she teaches him grammatically "correct" German and literacy both in Gothic and Latin letters (GP: 211); she reads newspapers and the standard works of classical literature with him (GP: 213) and invites him to reply to the sentimental and romantic letters that she sends him. When Schmul refuses to part with his sidelocks, Hermine cuts them off while he is asleep (GP: 214). Schmul has now been turned into a Sam, or rather a "Schmul-Sam" (GP: 224). Eventually, he is presentable enough to accompany her to a ball, wearing a second-hand modern suit. Schmul's deghettoisation and transformation are summed up in the following words:

> So war ein östliches Reis in eine verwandte, ihm nichtsdestoweniger doch nicht ganz verständliche Welt umgesetzt worden. Nach und nach gab er Gewohnheiten auf, die ihm ebensosehr Tradition bedeuteten wie die Bearbeitung seiner Bart- und Haupthaare. (GP: 218)[22]

Although Schmul now reads, in addition to the Talmud, also the works of Schiller and Goethe (GP: 218), two exponents of the enlightened humanism

---

[21] Ibid., 187.
[22] [Thus an Eastern seedling had been transplanted into a related, however, not quite understandable plot. Step by step he gave up old habits which symbolised as much tradition to him as the traditional treatment of his beard and hair.]

with which the urban Western Jew identified, his assimilation ultimately resembles the second-hand suit that he has been given. For what is conspicuously absent from Schmul's assimilation is the inner transformation or process of self-refinement and self-cultivation that is at the heart of the ideology of *Bildung* as paradigmatically spelt out by Meyer and Schönbein. And this of course means that Schmul only imitates the assimilation that he is subjected to. From the start Hermine's education of Schmul appears as a true parody of assimilation and its underlying assumptions. This parody brings out the double bind in which the Jew is locked: while Schmul was first despised for being a backward Eastern Jew, the scribe of the *Protokoll* now ridicules him for the opposite, namely his de-ghettoisation which is presented as a hopeless camouflage without essence.[23] We can see how the narrative mobilises all common anti-Jewish images in order to expose their imperviousness to empirical reality. The *Protokoll* thus highlights the semantic flexibility of the stereotype which manages to stigmatise all behaviour by Jews as essentially false, deceitful and deficient.

Drach gives his narrative one further ironic twist by sending his remade version of Schmul-Sam to Vienna where, with the help of Stengel and Himbeer, two ex-prisoners, he opens a shop. However, this new image of Schmul as an industrious and useful citizen is replaced by the old stereotype of the parasitic swindling Jew when it turns out that the shop turns over stolen goods.

Drach's narrative is thus a record of the various contested images of the Eastern Jew ranging from outright anti-Semitic stereotypes (underpinned by the anti-Jewish, racial, medical and Christian discourses), to the cult of the Eastern Jew at a time when the basic assumptions of assimilation had turned sour. The common denominator of all these conflicting images is that they essentialise the Eastern Jew as other. Regardless of the respective meanings of these images, they all rely on the category of Eastern Jewishness as a huge refuse bin for the waste that is produced in the formation of a fragile identity.

---

[23] On the "völkisch" interpretation of assimilation as a mere disguise see Aschheim, *Brothers and Strangers*, 67f.

File Style

What makes Drach's analysis of this discourse on the Eastern Jew so remarkable is his choice of genre, the judicial *Protokoll* which in *Das große Protokoll*, filters everything through the indirect speech of an official, in this case a trainee state prosecutor whose identity is only revealed towards the very end of the novel. In his laudatio on Drach, Wolfgang Preisendanz argues that the *Protokoll* produces an anaesthetising effect, which "selbst Paroxysmen des Unrechts, Unheils und Schreckens mit extremer Sachlichkeit, Emotionslosigkeit und Distanziertheit zur Sprache bringt"[24] [which articulates even paroxysms of injustice, calamity and horror in a distanced, matter-of-fact style, lacking any emotion]. While it is certainly true that the *Protokoll* distances the reader emotionally from the injustice it talks about, this does not, however, go hand in hand with objectivity. We will see that the trainee prosecutor uses a pervasive rhetoric of anti-Semitism which ridicules the Eastern Jew.

Drach repeatedly elaborated on his *Protokollstil* [file style]. Submitting his novel to Rowohlt publishing house, he explained in a letter of 13 December 1959 that the aim was not to persuade his readers but to win them over "durch Erzeugung von Widerspruch bei einer bis zum Ende gegen den Titelhelden gerichteten Darstellung"[25] [by provoking opposition through a style that until the very end, is directed against the protagonist]. Clearly, Drach radically breaks with the literary tradition as established in the age of sentimentality in the late eighteenth century, which defines the relationship between reader and protagonist as one based on empathy and identification. In a letter to André Fischer, dated 26 January 1989, he describes his position in the following way:

> Ich glaube, daß ich eine neue Position bezogen habe, wenn ich in der Epik alles Falsche und Schlechte zusammentrage, was gegen einen Menschen gesagt werden kann, damit er am Schluß Gelegenheit hat, sich seiner inneren Folgerichtigkeit gemäß zu behaupten oder zugrundezugehen. Er ist dann nicht verlorengegangen, wenn ein Licht von ihm übrigbleibt.[26]

---

[24] Wolfgang Preisendanz (1988), 'Die grausame Zufallskomödie der Welt'. Reprinted in: Gerhard Fuchs and Günther A. Höfler (Eds.), *Albert Drach*. Graz and Vienna: Droschl, 1995: 264.
[25] Quoted in Eva Schobel, 'Albert Drach oder das Protokoll als Wille und Vorstellung'. In: Bernhard Fetz (Ed.), *In Sachen Albert Drach*. Vienna: WUV Universitätsverlag, 1995: 12.
[26] Quoted in André Fischer, '"Der Zynismus ist ein Anwendungsfall der Ironie." Zum Humor bei Albert Drach'. In: G. Fuchs and G. A. Höfler (Eds.), *Albert Drach*, 32. [I believe that I have adopted a new position by collecting especially all those wrong and bad things that can be held against a human being so that in the end he has the opportunity either to stand his ground or to go under in keeping with his inner character. But he will not have been lost if a light of him remains.]

But for Drach his anti-identificatory *Protokollstil* only imitates life: "Das Leben nimmt keine Rücksicht, es schreibt in gleicher Weise hart gegen alle."[27] [Life has no regard (for the individual, A.F.), it is written in the same way against everybody.]

For this reason, Drach's *Protokollstil* rejects all those literary techniques which create the illusion of direct access to the protagonists' conscious and subconscious thought processes, ranging from the nineteenth century *style indirect libre*, the interior monologue first manifest in German in Schnitzler's *Leutnant Gustl* (1900) to stream-of-consciousness — in other words, all those techniques that achieve a confessional effect and create illusion and empathy for the protagonist are by-passed in favour of the indirect register of the official. Even Schmul's dreams are distanced from the reader with the same techniques that characterise the *Protokoll* as a whole: the trainee prosecutor's reported speech and his explanatory annotations undermine immediacy and suspend the reader's potential for unmediated identification with the protagonist. Günther A. Höfler has rightly pointed out that Drach's anti-psychological style poses an alternative to the simple dichotomy of perpetrator versus victim by exposing the very foundations of "die Logik und Dynamik der Rede über den Juden" [the logic and dynamic of language about the Jew].[28] Instead of empathising with Schmul, the reader has no option but to analyse the different filters which colour all representations of the Eastern Jew. In a curious way, this is a novel without a protagonist since our only access to Schmul is the citation of Schmul Leib Zwetschkenbaum in a number of conflicting judicial and medical reports which are all subsumed in the trainee prosecutor's great report against Zwetschkenbaum. Drach's refusal to give his readers a direct glimpse of Schmul thus directs them to the discourse which always stereotypes the meaning of the Eastern Jew prior to and irrespective of the particulars of the individual's existence. It is important to note here that Drach's point is not so much that the *Protokoll* represents Schmul wrongly, but rather that an unmediated, unfiltered representation of the Eastern Jew is impossible. Unlike Joseph Roth, Arnold Zweig and other ghetto writers of the early twentieth century[29] and unlike Jewish intellectuals such as Martin Buber

---

[27] Quoted in Günter Kaindlstorfer, 'Ratzeputz: Der Kanzleischreiber Gottes: Zum 90. Geburtstag des Schriftstellers Albert Drach'. In: Gerhard Fuchs and Günther A. Höfler (Eds.), *Albert Drach*, 274.

[28] Günther A. Höfler, '"Wenn einer ein Jud ist, dann ist das Schuld genug'. Aspekte des Jüdischen im Werk Albert Drachs'. In: G. Fuchs and G. A. Höfler (Eds.), *Albert Drach*, 185.

[29] On Roth's representation of Eastern Jewry see the previous chapter. A good example of the re-appropriation of the Eastern Jew after the turn of the century is Arthur Landsberger's edition of ghetto stories *Das Volk des Ghetto* (Munich: Georg Müller, 1916). Another prominent example of the nostalgic tradition is Arnold Zweig's *Das ostjüdische Antlitz* with illustrations by Hermann Struck (Berlin: Welt-Verlag, 1920). On the tradition of ghetto

who attempted to replace the negative stereotype of the Eastern Jew with the positive image of the Hasid, which they claimed to represent the true roots of Jewish identity, Drach disputes the very possibility of perceiving Schmul in original terms.[30] Irrespective of their positive or negative connotation, all images of the Eastern Jew are affected by the discourse on the Jew that precedes each individual appropriation.

Mimicry of Power: A Figure of Uncertainty

A good model for the analysis of *Das große Protokoll gegen Zwetschkenbaum* is provided by current post-colonial theory and its notion of mimicry. Homi Bhabha developed the concept of mimicry with reference to colonial discourse and its construction of knowledge of the colonised. At first sight, it may seem incongruous to apply post-colonial theory to Drach's work; after all, Germany's colonial history was relatively short and, in comparison with other colonial powers, such as Britain and France, fairly unimportant. However, it seems to me that Germany's and Austria's relationship with parts of Eastern Europe mirror many aspects of colonialism proper. I agree with Florian Krobb who has recently argued that "a broader concept of colonialism, one that does not exclusively focus on overseas territorial possessions populated mainly by non-Europeans and governed by a small European administrative, military and economic élite, can be applied to aspects of the history of German-speaking central Europe, to the Holy Roman Empire, Germany and Austria."[31] If one defines colonialism along the lines sketched out by Krobb and, following on from there, if one analyses the mechanisms used to construe a colonised other, then the racial, judicial and medical discourse on Eastern Jewry can be read

---

writing see Anne Fuchs and Florian Krobb (Eds.), *Ghetto Writing; Traditional and Eastern Jewry in German-Jewish Literature from Heine to Hilsenrath*. Drawer, Columbia: Camden House, 1999; Gabriele von Glasenapp offers a good survey of the various forms of ghetto stories in *Aus der Judengasse. Zur Entstehung und Ausprägung deutschsprachiger Ghettoliteratur*. Tübingen: Niemeyer, 1996.

[30] On the new cult of the Eastern Jew see Steven E. Aschheim, *Brothers and Strangers*, 185-214; and on Buber see Gilman, *Jewish Self-Hatred*, 271-286.

[31] Florian Krobb, 'Re-Claiming the Location: Leopold Kompert's Ghetto Fiction in Post-Colonial Perspective'. In: Anne Fuchs and Florian Krobb (Eds.), *Ghetto Writing*, 41. Krobb writes: "The so-called *Ostsiedlung* (eastward colonisation) during the Middle Ages shows hallmarks of the settlers' colonies in North America, New Zealand and Australia. The eastward expansion of both Prussia and Austria which brought regions without a native German-speaking population (parts of Poland and the Balkans) under Berlin's and Vienna's rule must be regarded as a colonising process. And even a degree of "internal colonisation", meaning the establishment of colonised communities inside a given national territory in the form of reservations or homelands, can be witnessed in German history (and indeed European history in general), if we consider Jewish ghettos as such reservations for people with diminished freedoms and civil rights." (Ibid., 42.).

as an example of colonial discourse. Drach's *Das große Protokoll* practices a mimicry of colonial discourse which effectively deconstructs it. By mimicking the discourse of power through the judicial *Protokoll*, Drach produces something which in Bhabha's terms is "almost the same, but not quite". This is a point which requires some elaboration.

In his essay 'Of Mimicry and Man', Homi Bhabha introduces mimicry as a new term capturing a fundamental ambivalence that characterises the construction of the colonial subject in certain forms of stereotyping. Mimicry is a type of camouflage through which the colonial subject imitates the coloniser — an example of this would be the educated Indian civil servant mimicking an Englishman, without, however, being one. What interests Bhabha is the difference between the "authentic" Englishman and the colonised mimic whom he describes as *"a subject of a difference that is almost the same, but not quite."*[32] Because camouflage only imitates without ever achieving identity with the authentic thing, it paradoxically ends up producing ambivalence and a subtle slippage which "becomes transformed into an uncertainty".[33] Mimicry is at best partial representation, for this reason it results in a sameness which is not quite the same. For Bhabha it is precisely this slippage between "white/not quite" which, in the colonial context, turns into the very menace of mimicry, ultimately disrupting the authority of colonial discourse.[34] The formula "white/not quite" encapsulates the displacement which takes place in this doubling: as partial representation, mimicry undermines the authority of the authenticity which it is supposed to imitate. The subtle displacement which occurs in this process disturbs the coloniser's authority to such a degree that in the words of Robert Young, "the imitation subverts the identity of that which is being represented, and the relation of power, if not altogether reversed, certainly begins to vacillate."[35]

Mimicry, a figure of displacement, is also latently a figure of irony, farce or comedy, mocking the authority which it mimics. According to Bhabha, colonialism speaks often "in a tongue that is forked, not false" and produces "a text rich in the tradition of *trompe-l-oeil*, irony, mimicry and repetition."[36] The irony Bhabha talks about is the product of the difference between the high ideals of the colonial imagination on the one hand and its low literary effects on the other. Looked at from this angle, the slippage of

---

[32] Homi K. Bhabha, 'Of Mimicry and Man'. In: Homi K. Bhabha, *The Location of Culture*. London and New York: Routledge, 1994: 86.
[33] Ibid., 86.
[34] Ibid., 88.
[35] Robert Young, *White Mythologies. Writing History and the West*. London and New York: Routledge, 1989: 147.
[36] Homi Bhabha, 'Of Mimicry and Man', 85.

mimicry is always a figure of parody. This is a crucial aspect of my reading of Drach's *Protokollstil* which helps to address the ironic subversion of authority which is so characteristic of Drach's file style.

On the basis of these theoretical deliberations this sub-chapter argues that the *Protokollstil* of *Das große Protokoll gegen Zwetschkenbaum* is a type of mimicry which, by miming the former authority of the Austrian Empire, mocks and de-authorises its speech-acts. It is in line with this that the entire *Protokoll* [statement of evidence] is written by a trainee prosecutor, i.e. by someone who is only in the process of learning and is therefore only mimicking the language and gestures of authority. Ultimately, the trainee prosecutor is in the same position as Bhabha's mimic man. His *Protokoll* produces precisely the slippage that Bhabha is talking about and that makes room for narrative irony.

There are two levels of irony: firstly, the ironic anti-Jewish comments that the trainee prosecutor quotes and also makes himself about Zwetschkenbaum, and secondly the irony which is the effect of mimicry. A few examples may help to illustrate the way in which irony reinforces anti-Jewish statements on a first level. At the beginning of the novel Zwetschkenbaum is asked about his family background and movements. His statement is rendered in the grammatical mode of reported speech which suggests impartiality and matter-of-factness. However, this objectivity is fundamentally undermined by the trainee prosecutor's insertion of 'explanatory' annotations in brackets which all cast doubt on the veracity of Zwetschkenbaum's statement. For instance, when Zwetschkenbaum tells the judge that his brother Itzik's spine was broken during a pogrom, the trainee prosecutor adds in brackets: "Anmerkung: vielleicht hat er sich dieses Übel auch anderweitig zugezogen." [annotation: perhaps he received this ailment in quite a different manner. GP: 8] Similarly, when Zwetschkenbaum states that his sister was making her living by working in Lemberg, the scribe comments "wahrscheinlich also durch Prostitution" [probably through prostitution, GP: 8].

In addition to these annotations, the trainee prosecutor keeps inserting all those grammatical particles which in the German language powerfully affect the illocutionary force of speech acts; one prominent example is the usage of particles such as "wohl" which insinuates that Zwetschkenbaum does not have the common sense shared by everybody else. For example, reporting Zwetschkenbaum's fear of the other prison inmates who, at this point, verbally abuse him, the trainee prosecutor states that the quiet acceptance of the prison regime "ist *wohl* das mindeste, das *billigerweise* von einem Verdächtigen oder Überwiesenen verlangt werden kann, und für einen 'Zellenbruder' kann *wohl* die Gesellschaft anderer Gefängnisbewohner nicht schlechter sein als seine eigene für dieselben" [is no doubt the very least that can be expected of a suspect or transferred prisoner; and the company of other prison occupants can hardly be worse for a prison inmate than his own is for the others, GP: 9]. Apart from such openly dismissive comments, ironic annotations and particles, the trainee prosecutor uses a racist register by interpreting Zwetschkenbaum's behaviour as "Ergebnis arteigentümlicher Überheblichkeit" [the product of an arrogance typical of his race, GP: 9]. Furthermore, Zwetschkenbaum's language is qualified as only partly comprehensible, his 'Jewish' gestures are emphasised and his ability to speak clearly is disputed.[37] He is described as "krumm" [crooked, GP: 16] and "orientalisch" [oriental, GP: 66] in appearance. The trainee prosecutor speculates that, due to his "Gemütsbeschaffenheit" [disposition of mind, mentality], he is unable "einem geradlinigen Gedankengang zu folgen, vielleicht auch wegen seines im Talmud verstrickten Denkens" [to follow a straight line of thought, perhaps also because his thinking is caught up in the Talmud, GP: 13]. These are just a few examples which illustrate to what extent the trainee prosecutor taps into common anti-Jewish stereotypes and prejudices.[38] Instead of simply quoting the anti-Jewish and anti-Semitic remarks of the other characters in the novel, as would befit a statement of evidence, he reinforces and universalises the anti-Semitism to the extent that it appears to be normal. Rather than objectifying the events, the trainee prosecutor's adherence to reported speech gives the *Protokoll* a monologic quality, lending authority to the anti-Semitism that it articulates. The absence of any dialogue in this novel therefore not only reflects the formal requirements of the *Protokoll* but it also mirrors the totalitarian quality of a system which excludes the notion of reciprocity as such. This is in line with Drach's statement that he wanted to provoke opposition through a style that until the very end is directed against the protagonist.

On the other hand, this normalisation of anti-Semitism is constantly challenged by the slippage and ambivalence produced by mimicry. As a figure of displacement, mimicry always disturbs and mocks the authority that it imitates. This is where the second level of irony comes into operation: while the first level apparently invites the reader to collude with

---

[37] Gilman, an expert in this field, showed the link between the neurological discourse of the nineteenth century and the stigmatisation of the Jew's language as pathological. Cf. S. Gilman, 'Zwetschkenbaum's Competence', 17ff; and Sander L. Gilman, *Freud, Race, and Gender*. Princeton: New Jersey Princeton University Press, 1993.

[38] A detailed analysis of the stylistic characteristics of the *Protokoll* is offered by Matthias Settele, *Der Protokollstil des Albert Drach — Recht, Gerechtigkeit, Sprache, Literatur*. Frankfurt am Main, Berlin, Bern: Peter Lang, 1992. While Settele's dissertation offers a good survey of the stylistic devices used by Drach, he does not have a theoretical model that would help illuminate the subversion of authority characteristic of Drach.

the pervasive anti-Semitism that characterises the discourse on the Jew, the second level displaces and, by implication, mocks all the gestures of superiority and authority on which the irony of the first level rests. It is precisely this unwanted slippage which makes mimicry an inherently carnevalesque and dialogic imitation in Bakhtin's sense of the word; for it opens the novel up to a second level of reception which counteracts the first.[39] By turning the imitation of authority into its parody, mimicry thus plays against the otherwise monologic quality of the *Protokoll*. It is important to note, however, that this carnivalisation of the *Protokoll's* monologic authority is never authorised by a superior omniscient narrator, as, for example, is typical of Thomas Mann's works, but that it is the subversive outcome of mimicry in Bhabha's sense alone. No superior voice legitimises the second type of irony as the proper level of reception because obviously such an authoritative gesture would run counter to the subversiveness of mimicry which rests exclusively on the continued slippage as discussed above. Instead of denouncing the anti-Semitic tenor of the trainee prosecutor's irony, Drach's *Protokollstil* forces his readers to vacillate between the two levels, as a result of which their collusion with the discourse of authority is exposed. Bhabha's analysis of the subversive dimension of camouflage offers a commentary on Drach's *Protokoll*: "Under cover of camouflage, mimicry, like the fetish, is a part-object that radically revalues the normative knowledges of the priority of race, writing, history."[40] *Das große Protokoll gegen Zwetschkenbaum* was written long after the demise of the Austrian Empire; it is a post-colonial narrative which, by miming authority, also exposes its allure. It seems to me that Drach's insistence on a style which remains directed against his protagonist gains particular virulence when read with reference to post-colonial theory. The project of Drach's writings is a radical revaluation of our normative knowledges of nation, race and culture.

---

[39] It seems to me that Bakhtin's theory of heteroglossia and carnevalisation complements Bhabha's theory of 'writing back' and mimicry extremely well. From a Bakhtinian angle, mimicry cannot but produce parody. Cf. Mikhail Bakhtin, *The Dialogic Imagination: Four Essays*. Ed. by Michael Holquist, Austin: University of Texas Press, 1981.
[40] Homi K. Bhabha, 'Of Mimicry and Man', 91.

Dissecting Women: >>Z.Z.<< das ist die Zwischenzeit

>>Z.Z.<< *das ist die Zwischenzeit, Unsentimentale Reise* and *Das Beileid* have been described as landmarks in the literature on the Third Reich because, unlike much of the autobiographical writing which deals with the experience of persecution, Drach uses irony to convey both the experience of a history which is devoid of reason as well as the utter fortuitousness of survival.[41] I agree with André Fischer's view that there is no other writer who relates the battle for survival and the psychological deformations suffered by history with the same lack of emotion and as much bitter wit as Drach.[42] Fischer argues that the ironic presentation of evil is more likely to mobilise a reaction in the reader than those representations which suggest that it is possible to make sense of and, by implication, to come to terms with the evils of the Third Reich and the genocide of the Jews. Such *Vergangenheitsbewältigung* [coming to terms with the past] is clearly rejected by Drach "als naive Harmonisierung des nicht Verarbeitbaren"[43] [naive harmonisation of that which cannot be rationally understood] in favour of the *Protokollstil*.

The same applies to the tradition of the modern confessional autobiography as established by Jean-Jacques Rousseau in his *Confessions*, where the illusion of immediacy and, coupled with it, that of the reader's direct access to an emotional truth are created.[44] In clear contrast to this confessional mode of writing, Drach places such a distance between his autobiographical alter egos and the reader that identification with the protagonists is made impossible. Both the son in >>Z.Z.<< *das ist die Zwischenzeit* and Peter Kucku in *Unsentimentale Reise* are shown to be engaged in a battle for survival which unhinges the enlightened and humanitarian ethos of sympathy and compassion and, moreover, deconstructs the opposition of good and evil. In the context of the inhumanity of the Third Reich, the likeability of the protagonists is simply irrelevant. As in *Das große Protokoll* Drach chooses a style that is directed against his fictional alter ego since, in his words, "man kann nur dann zugunsten eines Menschen wirken, wenn man alles das darstellt, was gegen ihn spricht und aus all dem, was gegen einen Menschen gesagt wird, folgert, was für ihn

---

[41] For a detailed analysis of humour and irony in Drach's autobiographies see André Fischer, *Inszenierte Naivität. Zur ästhetischen Simulation von Geschichte bei Günter Grass, Albert Drach und Walter Kempowski*. Munich: Wilhelm Fink 1992: 214-267.
[42] André Fischer, '"Der Zynismus ist ein Anwendungsfall der Ironie." Zum Humor bei Albert Drach'. In: Gerhard Fuchs and Günther A. Höfler (Eds.), *Albert Drach*, 45.
[43] André Fischer, *Inszenierte Naivität*, 216.
[44] Cf. Jean Starobinski, *Jean-Jacques Rousseau: la transparance et l'obstacle*. Paris: Gallimard, 1971.

vorliegt."⁴⁵ [One can only work in favour of a human being by representing everything that can be said against him, and then by deriving from all that which works against him that which works in his favour.] By refusing to present his protagonists in terms of innocence and goodness, Drach also draws attention to the immoral indifference of history and questions the validity of our moral criteria.

The first of Drach's autobiographical reports, >>Z.Z.<< *das ist die Zwischenzeit*, covers the years from his father's death in 1935 to his emigration some time after the so-called *Anschluß* of Austria in 1938. The book traces how the male protagonist, referred to throughout as "the son", tries to live up to the paternal legacy by establishing himself as a lawyer and taking care of his heart-broken mother, while at the same time harbouring literary ambitions. This conflict between his filial duties on the one hand and his personal ambitions on the other is set against the background of the imminent threat of the Nazis' take-over of Austria. It is this historical reference point and the son's awareness of what the annexation of Austria will mean for him as a Jew which creates the protagonist's cynical distance towards all human relationships throughout the report.

What is most striking about this account of a "Zwischendasein"⁴⁶ [interim existence], is the way in which sexuality is treated as a failing placebo of life. Throughout the book the hero is engaged in a series of sexual relationships which, although they are meant to compensate for the lack of meaning in the son's life, are presented as the antidote of lust and involvement. The son appears as a dispassionate Don Juan clinically detached from his sexual activities which turn out to be a mere masquerade of sexual drive:

> Die Frage, ob Sexus allein das Leben rechtfertige, konnte sich einem immer wieder stellen, der sonst nichts hatte, dem seine Hantierung, sein Alltag zuwider waren und den familiale Verpflichtungen weder mit Genugtuung noch mit Interesse speisten. (ZZ: 113)⁴⁷

This connection between the son's fixation on sexuality and a perceived lack in his own life is maintained throughout. He is always on the lookout for the ideal female body, an aesthetic icon of beauty and perfection which is completely deprived of any relation with life:

---

⁴⁵ Quoted in André Fischer, '"Der Zynismus ist ein Anwendungsfall der Ironie'", 34.
⁴⁶ Albert Drach, >>Z.Z.<< *das ist die Zwischenzeit*. Munich: Deutscher Taschenbuchverlag, 1996: 145. Henceforth cited as ZZ in brackets.
⁴⁷ [The question whether sex alone justified life could be asked time and again by one who had nothing else in life and who hated his job, his daily life and who did not derive any satisfaction from or have any interest in familial duties.]

> Dabei verstand er unter Schönheit nicht nur die aus dem Dargebotenen zu folgernde Vollendung der einzelnen Stücke, sondern auch deren Zusammensetzung und Einklang nebst einem Anziehungsmoment, das einen gewissen erotischen Reiz vermittelte und damals schon mit dem ungenauen Gemeinplatz Sex-Appeal schlecht umschrieben wurde. Denn es handelte sich keineswegs um eine weitverbreitete Eigenschaft, sondern um das Idealbild für einen Einzelgänger [...]. (ZZ: 30)[48]

The remarkable sterility of the language employed here highlights the fact that this ideal of beauty is devoid of any real desire. The son's cold analysis of female perfection in terms of well-fitting body parts conjures up the image of Olympia in E. T. A. Hoffmann's tale 'Der Sandmann' where the male protagonist Nathanael falls in love with the embodiment of female grace and harmony which, however, turns out to be a monstrous mechanical puppet. In both cases the ideal of beauty is exclusively defined with reference to technical perfection and harmony without any emotional attachment. The clinical language of Drach's description mimes a male gaze which is not really driven by desire but by the need to exclude and reject. In >>Z.Z.<<, this bloodless icon of beauty serves the son as an abstract ideal which legitimises and rationalises his enormous aggression towards the real women he meets and the majority of whom he attacks as being "ugly". Rapidly moving from woman to woman, he resembles less Don Juan than Jack the Ripper, as he metaphorically dissects women into isolated body parts which do not fit together properly. Two examples may suffice to illustrate the son's calculated attacks on woman as the abject other. Reflecting on his conquests the son finds·

> leichte oder schwere körperliche Mißstände, die nicht nur deren Gang und eine gewisse schlampige Busengestaltung anlangten, die man hierzulande häufig trifft, sondern außerdem und vor allem die Unregelmäßigkeit der Gesichtszüge, ein Nichtzusammenpassen der Einzelstücke, wie es weniger bei heimischen Naturdenkmälern, als viel häufiger bei Stadtsiedlungen, künstlerischen Erzeugnissen sonstiger Art [...] gang und gäbe ist [...]. (ZZ: 30)[49]

In what can be described as the economy of abjection (and misogyny), the ugly woman is a projection of the phobic male who constitutes his own

---

[48] [By beauty he did not just understand the perfection of the individual pieces but also their composition and harmony as well as a moment of attraction which referred to a certain eroticism that was even then badly captured in the cliché of 'sex appeal'. For this was hardly a common characteristic but rather the ideal of a solitary figure.]

[49] [slight or serious deformations which did not only refer to their gait and a certain sloppiness in their breast formation, which is common here, but moreover and above all refers to irregular facial traits, the individual parts of which do not properly fit together, all of which is less common in the native monuments of nature but more in urban settlements and other artificial products.] See also the scene in which he rapes a woman described as an old spinster. Here the dissecting view of the female body is paired with physical aggression. See ZZ, 62f.

territory through loathing. Such spasms of disgust and nausea help to demarcate the boundaries of his universe which remain, however, fluid. Since for this anti-hero 'woman' is ultimately some living waste on the border of death, she is first conquered and then cast aside. As a cadaver she symbolises what has to be abjected in favour of life — this is the logic of abjection which structures all sexual conquests in >>Z.Z.<<.

The first sexual conquest described in the narrative is a rape scene where the son is shown to be both a literal and metaphorical pervert: prior to the actual rape, there is a description of the woman which does not only tap into the common stereotype of the old maid but, moreover, uncannily evokes the image of the de-individualised, de-sexualised, emaciated female body which was to become a historical reality:

> Mit diesem alten Mädchen war er früher des öfteren zusammengekommen. Sie hatten miteinander zumeist über Literatur gesprochen, für die sich die Dame interessierte, weil sie körperliche Erlebnisse offenbar nicht hatte, denn sie war weder anziehend noch charmant. Ja, sie sah nicht so aus, als ob zwischen Knochen und Haut noch hinreichende Fleischteile eingeschmuggelt wären, um eine lohnende Kostprobe vorzuspiegeln. (ZZ: 61)[50]

The violence of the ensuing rape is recorded with complete detachment and without any traces of emotional involvement. This technique of deliberately repressing the trauma of the rape-scene mobilises a strong reaction in the reader who cannot but perceive the enormous gap between the experience of violence and its representation.[51] In addition, this anaesthetising style reinforces the complete absence of any emotional investment from the son's sexual conquests. This anti-hero is a metaphorical Jack the Ripper who, before or after the act, enjoys dissecting his women through language. Equipped with his clinical gaze, he dismembers the "ugly female" in order to reinstate his fetish-object, the quasi-religious icon of the beautiful woman purified of all affective and somatic impulses, in short: of all life. In an interesting study of the functionalisation of the female body in Drach's work, Gerhard Fuchs interprets these attacks on the "ugly female" as the protagonist's projection of his own sense of deficiency onto a colonised other:

---

[50] [He had met up with the old maid quite often in the past. They had mainly talked about literature, for which the lady had an interest because she did not seem to have any physical experiences, for she was neither attractive nor charming. She did not look as if enough fleshy parts had been smuggled in between her bones and skin to have turned her into a worthy dish.]
[51] Cf. Wolfgang Preisendanz on this point, 'Die grausame Zufallskomödie der Welt', 265.

> Diese Ausstoßung einer das Selbst gefährdenden Körper-Repräsentanz (des Signi-
> fikanten für Schönheit) ermöglicht eine entschiedene Grenzziehung und Ablehnung
> sowie das Zulassen der damit verbundenen Emotionen wie Haßgefühle und Ekel.[52]

This captures the economy of abjection well and the logic of exclusion which structures the son's life, which wavers between self-aggrandisement and the loss of all meaning in life.[53]

The son's life is marked by the awareness that he is moving in a political and historical interim period which comes to an end only with the annexation of Austria. In this historical context, there is no room for real desire but only for the self-conscious mimicry of desire: "Und schließlich waren auch die sogenannten Liebesgenüsse des Sohnes, zu Unrecht einer echten und achtbaren Einigungskraft unterstellt, bloße Verschlingungen und Verrenkungen, die für Sekunden Lustersatz vortäuschten." [And, the son's so-called pleasures of love, wrongly attributed to a real and admirable desire for copulation, were, after all, nothing but contortions which faked passion for a few seconds. ZZ: 192] As a type of camouflage this mimicry barely masks the underlying fear of the son who feels that his movements resemble "ein Zickzackfliehen in der Dunkelheit vor einem Schützen, der bei Gelegenheit auf ihn anlegen würde" [a zigzag flight in darkness avoiding a marksman who would eventually target him, ZZ: 125].[54]

---

[52] Gerhard Fuchs, 'Männer, Mütter, Mädel. Die Funktionalisierung des Weiblichen bei Albert Drach'. In: G. Fuchs and G. A. Höfler (Eds.), *Albert Drach*, 79-121; here 92. [The abjection of a physical representation (the signifier of beauty) which endangers the self makes it possible for the self to draw strict boundaries and to act out rejection while allowing for feelings of hatred and disgust.]

[53] Cf. Julia Kristeva, *Powers of Horror*, 18.

[54] However, the economy of abjection is not only set in motion by the interim period and the doom of fascism but also by the intensive and angst-ridden relationship with his mother which he resolves abruptly in the end by leaving her behind when he finally flees. The mother-son relationship will be discussed with reference to *Unsentimentale Reise* later.

A Pedlar who may be God

Halfway through Drach's autobiographical report, there is an encounter with an Eastern Jew which, although it is recorded in the *Protokollstil*, differs in tone and style quite significantly from the rest of the book. One day the son is visited by a pedlar who is described as a typical wandering Eastern Jew (ZZ: 137). The son is struck by something special about this man which he cannot explain alone with reference to the man's "Zaudern, offensichtliche Einsamkeit, Nirgendszugehörigkeit und Gebeugtheit" [hesitation, apparent loneliness, belonging nowhere and stooped appearance, ZZ: 137]. What makes this episode so interesting in this context is not so much the image of the wandering Jew and the role it played in the reappropriation of Eastern Jewishness after the First World War[55] but the uncommon display of emotional engagement in what is otherwise a story of abjection. This precursor of Zwetschkenbaum engenders a rare emotional reaction in the son:

> Der Sohn hatte vielmehr einen Augenblick das Gefühl, als stünde eine geheimnisvolle Gestalt vor ihm, die sich des Äußeren eines kleinen und krummen ostjüdischen Hausierers bediente, um ihn an Dinge zu erinnern, die er längst vergessen hatte [...]. (ZZ: 138)[56]

The mysteriousness of this encounter is reinforced when the stranger eventually replies to the son's question what he wants: "Ich bin gekommen, um dazusein" [I have come in order to be here, ZZ: 139], a startling reference — and the only example of direct speech in the entire book — which introduces messianic hope as a theme to the narrative.

Prior to this encounter, the son's attitude to life is characterised by a distinct lack of belonging. He defines himself as a Faustian character who, in search of a "Lebenszweck" [purpose in life, ZZ: 140], rushes from religion to religion and from philosophy to art until he seems to have exhausted all possibilities of identification with life based on belief. Typically, this quest for a lasting belief system is exclusively driven by the intellect without any reference to the subject's emotional make-up. When this intellectualised search for identification fails, the son accepts "daß sein Dasein in Stunden unterteilt war, die der Arbeit gehörten, und andere die der Erbauung dienten. Dazwischen lagen Essen und Trinken, das ihm die Mutter als auch die Schwester so gut als möglich zurichteten" [that his existence was divided up into those hours, which were dedicated to work, and those which

---

[55] See Steven Aschheim, *Brothers and Strangers*, 139-184.
[56] [But the son had for a second the feeling that a mysterious figure stood in front of him which used the appearance of a small and stooped Eastern Jewish pedlar in order to remind him of things that he had forgotten a long time ago.]

belonged to edification. In-between there was the food and drink prepared by his mother and sister as best as possible, ZZ: 140]. The precision with which the son formally adheres to notions of professional and familial duty highlights yet again the absence or, rather, violent suppression of any emotional attachment. His pursuit of identifications leaves him with the experience of a ghost-like existence, devoid of all affect. In Kristeva's terms this phobic subject resembles a "fortified castle". And her analysis of the space occupied by the abject self reads like a commentary on the son in Drach's >>Z.Z<<:

> The constituting barrier between subject and object has here become an unsurmountable [sic] wall. An ego, wounded to the point of annulment, barricaded and untouchable, cowers somewhere, nowhere, at no other place than the one that cannot be found. Where objects are concerned he delegates phantoms, ghosts, 'false cards': a stream of spurious egos and for that very reason spurious objects, seeming egos that confront undesirable objects. Separation exists, and so does language, even brilliantly at times, with apparently remarkable intellectual realizations. But no current flows — it is a pure and simple splitting, an abyss without any possible means of conveyance between its two edges.[57]

Since the abject character does not have a true object as his correlative, he must experience all object relations as false. We are in the realm of the borderliner who is capable of producing an intellectualised language which, because of its abstractions and precisions, Kristeva describes as the "shell of ultra-protected signifier".[58] This language is based on the disconnection between verbal sign and drive representation; it thus reflects the lack of desire and, also, object relations, in the abject character's life. It is a sterile language, cut off from any affect. Kristeva's analysis helps to illuminate the meticulous language of the *Protokoll*, which, with its abstract intellectualisations, testifies to the power of the symbolic order that keeps abjection at bay, albeit at the price of a complete disconnection between signification and affect.

The appearance of the Eastern Jew, however, disturbs this economy. The fact that this pedlar does not beg or sell anything, that he has simply come in order to be there, cannot be rationalised by the son with reference to his functional understanding of all relations in life. The pedlar who does not want anything but to be present thus symbolises the want in the son's own life. In a rare moment, true desire is experienced by the son who is so emotionally touched by this encounter that he sees the pedlar as an icon of messianic hope and tries to touch him: "Und wie er nach ihm griff, um zu fühlen, ob er körperlich sei, erhob sich der verhinderte Hausierer sofort,

---

[57] Kristeva, *Powers of Horror*, 47.
[58] Ibid., 49.

denn er war offenbar greifbar und daher auch tatsächlich vorhanden" [and as he was touching him in order to feel if he was physically real, the pedlar manqué immediately got up, for apparently he was touchable and, by implication, physically present, ZZ: 139]. Although the irony of the *Protokollstil* again creates distance towards this quasi-religious gesture and its symbolism, the episode stands out from the rest of the narrative because of the unique display of spontaneous affect, which conjures up images of the Messiah. After the pedlar has left, the son is ashamed at his inability to abandon the thought that this poor Eastern Jew may have been God (ZZ: 141). He finally breaks the aura of the divine by giving the pedlar an ugly name:

> Er gab ihm zwar in der Erinnerung einen häßlichen Namen, rein willkürlich, wie österreichische Beamte im galizischen Kronland die ihnen vorgeführten Beschnittenen benamsten, die nicht für bessere Namen bezahlen konnten. Damit war zwar ein Dreckwurf nach der Erscheinung gezielt, aber keine völlige Entgötterung erreicht worden. (ZZ: 141f.)[59]

The son refers here to legislation introduced in the Enlightenment period which required Jews to adopt German-sounding family names. This requirement was an integral part of the Josephinian policies which aimed at providing the Empire with uniform administrative laws.[60] Although Joseph's *Toleranzedikt* of 1782 had removed many restrictions from the lives of Jews, his reforms were also a colonial gesture in that they removed Jewish autonomy. In 1784 Jews lost their judicial autonomy, and in 1788 they were ordered to adopt the family names and to stop using Hebrew and Yiddish for public and commercial purposes.[61]

In the above-quoted passage, the son mimics this colonial gesture by not only naming the pedlar who may be God, but, in addition, by giving him an ugly name in the same manner as the Austrian officials were reputed to do unless they were paid a bribe.[62] From a Jewish perspective this is an act of

---

[59] [Although in his memory he attached an ugly name to him, on an arbitrary impulse, just like the Austrian civil servants who in the Galician crownland had named the circumcised they were presented with and who could not pay for a better name; although some dirt was thrown at the apparition in this manner, a complete profanation was not achieved.]

[60] For more details on this see Robert S. Wistrich, *The Jews of Vienna in the Age of Franz Joseph*. Oxford: Oxford University Press 1989: 16f.

[61] Robert S. Wistrich, *The Jews of Vienna*, 17.

[62] In his study on Jewish names Dietz Bering claims that the choice of name was always left to the Jews. He mentions only one uncertain case of enforced naming in Western Galicia in 1805. However, in my view this does not prove that bribes were not taken by officials — after all, they would hardly have recorded it in their official registers. Cf. Dietz Bering, 'Der "jüdische" Name. Antisemitische Namenspolemik'. In: Julius H. Schoeps and Joachim Schlör (Eds.), *Antisemitismus. Vorurteile und Mythen*. Frankfurt am Main: Zweitausendundeins: no year: 153-166, here 156.

blasphemy which breaks the taboo not enunciate the name of God.[63] For the son it is a gesture with which he tries to re-establish his sense of control and authority through a figure of farce. However, although he attempts to degrade the pedlar even further by using this name as a code word for his bank account (ZZ: 147), the aura of their encounter remains largely unaffected by this. As before, mimicry produces an unwanted slippage defying the gesture of authority which it imitates. Unable to master this encounter through defamation and rationalisation, the son starts taking notes on the appearance of the pedlar, thus sublimating fear through writing. Later on in the narrative, the son hears of a pedlar without goods who was captured by the Gestapo and sent to Buchenwald concentration camp,

> wo man ihn zu Tode gepeitscht hatte, bloß weil er auf die Frage nach seinem Daseinszweck erklärte, er sei gekommen, um dazusein, da hatte der Sohn den Eindruck, es müsse sich um den Mann gehandelt haben, dem er glaubte in seiner Kanzlei einmal begegnet zu sein und den er jetzt wie damals noch für etwas anderes hielt als bloß für die Verkörperung eines Hauszuhaushändlers. (ZZ: 308)[64]

The story of the Eastern Jewish pedlar thus does not only tell the story of the genesis of *Das große Protokoll gegen Zwetschkenbaum,* but it also reveals the hidden underside of Drach's writing: the existential fear that there is no escaping from the dehumanisation of the Nazi period. Paradoxically, the language of the *Protokoll* is both an expression of that fear and its disguise. Drach's controlled language, which always channels the protagonist's affective impulses into cynical detachment, has fear as its terrifying referent. In this instance it is the fear that, if God were really whipped to death, a coming alive through writing can be nothing but a fetish for the loss of messianic hope. Looked at from this angle, modernism appears as self-conscious fetishism and a parody of meaning.

---

[63] Cf. 'Tetragrammaton'. In: Alan Unterman, *Dictionary of Jewish Lore & Legend.* London: Thames & Hudson, 1991: 198.
[64] [where he was flogged to death merely because he declared when asked about his purpose in life that he had come in order to be there, the son had the impression that it had to be the same man he believed to have met in his office one day and who he believed then and now to have been more than just the embodiment of a common pedlar.]

Mastering the Mob

In his recent study of literary representations of pogroms, Joachim Beug shows how nineteenth century writers of ghetto fiction tended to portray pogroms as events of the past because these authors believed in the lasting influence of Enlightenment ideas. With the resurgence of pogroms from the 1880s onwards a new generation of writers emerged which was willing to articulate anti-Jewish violence in their texts, using "more disruptive forms" of literary representation.[65] Beug summarises his findings thus:

> Narrative techniques adopted for the representation of pogroms range from omission of the events proper in favour of substitution or reflection to stark realistic and factual descriptions which deal directly with the horror of the pogroms. Similarly, the role of individual characters, heroes or villains, becomes insignificant when the anonymity of perpetrators and victims is emphasised. The progression of events and the irrational drift of such mob-action defies both meaningful plot and an ending that resolves or redeems what happened. A sense of unfinished business prevails throughout and a gap remains open that no literary stratagem can bridge.[66]

Set against this tradition, the detailed portrayal of a local pogrom towards the end of >>Z.Z<< is quite startling in that Drach does not only omit any reference to the emotional trauma of this attack but, moreover, uses a highly ironic style which carnevalises the events. Drach's description of this orchestrated attack starts with a mob of people gathering outside the family home where the son and his mother are having lunch. When the rioting mob is about to break into the house, the son hides in the bathroom, equipped with his favourite desert, leaving his mother to deal with the ringleaders. This image of the desert-eating son deliberately undermines the reader's expectations of heroism in favour of a detached and detailed depiction of the events highlighting the absurdity and senselessness of the attack. The report records not only how some thirty-five men gather around his mother and threaten her, but also how all this is observed by the son through the keyhole (ZZ: 258). Eventually he makes his appearance when one of the SA men is about to rape the maid. He is then escorted outside where it transpires that the ringleaders' original plan to force him to write "Jude" [Jew] on the plaque on his door has to be aborted because someone else has already written "nichtarische Kanzlei" [non-Aryan legal practice, ZZ: 259] over it. Instead he is forced to carry a ladder across the road in order to write "Nur ein Schwein kauft bei Juden ein" [only a pig buys from Jews, ZZ: 260] over the business plaque of a Jewish shopkeeper. What is striking

---

[65] Joachim Beug, 'Pogroms in Literary Representation'. In: Anne Fuchs and Florian Krobb, *Ghetto Writing: Traditional and Eastern Jewry in German-Jewish Literature from Heine to Hilsenrath.* Columbia: Camden House, 1999: 84-97.
[66] Ibid.,96.

about Drach's representation of the pogrom is the extremely formal control of language that creates here the highest possible degree of irony and, by implication, a vast distance between signification and signified, namely between the *Protokoll's* controlled language on the one hand and the depicted violence of the scene on the other. The effect of this technique is a reversal of the relationship between degrador and degraded: while on the level of plot, the mob does everything in its power to degrade the son, the irony of the report highlights the degradation of the ringleaders and their mob in their acts. From the start the pogrom appears as a carnevalesque farce.

What can be described as a carnevalisation of the pogrom is also achieved through mimicry and the son's adoption of the kind of attitude to the events which Bhabha describes as "sly civility". One powerful example of mimicry is the scene where the son is forced to carry a ladder on his back (ZZ: 260): here explicit allusions are made to the iconography of Christ's crucifixion. This is not in order to enhance meaningfulness of this scene, but — on the contrary — to create a gulf between a theological view of history which contains the promise of Christ's return and the actual experience of history in terms of senseless mob power.

Similarly, "sly civility" is a form of civil disobedience masquerading under the disguise of civility. In his essay 'Sly Civility', Bhabha demonstrates how, for instance, in the process of transporting the instructions of the East Indian Company from London to India, a slippage was produced, affecting their local implementation to such an extent that a loss of control occurred on the part of the coloniser.[67] Thus this process produces ambivalence and "re-inscribes both colonizer and colonized in a different relation of power with the result that authority cannot be maintained."[68] Something similar happens in Drach's pogrom scene where the son adopts an attitude of sly civility which subverts the relationship of power completely. When he is asked to write the offensive anti-Semitic slogan on the shopfront of another Jewish businessman, he appears to be so clumsy that both the onlookers and the SA men begin to help and in so doing slip into the role of the victim:

> So kam es, daß sowohl SA als auch Zivilisten ihm bei seiner Vorleistung behilflich sein, ja sie sogar an seiner Statt übernehmen mußten. Schließlich ergab sich eine Lage, bei der ein SA-Mann den Farbtiegel hochob (sic), ein anderer den Pinsel eintauchte,

---

[67] Homi K. Bhabha, 'Sly Civility'. In: Homi K. Bhabha, *The Location of Culture*, 93-101, here 97.
[68] Robert Young, *White Mythologies*, 150.

während ein Zivilist die Leiter ansetzte, auf welcher der Sohn dann gemächlich hinaufstieg. (ZZ: 261)[69]

Subsequently, the implementation of the degrading task is further subverted when the son paints the first letter of the first word of the anti-Semitic slogan so large that not enough space is left for the remaining words. Ordered to use smaller letters, he carries this to the extreme by using such minute writing that it can hardly be made out any longer. Such literal implementation is a form of resistance which sets the master-slave dialectic in motion in that the master becomes the slave's helper. Sly civility is thus a subversive perversion of authority, which, in this instance, carnevalises the ringleaders' strategy of surveillance:

> Als daraufhin der Schlosser auch diese Schriftart beanstandete, erklärte der Sohn, möglicherweise nicht ohne Beziehung im Tonfall auf den herrschenden Zeitgenossen, welcher derlei Metier aus früherer Ausübung beherrschte, daß er seinerseits eben kein gelernter Anstreicher sei, daher die einschlägigen Maßstäbe anzuwenden nicht in der Lage sei. (ZZ: 261)[70]

The son's overt reference to Hitler as a trained "Anstreicher" with its connotation of a failed painter who only barely manages to disguise reality, upsets the ringleaders to such an extent that they call the party office for further instructions. Their attempt to reassert authority by deference to the party headquarters fails, however, because their call is answered by the granddaughter of the local party leader who knows the son and orders his immediate release. The scene thus ends with a complete loss of control on the part of the Nazis. What was intended as a display of Nazi power turns into a figure of farce orchestrated by the son's sly civility and the ironic detachment of the report.

The reader is subsequently told of other attacks on Jews where the victims were not as lucky as the son: there is the story of a Jewish fur trader who, after being forced to smear anti-Semitic slogans on his shop-front, committed suicide (ZZ: 263); or that of a greengrocer who loses his mind after similar attacks and degradations (ZZ: 264); further cases are reported where degrading pictures were taken of so-called 'ugly' Jews (ibid.). These

---

[69] [So it happened that both the SA as well as the civilians did not only have to help him withthe performance of his task, but had to take over from him. Eventually, a situation was arrived at in which a SA man had to pass him the paint bucket, while another one dipped the brush into it and a civilian positioned the ladder which the son then climbed without haste.]

[70] [When the locksmith then criticised this type of writing too, the son explained, probably not without slightly imitating the inflection of the ruling contemporary who, due to earlier professional experience, would master this job perfectly, that he himself, however, was not a trained painter and therefore not in a position to apply the usual guidelines.]

episodes highlight the episodic character of the son's victory over his aggressors. >>Z.Z<< does not present sly civility as a political form of opposition — this would be a naive reading of fascism — but rather as the individual's resistance to authority which, temporarily, creates enough slippage of power to subvert the intended degradation.

Reality as Labyrinth: From Sterne's *Sentimental Journey* to Drach's *Unsentimentale Reise*

In Laurence Sterne's *Sentimental Journey through France and Italy* (1768), Yorick, the travelling protagonist, sets out on a "quiet journey of the heart in pursuit of NATURE, and those affections which rise out of her, which make us love each other."[71] Yorick plays the part of an anthropologist full of grandiose feelings who effaces all objectivity in order to write what I have called elsewhere "the grammar of the heart".[72] His journey is conceived as a series of experiments on man's good nature, which, in his own words, attempts to overcome "the difference in education, customs and habits", the "impediments in communicating our sensations out of our own sphere" (SJ: 9). For the sentimental traveller communication as the trading of sentiments between self and other is the only valid target of a journey which is defined as an "assay upon human nature" (SJ: 28). These programmatic statements highlight Yorick's unique role as a sentimental anthropologist who considers the formal features of the other culture as a mere disguise behind which the sole object of his study has to be discovered, namely the universality and goodness of human nature (SJ: 84).

Like all anthropologists Yorick needs a methodology for his quest which is dealt with during an episode with a French officer whom he meets in the opera in Paris. Yorick observes how, upon his arrival in their shared box, the officer puts a pamphlet he has been perusing in his pocket. Yorick comments on this incident in the following way:

> Here's a poor stranger come into the box — he seems as if he knew nobody; and is never likely, was he to be seven years in Paris, if every man he comes near keeps his spectacles upon his nose — 'tis shutting the door of conversation absolutely in his face — and using him worse than a German.

---

[71] Laurence Sterne, *A Sentimental Journey through France and Italy by Mr. Yorick*. Ed. Ian Jack, Oxford: Oxford University Press, 1984: 84. Henceforth cited as SJ in brackets.

[72] Anne Fuchs, 'Laurence Sterne's *Unsentimental Journey* and Goethe's *Italian Journey*: Two Models of the Non-Perception of Otherness'. In: *New Comparison* 1993: 27. What follows is based on my earlier article '"... da Hitler zu Ermordungszwecken nach und nach alle Juden dringend braucht": Labyrinth und Abjektion in Albert Drachs *Unsentimentale Reise*'. In: *German Life and Letters* 49 (1996): 223-235.

And he continues:

> There is not a secret so aiding to the progress of sociality, as to get master of this *short hand*, and be quick in rendering the several turns of looks and limbs, with all their inflections and delineations, into plain words. For my own part, by long habitude, I do it so mechanically, that when I walk the streets of London, I go translating all the way.(SJ: 57)

By affirming to be a master of this "short hand" and "to go translating all the way" Yorick claims to be an experienced anthropologist with a working model of how to read the stranger's acts and gestures. Both his translation exercise and the metaphor of the "short hand" suggest that, for him, man's gestures form a natural grammar of the heart, indicating human motivations in a less distorted way than discourse. It is Yorick's fundamental axiom that the non-verbal gesture, particularly the tear and the sigh, is by its very nature an immediate reflex of man's goodness. For this reason, the novel carefully evokes body movements, touching, sighing and other paralinguistic gestures. In Yorick's view, they provide immediate access to man's finer sensibilities without the distortions caused by the figurative and rhetorical nature of language. Abandoning the traditional tour in favour of a travel route and narrative style full of digressions, coincidental meetings, and seemingly trivial observations, Yorick and his author Laurence Sterne thus explore the goodness of human nature in a playful manner. The underlying assumptions of this exploration are, however, never questioned: firstly, that human nature is good, and secondly, that empathy is an ability shared by all human beings.

Such humanitarian and epistemological optimism is completely undermined in Albert Drach's *Unsentimentale Reise* [Unsentimental Journey, 1966], a dialectic anti-narrative to Sterne's *Sentimental Journey,* in which Drach articulates the traumatic experience of persecution in Vichy-France.[73] In the context of Nazi barbarism and the complicity of the Vichy government, all the basic assumptions of the Enlightenment period no longer make sense. Where Yorick's journey appears as a series of exploratory digressions illuminating the richness of human nature, that of Drach's autobiographical alter ego, Peter Kucku, consists of a labyrinthine movement through a space of anxiety which always ends and starts in Nice where another deportation order is awaiting him. The protagonist remains trapped in what Ernestine Schlant has called the "magnetic field of the *universe* [sic] *concentrationnaire*".[74] In Peter Kucku's world the contingencies and coin-

---

[73] Quotations in the text refer to the following edition: Albert Drach, *Unsentimentale Reise. Ein Bericht.* Munich and Vienna: Carl Hanser, 1988. Cited as UR with page references.
[74] Ernestine Schlant, 'Albert Drach's *Unsentimentale Reise*: Literature of the Holocaust and the dance of Death', *Modern Austrian Literature* 26 (1993), 45.

cidences of life are therefore not registered as proof of the universality and diversity of human nature, but only as evidence of a senseless and disorientating movement through history which renders useless the humanitarian notion of growth through experience.

The novel opens with the image of the protagonist's labyrinthine journey through the space and time of history: "Ich bin in voller Fahrt. Wohin es geht, weiß ich nicht. Ich strebe nirgends hin, liege auch. Niemand hat mich um das Fahrtziel befragt. Ich erinnere mich nicht, eine Fahrkarte gelöst zu haben." [I am travelling at top speed. I do not know the destination. I am heading nowhere, after all I am lying flat. Nobody asked me for my destination. I don't remember buying a ticket. UR: 7] When Kucku wakes up and finds out that he and his fellow travellers are on their way to the camp in Rives Altes, where deportation to Auschwitz is awaiting them, he decides to escape.

The account of this journey is interrupted by one of many flashbacks which deliberately disrupt the chronology of events thus adding a temporal labyrinth to the spatial one. In this flashback we learn how Kucku escaped deportation before, when he managed to persuade the prefect of Nice to withdraw a deportation order signed by the anti-Semitic Fräulein Felice. However, unlike in Yorick's world, where such an act would have been registered as proof of man's innate goodness, in Peter Kucku's universe such a reading would be highly fallacious, since the prefect's decision to grant Kucku's request merely follows an impulse triggered by a bourgeois spleen, namely his liking of Kucku's academic title: Dr. Kucku. Although this intervention helps Kucku survive temporarily, it does not appear as a humanitarian act derived from man's anthropological make-up, but as a personal whim which highlights once more the arbitrariness of survival which is one of the central concerns of this report.

The labyrinthine structure of Drach's *Unsentimentale Reise* is thus an epistemological comment on the unreadability of both personal and macro-history. Throughout the report the protagonist remains caught up in a labyrinth *in malo* where he is faced with an endless series of disorienting bifurcations which all lead him potentially to his death. Although he manages to escape deportation, his survival is not presented as a learning experience composed of meaningful and patterned human interaction, but as the outcome of unreadable chance, unpredictable personal idiosyncrasy as well as the protagonist's anaesthetising detachment from the trauma of history. Throughout this unsentimental journey, Peter Kucku is engaged in a decision-making process which disallows the interpretation of the here and now in terms of a meaningful past. But this readability of past events is the pre-condition of the very notion of experience. This space of anxiety engenders no growth but only the experience of abjection. The negativity of history after Auschwitz is captured in the final image where Kucku is about to commit suicide by gassing himself after France's liberation by the Allies:

> In meinem Zimmer, das eng ist wie ein Sarg, liege ich und möchte weinen. Aber Tote weinen nicht, und Tränen sind überhaupt nicht erlaubt auf einer unsentimentalen Reise. Ich weiß nicht, ob ich die Gashähne geschlossen habe, als wir nach dem halbrohen Abendessen noch Tee bereiteten, aber ich erhebe mich nicht, um nachzusehen. Das Zimmer scheint nach Gas zu riechen.
> Sagt Dr. Honigmann. 'Wo wir jetzt nackt sind als die letzten, und man hat schon begonnen, das Gas einzulassen, Sie haben nichts erreicht und die andern auch nicht. Draußen liegen der Schuster, Agnes, Stieglitz, Ehrlich. Wohin haben Sie gewollt mit ihrem Traum?'
> 'Hinaus', sage ich. (UR: 368)[75]

Kucku's labyrinthine movement through history ends with this vision of his fellow Jews whom he met on the train at the beginning of the narrative and all of whom were murdered in Auschwitz; the report thus condenses the negativity of history into a final image which highlights the illusory nature of the notion of liberation. Negating all teleological and utopian models of historiography, this vision of Kucku's gassed fellow travellers emphasises the trauma of abjection which is a major theme of this unsentimental journey.

Existentially dislocated and astray, Peter Kucku experiences all life as empty, puppet-like and void. Without a sense of orientation he glides through a space of anxiety where the boundaries between inner and outer world are constantly threatened by the invasion of the abject and where no true objects of desire can exist. Trapped in this space of anxiety Kucku has lost all ability to identify with an other, even with his own Jewishness. A first example of the abjection of self and other is the laconic and detached manner in which Kucku registers the conversations of his fellow-travellers during their journey to Rives Altes which revolve around the all too human hope that they might escape deportation to the extermination camps. Here the first-person narrator highlights the grotesque discrepancy between the formality with which the passengers of the doomed train journey introduce themselves to each other and an earlier incident where a prisoner who tried to escape was beaten to death: "Der Kopf des verhinderten Flüchtlings schlägt springend wie ein Ball an die Wagenwand

---

[75] [I'm lying in my room, which is as narrow as a coffin, and would like to cry. But dead bodies do not cry, and tears are not allowed on an unsentimental journey. I do not know if I turned the gas off when we were making tea after our half-cooked supper, but I am not getting up to check. The room seems to smell of gas. Says Dr. Honigmann, 'Now that we are naked and the last ones left, and they have already started letting the gas in, you have achieved nothing and neither did the other ones. Schuster, Agnes, Stieglitz, Ehrlich are lying outside. Where did you want to get to with your dream? 'Away', I reply.]

und macht dort Lärm. Das Ergebnis wird zugedeckt weggetragen." [The head of the would-be fugitive bounces against the carriage wall like a ball and makes a loud noise. The result is covered up and carried away. UR: 19] With ironic detachment Kucku summarises his fellow-travellers' ensuing conversations as follows: "Die Hinterbliebenen glauben einander nähergekommen zu sein, seit jeder den Namen des andern weiß [...]." [The survivors believe that they are more familiar with each other now that everyone knows each other's name. UR: 21] The immediate juxtaposition of a barbarous murder with a normalised conversation that is informed by notions of status, formality and familiarity underlines the grotesque incongruence between the individual's expectation of meaning in life, and a destructive macro-history that violates *all* notions of civilisation. Perceived against the latent backdrop of the gassings, all basic forms of human interaction appear in Kucku's eyes not only as pointless but also as inherently absurd.

Throughout *Unsentimentale Reise* the detachment of the *Protokollstil* therefore highlights the unbridgeable abyss between the assumption of a shared civilisation, based on inalienable human rights on the one hand, and the barbarity of a reality on the other, which cannot be read from a humanitarian viewpoint any longer. This nullification of the "universal" ethics of the Enlightenment is implied in Kucku's letter to his sister, where he notes laconically, "daß die Polizei der Regierung von Vichy Judenrazzien durchführt, da Hitler zu Ermordungszwecken nach und nach alle Juden dringend braucht." [That the police of the Vichy-government is carrying out raids on Jews because Hitler urgently requires all Jews for the purposes of extermination. UR: 23] Imitating the tone and grammatical features of German judicial discourse, in particular the "Nominalstil", Kucku points here to the bureaucratic authorisation and routinisation that characterised the deportations.[76] The reference point of Kucku's mimicry of the legalistic language of the deportation orders is what Zygmunt Bauman has aptly called "the social production of moral invisibility", based on the psychic and physical distance between the act and its consequences.[77] Kucku's detached and legalistic style thus draws attention to the disturbing detachment of rationality from moral inhibitions.

On the other hand, Kucku's cynicisms, ironies and distancing devices are always an expression of the abjection of self which culminates in his suicide at the end of the report. This theme is first made explicit in the motif of the "stolen life" in Rives Altes where Kucku observes a group of young Eastern

---

[76] Another important condition for a successful erosion of moral inhibitions is the dehumanisation of the victims. Cf. Zygmunt Bauman, *Modernity and the Holocaust*. Cambridge: Polity Press, 1989: 21ff.

[77] Zygmunt Bauman, *Modernity and the Holocaust*, 24f.

European Jews dancing Horah (UR: 57). Ernestine Schlant has rightly observed that in this scene Kucku's language "assumes a rare solemnity, commensurate with what he sees."[78] The dance creates an aura that leaves the murderous reality at least momentarily behind and, in Kucku's own words, symbolises a dignity and:

> Willen zum Tanz angesichts ihres Todes — wie Jephtahs Tochter noch im Kreis ihrer Gefährtinnen tanzte, als ihr Vater angekündigt hatte, er würde sie für sein Gelübde der Gottheit zur Sühne und zum Opfer bringen. (UR: 83)[79]

This is one of the few passages in which Kucku manages to identify with his Jewishness and where he interprets Jewish history as intrinsically meaningful with reference to biblical tradition and exegesis. However, this identification cannot be transported beyond the aura of the dance; in the end Kucku reverts to the abjection of self and other: "Ich betrachte den Tanz, der nicht mehr zu mir gehört." [I watch the dance, which does not belong to me any more. UR: 83]

As a stray subject he suffers from a "splitting, an abyss without any means of conveyance between its two edges", thus remaining cut off from all identification with life. [80] When he learns that he is among the few prisoners who will be released from Rives Altes, he is overcome by feelings of abjection and worthlessness:

> Ich weiß sehr wohl, daß ich mein Leben stehle, daß es ebenso verfallen ist wie das der anderen, und ich weiß sehr wohl, daß andere würdiger wären an meiner Statt zu gehen, die kräftiger und selbstloser sind und durch stärkere Bindungen mit dem Leben verknüpft scheinen als ich [...]. (UR: 83)[81]

Although this abjection of the self is clearly an example of survivor-guilt, it precedes this episode and underlies the report as a whole. In one of the flashbacks a link is created between the violent abjection of the self and the loss of the maternal *chora* which is a theme running through both >>Z.Z.<< and *Unsentimentale Reise*. Kucku notes here: "Meine Mutter habe ich nicht sterben sehen. Ich habe sie bloß ermordet." [I did not see my mother die. I only murdered her.] And he continues:

---

[78] Schlant, 49.
[79] [will to dance in the face of their own death — like Jephtah's daughter who kept dancing in the circle of her friends after her father had told her that, obeying his vow, he would sacrifice her to God as an act of repentance.]
[80] Kristeva, *Powers of Horror*, 47.
[81] [I know very well that I am stealing my life, that it is just as invalidated as that of the others, and I know very well that others would be worthier to go than me, people who are stronger and less selfish and have stronger connections with life than I.]

> Ich habe sie zurückgelassen unter Hitlerschurken und -banden in dem Land, das einmal meine Heimat war, für dessen Volk ich nurmehr die tiefste Verachtung aufbringe, wie jetzt in diesem Augenblick für mich selbst, der auch ich diesem Volk angehöre, wenn ich außerdem ein Jude bin. Ich habe ihre Schreie nicht gehört, als sie starb. Ich wollte auch ihre mütterlichen Worte nicht hören, als sie noch lebte. Sie hat mich gelehrt, meinen Vater als etwas Großes zu ehren. Sie versorgte alles, liebte ihren Dienst und lebte und starb in seinem Schatten, obgleich sie in Haltung und Ausdruck eine Königin war. (UR: 73)[82]

While the style of the report is generally characterised by distancing devices that refuse to validate identification, here the detachment of the report is momentarily suspended in favour of the expression of an unusually strong affect that is otherwise suppressed. At the centre of this passage is the image of an original motherly care which reflects Kucku's strong attachment to the maternal sphere, what Kristeva calls the *chora*, a "self-contemplative, conservative, self-sufficient haven"[83] which, although it is repressed in the economy of the subject, is always mourned and desired. The subject "normally" manages this loss through identification with the symbolic order and its objects. Kucku, however, is a subject trapped in abjection. Such inability to identify with the paternal metaphor is always anchored in the subject's archaeology and the "reluctant struggle against what, having been the mother, will turn into an abject."[84] It is important to note here that this crisis of subjectivity can be significantly aggravated by a historical crisis of the paternal metaphor, which in the Germany of the Thirties was channelled into the vulgar phallic ideology of Aryan superiority and a phobic social order that constituted its boundaries through the abjection of a stigmatised other, the Jew. It is therefore hardly surprising that the Austrian Jew Kucku has lost the ability to identify with an other. His only remaining link to the symbolic sphere is a strong super-ego producing self-loathing and a permanent sense of guilt for having "murdered" his mother.

Unsentimentale Reise is thus also a pre-oedipal story about a mother-son relationship, its subtext gives expression to "the violence of mourning for an 'object' that has always already been lost."[85] It is a journey that takes "the ego back to its source on the abominable limits from which, in order to be, the ego has broken away."[86] Kucku's violent mourning for the lost mother

---

[82] [I left her behind among Hitler henchmen and gangs in the very country that used to be my home, and for whose people I have no other feeling than contempt, including myself at this very moment, I who also belong to this people, even if I am also a Jew. I did not hear her cries when she died. I did not want to hear her motherly words either when she was still alive. She taught me to honour my father as someone mighty. She cared for everything, loved her duty and died in his shadow, although she was in posture and expression a queen.]
[83] Kristeva, *Powers of Horror*, 14.
[84] Ibid., 13.
[85] Ibid., 15.
[86] Ibid., 15.

also helps to explain the many sexual affairs which are reported both with a high degree of chauvinism à la Hemingway and considerable cynical irony. *Unsentimentale Reise* thus continues the theme of sexual conquest of >>Z.Z.<< that I have already discussed. As before Kucku's erotic cult is not driven by any real desire but by abjection. A good example of his sexual aggression, in its link to abjection barely covering an original want, is an episode in Rives Altes where he takes a sixteen year old girl for a walk:

> Ich möchte sie trösten, was schier unmöglich ist, und habe dabei Lust von ihr Besitz zu ergreifen. In einem verborgenen Winkel versuche ich, sie zu entkleiden. Sie leistet etwas Widerstand. Das Schamgefühl oder Koketterie, die beide keinen Sinn mehr haben, meldet sich noch. Ich weiß, daß es bei ihr niemand mehr schaden kann, und habe doch das Gefühl niedriger Gesinnung. (UR: 83)[87]

Faced with the utter bleakness of death in the camps, Kucku cannot follow his initial impulse to comfort the girl. Instead he transforms this sentiment into an act of abjection: aggressively trying to conquer the girl, he just stops short of what he calls a "Leichenschändung" [desecration of the corpse, UR: 85] when her resistance is broken. His chauvinistic bravado and aggression thus reflect the inability of the dislocated subject to relate to another and also the despair with which he hangs on to the erotic cult as a symbol of life. However, unlike in >>Z.Z.<<, where the son has serialised sex, in *Unsentimentale Reise* Kucku's sexual aggression hardly ever translates itself into a sexual act; his violent attempts to conquer women barely mask his psychic impotence rooted in self-loathing and, by implication, a sense of guilt towards the dead mother. Towards the end of the report Kucku confesses: "Im Grunde genommen sind alle Frauen für mich anonym." [All women are fundamentally anonymous for me. UR: 330] And elsewhere he elaborates the economy of abjection that dominates his life thus:

> Ich wollte Ilse noch vor der Vergasung haben, dazu kam es nicht mehr. Ich wollte nach meiner Rückkehr Jeanne Varien. Ich habe alle Gelegenheiten versäumt. Ich war in Darling Whithorse verliebt, habe mit Veronica geflirtet und beinahe vor den Augen ihres Gatten die häßliche Frau des schönen Gendarmen in Besitz genommen. Ich werde es bestimmt nie wieder tun, weder nüchtern noch betrunken. (UR: 268)[88]

---

[87] [I want to comfort her, which is nigh impossible, and want to conquer her at the same time. In a hidden corner I try to undress her. She resists a little. A sense of coyness or coquetry neither of which make sense any more are coming through. I know that it does not make a difference for her any more, but I still feel base.]

[88] [I wanted to have Ilse before her gassing, it did not come to that. After my return I wanted Jeanne Varien. I have missed all opportunities. I was in love with Darling Whithorse, flirted with Veronica and nearly took possession of the ugly wife of the beautiful policeman right under his eyes. I will never do it again, neither sober nor drunk.]

An emptiness and want have taken the place of desire, driving Kucku from woman to woman. With the loss of the motherly *chora* he has lost his only bond with life. Bereft, Kucku moves phantom-like through a labyrinth in search of a symbol of life, which, in the final part of the report, he believes to have found in Darling Whithorse. This hope that he might be regenerated through her turns out to be misfounded since Darling is also caught up in the crisis of abjection which is the major theme of this book.

With her formal beauty, reminiscent of antiquity, Darling Whithorse represents to Kucku for a long time the "Sinnbild edlen Ebenmaßes, an das die Zeiten und Völker glauben, seit sie sich des Schönen bewußt sind" [the symbol of all noble harmony in which all people at all times have believed for as long as they have had a sense of the beautiful, UR: 308]. As in >>Z.Z.<< this ideal of beauty is a quasi-religious icon, a fetish object purified of all affective and somatic impulses, in short: of all life. However, while in >>Z.Z.<< this ideal of female perfection remains unchallenged, in *Unsentimentale Reise* it takes a tumble when Darling turns out to be just as beset by abjection as the protagonist. Not only does she jeopardise Kucku's life by attaching a note to Paul Lebleu's house "maison juive" [Jewish house] but, moreover, after the liberation by the Allies she returns one day from the forest carrying "etwas Weißes, Glänzendes" [something white and shining] which turns out to be the teeth of dead German soldiers. She explains to a shocked GI that she is going to wear them as a necklace since "ein Toter ist doch nichts anderes mehr als eine Puppe." [A corpse is nothing other than a doll. UR: 318] Darling's view of the dead body as a piece of waste or a broken toy to be dismembered and recycled for further usage mirrors the desecration of human life, for which the name Auschwitz stands, and shatters Kucku's only remaining hope of a life unaffected by abjection. Once abjection has encroached upon the embodiment of beauty and perfection, there is no escape for Kucku from this labyrinth *in malo*. Kristeva puts it like this:

> In the dark halls of the museum that is now what remains of Auschwitz, I see a heap of children's shoes, or something like that, something I have already seen elsewhere, under a Christmas tree, for instance, dolls I believe. The abjection of Nazi crime reaches its apex when death, which, in any case kills me, interferes with what, in my living universe, is supposed to save me from death: childhood [...] among other things.[89]

---

[89] Kristeva, *Powers of Horror*, 4.

Bad Boys and Evil Witches: Gender and Abjection in Edgar Hilsenrath's *Der Nazi & der Friseur*

Hansel and Gretel Revisited

In Grimms's famous fairy-tale 'Hansel and Gretel' the protagonists find themselves abandoned and lost in the deep forest. They wander around by themselves until they reach a cottage made of bread and cake. Breaking away chunks of cake from the roof and windows, they are caught by a witch who beckons the children to step inside. The witch imprisons Hansel in a cage where he is to be fattened up for slaughter. But clever Hansel offers her a chicken bone instead of his fat finger. When she decides to slaughter the boy it is Gretel's turn to outwit the evil witch by shoving her into the oven where she burns to death. The children are free to return home laden with golden coins. They find their kind father alive and their bad stepmother dead and buried. Poetic justice has been restored.

Now, imagine this: a man, all by himself, lost in a wintry forest which looks like a "deutscher Märchenwald" (NF: 94), a forest from a German fairy-tale.[1] He too wanders around until he comes across a thatched cottage which is inhabited by an old hag. "So wie bei Hänsel und Gretel" [just like in Hansel and Gretel, NF: 101] she appears at the door and beckons our Hansel inside where, as in Grimms's tale, he is fed and afraid of being eaten:

> Dachte unwillkürlich an einen Riesenkochtopf, in dem mein Hintern schwimmt ... rosarot ... fertig zum Anschneiden ... sah meine Froschaugen losgelöst in der Brühe schwimmen. Und meine Augen sahen ihr Gesicht, das grinsende Gesicht eines Hutzelweibes ... über den Kochtopf gebeugt. (NF: 101)

But our protagonist's childish fear that he might be trapped in a fairy-tale where bad witches threaten to devour innocent children is of course unfounded. The setting is not the German forest of the fairy-tale but Poland

---

[1] Edgar Hilsenrath, *Der Nazi & der Friseur*. Munich and Zurich: Piper, 1990. Cited as NF with page numbers. [I could not help thinking of a huge saucepan, my bottom swimming in it, pink, ready for carving, I saw my frog's eyes swimming in the broth. And my eyes saw her face: the grinning face of a shrunken old witch bent down over her pot.]

in January 1945, and the protagonist of this (post-)Shoah narrative is Max Schulz, SS man and mass murderer, currently on the run from the approaching Russian army.

Schulz is the anti-hero of Hilsenrath's novel *Der Nazi & der Friseur* [The Nazi & the Barber, 1977] and the embodiment of a moral degradation which goes unpunished: the old woman Veronja takes Schulz in and feeds him. When she discovers a box full of gold teeth, the gruesome booty of Schulz's murders, she attacks him with a hatchet but is killed by Schulz who hacks her to death (NF: 116F.). In Hilsenrath's anti-fairy-tale the reward for innocence and goodness, the golden coins that Hansel and Gretel take home, has turned into a terrible symbol of the utter moral depravity for which Schulz stands. Later on in the story the gold teeth buy Schulz the Jewish identity of one of his victims — a gruesome twist that highlights once more the abyss between the moral romanticism of Grimms's fairy tale and the ethical vacuum created by the Shoah.

Hilsenrath's narrative does not simply reverse the roles of Grimms's story but furthermore it deconstructs the dichotomy of good and evil that structures the fairy-tale. Although Schulz is a mass murderer and undoubtedly evil, his victim Veronja is hardly a suitable representative of innocence and goodness since her original impetus to punish Schulz for his evil deeds quickly deteriorates into a sadistic orgy and power-game with beatings, torture and violent sex. Ironically, she ends up acting out a depravity similar to that of Schulz. While in Grimms's world goodness and innocence win, in Hilsenrath's universe moral categories have become obsolete, or rather, their place has been usurped by the category of survival. Hilsenrath's modern anti-fairy-tale thus illustrates an uncomfortable truth which is the theme of the novel as a whole: namely, the inability to interpret history (after Auschwitz) in moral categories.

It is noteworthy here that it is Schulz himself who tells his tale to the widow of the SS murderer Günter, shot dead by Polish partisans. This one-legged woman, who inhabits the basement of a bombed house in Berlin in 1945, is ironically called Frau Holle, thus referring the reader once more back to the world of Grimms's fairy-tales. Needless to say, Hilsenrath's Frau Holle has little in common with her famous predecessor: when Schulz tells her about the killings in the concentration camp, she displays no emotional reaction to the moral degradation but merely follows the story with a titillation that mirrors the response to an action-packed thriller. At the end of Schulz's gruesome story she praises his narrative talent in the following words:

'Wissen Sie, daß Sie manchmal wie ein Dichter reden! 'Das kann ich manchmal', sagte Max Schulz ... 'wenn auch nicht immer ...'
'Gar nicht wie ein Friseur', flüsterte Frau Holle. 'Und schon gar nicht wie ein Massenmörder. So wie ein Dichter.' (NF: 119)[2]

Hilsenrath's grotesque reference to Frau Holle, the icon of goodness in Grimms's tale, in a morally depraved environment, implicitly also questions a model of story-telling which fulfils the reader's expectation that the bad will ultimately be punished. Although Frau Holle dies in Hilsenrath's novel when she steps on a land mine, her death is not an act of punishment but an accident typical of its times.

Humour in Holocaust Fiction

Edgar Hilsenrath's satirical novel *Der Nazi & der Friseur* relates the story of "Max Schulz, unehelicher, wenn auch rein arischer Sohn der Minna Schulz ... zur Zeit meiner Geburt Dienstmädchen im Hause des jüdischen Pelzhändlers Abramowitz." [Max Schulz, the illegitimate but purely Aryan son of Minna Schulz, who at the time of my birth was a maid in the service of the Jewish fur-trader Abramowitz. NF: 7]. What is immediately striking about this opening sentence is the grotesque contrast between Schulz's Aryan aspirations on the one hand and his illegitimate background on the other.[3] This sets the tone for the novel as a whole which communicates what one may call the incongruity of historical experience through a register that favours the grotesque and the satirical. Hilsenrath's satirical portrayal of the fascist petty bourgeois is comparable to Günter Grass's classic *Die Blechtrommel* [The Tin Drum, 1959] in that — as Andreas Graf has noted — both authors favour black comedy to articulate the horrors of the Third Reich and both authors present parodies of the tradition of the German *Bildungsroman* which, on the basis of the humanitarian ideals of the Enlightenment period, traced the genesis of subjectivity in and through society.[4] However, one crucial difference between Grass's *Blechtrommel* and Hilsenrath's *Der Nazi & der Friseur* must not be overlooked, namely that the latter breaks a taboo by depicting a mass murderer with comic means.

---

[2] ['Do you realise that, sometimes, you talk like a poet!' 'Sometimes I have that talent' replied Max Schulz ... 'although not always'. 'Not at all like a barber', whispered Frau Holle. 'And definitely not like a mass murderer. Just like a poet.']
[3] Cf. my previous article, 'Edgar Hilsenrath's Poetics of Insignificance and the Tradition of Humour in German-Jewish Ghetto Writing'. In: Anne Fuchs and Florian Krobb (Eds.), *Ghetto Writing* : 195-209.
[4] Andreas Graf, 'Mörderisches Ich. Zur Pathologie der Erzählperspektive in *Der Nazi & der Friseur*'. In: Thomas Kraft (Ed.), *Edgar Hilsenrath. Das Unerzählbare erzählen*, Munich: Piper, 1996: 141.

This point was made by the German critics who commented on the fact that Hilsenrath had done the unthinkable and written a black comedy about a mass murderer. The influential magazine *Der Spiegel*, for instance, described the novel as "ein blutiger Schelmenroman, grotesk, bizarr und zuweilen von grausamer Lakonie."[5] While for the *Spiegel* Hilsenrath's Jewishness and his first-hand experience of persecution legitimise the application of black comedy to his subject matter, Gert Sautermeister takes exception to this hotchpotch of different traditions and styles, ranging from the German *Bildungsroman*, the picaresque novel, romantic elements, fairy-tales to satire. He argues that this mode of communication ultimately trivialises the enormity of the Shoah.[6]

That humour and the Shoah are perceived to be incompatible is hardly surprising. In an article on humour and laughter in German Holocaust literature Rüdiger Steinlein also deals with the relatively novel emergence of a new type of German Holocaust fiction that not only breaks the taboo of fictionalising the Holocaust, a debate which has been rekindled since Spielberg's *Schindler's List,* but also the even greater prohibition against portraying the Holocaust with comic means.[7] Steinlein rightly argues that literary humour always has the tendency to reduce the sacred and the terrible to a human level,[8] and that, in the case of the unthinkable horror of Auschwitz, this contains the danger of belittling the suffering of the victims as well as of playing down the enormity of the Nazis' transgression against the most basic understanding of a shared humanity. On the other hand, it seems to me that the silent *Betroffenheit* [consternation, sense of guilt] that characterised much of the postwar cultural climate in Germany has had the undesirable side-effect of contributing to collective repression. Klaus Laermann comes to a similar conclusion in a recent article on the impact of Adorno's famous verdict of 1949: "Nach Auschwitz ein Gedicht zu schreiben, ist barbarisch"[9] [Writing a poem after Auschwitz is barbaric]. Arguing that Adorno's sentence was interpreted as a taboo that helped to erect a negative but sacred boundary around Auschwitz, Laermann points out that Adorno corrected his position later in *Negative Dialektik* [Negative Dialectics, 1966], and

---

[5] Cf. Fritz Rumler, 'Max & Itzig'. In: *Der Spiegel* No. 35 (22. 8. 1977), reprinted in Thomas Kraft, *Edgar Hilsenrath*, 69-72, here 69. [A picaresque novel full of blood, grotesque, bizarre and at times full of a cruel matter-of factness has now come out on the German market, the novel reports of dark times with black humour: *Der Nazi & der Friseur*. The author knows his subject: Edgar Hilsenrath, 51, is Jewish.]
[6] Cf. Gert Sautermeister, 'Aufgeklärte Modernität — Postmodernes Entertainment', 236f.
[7] Rüdiger Steinlein, 'Das Furchtbarste lächerlich? Komik und Lachen in Texten der deutschen Holocaust-Literatur'. In: Manuel Köppen (Ed.), *Kunst und Literatur nach Auschwitz*. Berlin: Erich Schmidt, 1993: 97-106.
[8] Ibid., 99.
[9] Theodor Adorno, 'Kulturkritik und Gesellschaft'. In: Theodor Adorno, *Prismen*. Frankfurt am Main: Suhrkamp, 1987: 26.

concludes with the question: "Wo denn wären die Millionen zu begraben, wenn nicht in Gedichten?"[10] [Where else could the millions be buried if not in poetry?]

The paralysing effect of the cultural climate in postwar Germany can be illustrated with reference to the bizarre detour that Hilsenrath's satirical novel *Der Nazi & der Friseur*, written in 1968, had to take before it could appear in Germany: while the American translation of the novel was fairly quickly published by Doubleday in 1971, it took another six years before the German original appeared in 1977 in the relatively obscure Cologne-based publishing house Hermann Braun.[11] In the meantime, more than a million copies had been sold abroad.[12] This episode shows that despite the "writing-after-Auschwitz" debate and the impact of the students' revolution of 1968, the Shoah had ultimately remained a taboo subject in Germany.

In a recent discussion with the provocative title 'Holocaust and Entertainment' Hilsenrath explained why he felt that he had to find a new mode of communication after the Second World War:

Nach dem Krieg sind Tausende und Tausende von Büchern erschienen, meistens sehr schlecht geschrieben, von Überlebenden, die etwas aufgezeichnet hatten. Es war eine derartige Überschwemmung, daß mir schon 1948 ein deutsch-jüdischer Schriftsteller, dem ich erzählte, daß ich etwas über das Ghetto schreiben wolle, riet: 'Um Gottes willen, schreiben Sie lieber etwas über Walfische oder Kanarienvögel. Kein Mensch will das lesen.' Aber erstens war das mein stärkstes Erlebnis, und ich wollte darüber schreiben. Zweitens war es auch wichtig, daß das Thema nicht vergessen wurde. Also mußte ich einen neuen literarischen Weg finden. [...]
  Mir hat mal eine Zeitung bescheinigt, daß ich zwar satirisch schreibe, aber die Würde der Opfer unangetastet lasse. Das heißt, das Satirische bezieht sich auf den Zeitgeist, auf das, was jenseits der Vorstellung ist, das, was man realistisch eigentlich gar nicht begreifbar machen kann. [...]
  Es kommt nicht darauf an, Auschwitz zu fotografieren, oder über Auschwitz zu schreiben. Mir geht es darum, den Zeitgeist darzustellen.[13]

---

[10] Klaus Laermann, "Nach Auschwitz ein Gedicht zu schreiben, ist barbarisch:' Überlegungen zu einem Darstellungsverbot'. In: Manuel Köppen (Ed.), *Kunst und Literatur nach Auschwitz*, 14.
[11] Helmut Braun, 'Erinnerung'. In: Thomas Kraft (Ed.), *Edgar Hilsenrath: Das Unerzählbare erzählen*, 43-50.
[12] Susanne Möller, 'Zur Rezeption – Philosemiten und andere – die Verlagsstationen Edgar Hilsenraths'. In: Thomas Kraft (Ed.), *Edgar Hilsenrath*, 109-10.
[13] 'Holocaust und Unterhaltung: Eine Diskussion'. In: *Kunst und Literatur nach Auschwitz*, 108. [After the war thousands and thousands of books appeared, most of them badly written, by survivors who had jotted something down. It was such a flood that in 1948 a German-Jewish writer said to me, when I told him that I wanted to write about the ghetto: 'Dear God, you would be better off writing about whales or canaries! Nobody wants to read this stuff.' But, first of all, this was the formative experience of my life, and I wanted to write about it. Secondly it was important that this theme was not forgotten. For this reason I had to find a new literary voice. Once a newspaper wrote about me that, although I write in a satirical mode, I leave the dignity of the victims undisturbed. This means that my satire is directed

Hilsenrath's statement makes it clear that for him the moral yardstick for all satire and humour in Holocaust fiction is the integrity and dignity of the victims. It follows from there that satirical and humorous techniques in Holocaust fiction must provoke what Steinlein calls a "Katastrophenlachen"[14] [catastrophic laughter]: a bitter and unappeased response to the failure of reason to enlighten the world. Humour in this sense of the word hovers over the abyss and communicates a negativity that cannot be reasoned away.

The Scandal of Mimicry: A Nazi Imitates a Jew

In *Der Nazi & der Friseur* Hilsenrath applies the schema of the developmental or educational novel to a mass murderer, relating Schulz's development from birth to death in six books: book one covers the period between 1907, the year of Schulz's birth, until 1937 when Schulz has long joined the Nazi party and engages in anti-Semitic activities. Book two is set after the Second World War, starting in 1945 with frequent flashbacks depicting Schulz as SS officer in concentration camp Laubwalde. Book three provides a crucial turning point in that it relates how Schulz, now a black market dealer in Berlin in 1946/47, decides to escape justice by adopting the identity of one of his victims, namely that of his former childhood friend Itzig Finkelstein who was murdered by Schulz himself in Laubwalde. This change of identity is made plausible by Schulz's early exposure to Yiddish and Jewish rituals when, as a child and youth, he was still friends with the Finkelsteins and apprentice in Finkelstein's barber shop "Der Herr von Welt". Collecting further evidence for his masquerade, Schulz has an Auschwitz number tattooed on his arm and a circumcision carried out. Equipped with these credentials and, above all, a physical appearance which is the living embodiment of the anti-Semitic stereotypes — while his Jewish friend Itzig Finkelstein was blond and blue-eyed, Schulz "hatte schwarze Haare, Froschaugen, eine Hakennase, wulstige Lippen und schlechte Zähne" [had black hair, protruding eyes, a crooked nose, thick lips and bad teeth, NF: 24] — he appears before a committee for surviving victims of Nazi crimes which examines the Jewish identity of the applicants. Unlike the other victims he does not have to prove his Jewish identity because he is immediately identified as a Jew. Hilsenrath's inversed projection of racial stereotypes and obsessive fantasies of Aryan maleness does not only allow

---

towards the *Zeitgeist*, it evokes that which seems unimaginable, that which cannot be made comprehensible in realistic terms. It is not important to photograph Auschwitz or to write about Auschwitz. For me it is more important to portray the *Zeitgeist*.]

[14] Rüdiger Steinlein, 'Das Furchtbarste lächerlich?', 105.

him to motivate Schulz's abrupt change of identity, but furthermore, to examine the continued presence of the same stereotypes after the demise of fascism. The committee's application of the racist stereotypes to the survivors thus highlights the underside of the emerging philo-Semitism in postwar Germany, namely the anti-Semitism of old.[15]

Book four depicts Schulz-Finkelstein on board the "Exitus" which, in a clandestine operation, transports Jewish survivors to Palestine in 1947.[16] Book five covers the time from Schulz's arrival in Palestine to Israel's independence: Schulz not only manages to establish himself as a successful barber, he also turns himself into a respected citizen: his masquerade as a survivor of Auschwitz, his fervent support of Zionism, his involvement with Jewish underground movements, including the Haganah, his marriage with Mira, a survivor of the camps — in the eyes of his environment all this makes him a model Jew.

In book six, which covers the time from 1950 to 1968, the year of Schulz's death, Schulz is increasingly haunted by the memories of his deeds. Eventually, he tries to confess his past to Wolf Richter, a German Jew and former judge, who is asked by Schulz to sit in judgement on him. At the end of a mock-trial, Richter finds Schulz guilty and sentences him to death by hanging. The question arises as to how many times Schulz should be hanged. Agreeing on a figure of ten thousand murders, Richter sentences him to "10000mal aufhängen" [ten thousand times hanging, NF: 312]. The absurdity of Richter's sentence leads to his and Schulz's realisation that no punishment fits the crime. The episode ends with Schulz's imaginary "Freispruch" [acquittal]: Schulz is guilty but free to go because justice cannot be done.

When Schulz is about to die of a heart attack, Richter comes up with a different solution: he now refers Schulz's case to God. Although Schulz replies that God may not exist, he is all of a sudden engulfed by a fear of death, which, according to Richter, resembles that of his victims. "'Soll das die gerechte Strafe sein?' 'Nein.'" ['Is this supposed to be my fair punishment?' 'No.' NF: 319].

The real scandal of Hilsenrath's novel is caused by what Andreas Graf rightly calls the pathology of the narrative perspective. Unlike Hilsenrath's earlier novel *Nacht* [Night, 1964] which relates the battle for survival in the Romanian camp Moghilev-Podolsk from the viewpoint of one of the interned Jews, Ranek, *Der Nazi & der Friseur* forces the reader to adopt the

---

[15] Cf. Sander Gilman, 'Hilsenrath und Grass Redivivus'. In: Thomas Kraft (Ed.), *Edgar Hilsenrath. Das Unerzählbare erzählen*, 122f.
[16] The name alludes to the 'Exodus' which transported Jews from Europe to Palestine in 1945. However, the passengers of the real Exodus were not allowed to disembark. The British authorities sent the ship via Cyprus back to Europe.

perspective of the mass murderer Max Schulz throughout. With the exception of book two where an omniscient narrator relates Schulz's arrival in Berlin, the entire novel is conceived as a first-person narrative and confessional in the tradition of Jean Jacques Rousseau's *Confessions*. But whereas Rousseau's autobiography and the ensuing literary tradition articulate the genesis of an innocent and authentic subjectivity which is constituted through the act of writing, Hilsenrath's satirical novel undermines such an idealistic conception: not only does he deal with a mass murderer who does not even know how many people he murdered but, and that is the real scandal, he allows his anti-hero to successfully undergo his opportunistic metamorphosis into a survivor. Andreas Graf's observation that Hilsenrath's combination of the perpetrator's perspective with a victim's identity poses a challenge to the reader is certainly correct.[17] However, it seems to me that Hilsenrath's novel poses a further challenge in another respect: not only is the reader forced to maintain the perspective of the mass murderer, not only does this mass murderer live a successful life, but in addition there is an increasing and perhaps unbearable sense of uncertainty as to whether Schulz's transformation is in the end still nothing more than role-play.[18] But it is less the fact that Hilsenrath allows his character to undergo change — one indication of this is his growing sense of guilt and his need to confess his past to judge Richter — which is so disturbing but the subtle effect Schulz's mimicry has on that which is being mimicked, namely Jewish identity after the Shoah.

In order to elaborate on this point it may be useful to recall the main tenets of Homi Bhabha's concept of mimicry as first discussed in chapter four: Bhabha introduces mimicry as a key concept in the relationship between colonised and coloniser.[19] Mimicry is a type of camouflage through which the colonial subject imitates the coloniser without ever achieving identity with the imitated object. Mimicry therefore produces a subtle slippage and displacement that ultimately undermines the authority of the authenticity which it is supposed to imitate. As an act of camouflage, mimicry is always a form of mockery and irony.

We have seen in chapter four how the main protagonist in Drach's >>Z.Z.<< subtly exploits this subversive potential of mimicry in order to undermine the authority of the local Nazis who intend to degrade him publicly. This episode in Drach's book can be read from the viewpoint of

---

[17] Andreas Graf, 'Mörderisches Ich', 137.
[18] See also Katharina Gerstenberger and Vera Pohland, 'Der Wichser. Edgar Hilsenrath — Schreiben über den Holocaust, Identität und Sexualität'. In: *Der Deutschunterricht* 3 (1993): 74-91.
[19] Homi K. Bhabha, 'Of Mimicry and Man. The Ambivalence of Colonial Discourse'. In: Homi K. Bhabha, *The Location of Culture*. London and New York: Routledge, 1994: 85-92.

post-colonial theory because the relationship between the son and the Nazis mirrors that of the colonial subject to the coloniser, with the former defying the authority of the latter. The juxtaposition of Drach's >>Z.Z<< and Hilsenrath's *Der Nazi & der Friseur* helps to highlight the real challenge of Hilsenrath's satirical novel: in *Der Nazi & der Friseur* it is not the colonial subject who imitates the coloniser, thus disrupting the authority of the latter, but the coloniser who imitates the colonised. If we accept this, then this raises the question of what effect this inverted constellation has on Jewish identity in the novel. Doesn't Schulz's successful camouflage produce the very slippage that, according to Bhabha, always subtly mocks the authority and authenticity of the imitated identity? And if so is this figure of farce not highly cynical, in fact insulting to the survivors in that it erodes the moral abyss between perpetrators and victims?

But this is precisely the point: the displacement of Schulz's scandalous mimicry is of course perceived by the reader who cannot reconcile the rupture between Schulz's past and his disguise as Finkelstein in the present. Although outwardly successful, Schulz-Finkelstein remains a subject of difference, who, despite his growing identification with Finkelstein's Jewishness, does not develop a new identity. Whereas, after Freud, identification usurps the place of identity, in Hilsenrath's post-Shoah world, camouflage replaces both identity and identification. Hilsenrath's novel is thus the modern version of another fairy-tale: that of the wolf in sheep's clothing.

Eating Monsters and Waste Factories: Female Abjection

Many critics have commented in passing on the chauvinism and vulgarity that characterise Hilsenrath's descriptions of sexuality. However, there has been only one attempt to explore the connection between Hilsenrath's concern with the holocaust and his depiction of sexuality. Following Sander Gilman's analysis of sexual and racial stereotypes, Gerstenberger and Pohland ask why Hilsenrath's portrayal of sexuality is nearly always characterised by images of violence.[20] With reference to *Der Nazi & der Friseur* they argue that Hilsenrath's representation of sexuality has to be understood in the context of collectively shared fantasies of the Jew's circumcised body. Sander Gilman has shown how in the phobic discourse of the Christian male, the marked body of the circumcised Jew paradoxically produced two opposing fantasies: that of the hypersexual and that of the effeminate, menstruating Jew.[21] According to Gerstenberger and Pohland, Hilsenrath cites phobic fantasies and projects them onto his non-Jewish male characters, thus exposing the sexual stigma attached to the male Jewish body.[22] One striking example of this is Schulz's description of Günter's dead body, the SS murderer who was killed by Polish partisans:

> 'Ich kratzte den Schnee von den Gesichtern herunter ... von einigen nur ... auch von ihren Körpern ... entdeckte schließlich Günter ... Günter ... ohne Schädeldecke und ohne Schwanz.'
> 'Wie sah Günter aus ... ohne Schwanz?' fragte Frau Holle.
> 'So wie eine menstruierende Frau', sagte Max Schulz ... 'mit einem roten Loch zwischen den nackten Beinen.' (98)[23]

This description of the castrated and feminised male body undoubtedly gives expression to the castration anxiety of the Aryan male. But it seems to me that it also points to an economy of desire which registers the female body primarily in terms of abject otherness. There is a pathological undercurrent in Hilsenrath's equation of the menstruating woman with a "red hole" between naked legs which requires further analysis.

Hilsenrath depicts two types of female characters in *Der Nazi & der Friseur*: the fat woman, who is always desired by the protagonist, and the ugly old hag. While these types seem at first to be diametrically opposed, a

---

[20] Cf. Katharina Gerstenberger and Vera Pohland, 'Der Wichser. Edgar Hilsenrath', 74-91.
[21] Cf. Sander L. Gilman, *Difference and Pathology*. Ithaca and London: Cornell University Press, 1985.
[22] Cf. Katharina Gerstenberger and Vera Pohland, 'Der Wichser', 83.
[23] [I scratched the snow off their faces .. but only of some of them .. also off their bodies .. and eventually I discovered Günter .. Günter without a scull and without a dick.' 'What did Günter look like ... without a dick?', asked Frau Holle. 'Just like a menstuating woman', said Max Schulz ... 'with a red hole between his naked legs'.]

closer analysis reveals that they are in fact only two expressions of the same desire. Irrespective of their actual physical appearance, all women are eating monsters and waste factories that threaten male identity.

Compare for instance Schulz's mother Minna with Veronja, the old hag, and Frau Holle. Minna is described as "ein wandelndes Bierfaß auf Stelzen" [a walking beer-barrel on stilts, NF: 13] with blond hair, blue eyes, a wart on her chin and strong white teeth. In clear contrast, Veronja is described as a "Hutzelweib" [an old hag, NF: 101] with dried-up breasts, warts, and wrinkly hands with long-finger-nails that torture the male genital (NF: 109). Frau Holle occupies a place in-between the desirable fat woman and the decaying female body: she is one-legged, emaciated and ageing, grey-haired and has a set of big, protruding yellow teeth (NF: 60).

While on the surface Schulz's mother Minna appears to be the embodiment of female desirability — she has so many lovers that she does not know which one is Schulz's father —, she too symbolises what threatens male identity:

> 'Mensch Minna, wenn ich deine Zähne seh', dann krieg ich immer gleich Angst, daß du mir den Schwanz abbeißt.' Und dann pflegte meine Mutter zu sagen: 'Ach Quatsch, Hubert, das konnte mir nur bei dem Hausdiener Adalbert Hennemann passieren, weil das bei dem so schlaff ist. Was stahlhart ist, das beiß ich nicht an.' (NF: 14)[24]

This exchange between Minna and the butcher, one of her lovers, reveals the phobic character of the male fantasies of virility. Phobia shapes nearly all sexual encounters in the novel in that they are not an expression of desire but a counterphobic activity. This also explains why the male characters are obsessed with counting the number of sex acts they perform. Their desire barely masks a loathing which maintains the fragile boundary between self and the devouring mother.

In *Der Nazi & der Friseur* desire easily switches over into loathing and back again because ultimately loathing and desire are only the two sides of the same libidinal economy which preserves a fragile male identity by abjecting the castrating (m)other. Recall that at the beginning of the narrative, Schulz's mother nearly castrates her son when, mistaking circumcision for dismemberment, she nearly cut his genital off. Again this crass episode highlights the Aryan sexual obsession with circumcision as well as the fragility of male identity. Ultimately, Minna, Frau Holle, Veronja and Gräfin von Hohenhausen are variations of one type: the female vampire

---

[24] ['Believe me, Minna, when I see your teeth I always get frightened that you might bite off my dick.' And my mother used to reply: 'Nonsense, Hubert, this could only happen to me with the caretaker Adalbert Hennemann because his dick always hangs limp. If it's hard as steel I don't bite.]

who threatens to suck the male empty by means of the very activity through which he tries to reinstate the boundaries between self and other: sex.

One striking example of Hilsenrath's coupling of desire and loathing is the episode with Frau Holle's wooden leg which she is shown to take off and put on again throughout book two. We learn that, in 1933, the day Hitler rose to power, her real leg was amputated because it was "verfault" [rotten, NF: 71]. Hilsenrath clearly alludes here to anti-Semitic imagery, thus exposing the pathological character of these stereotypes. However, there is an obsessive quality to the narrator's continued comments about the wooden leg which cannot be explained alone as a critique of the discourse on the Jew. In the ensuing story with the American Major the wooden leg is fetishised: excited by Frau Holle's handicap, the Major dies of a heart attack after "sieben Nummern" [seven sex acts, NF: 75] with the wooden leg. Here and elsewhere there is an undercurrent that stigmatises the female body in a similar way as the Aryan phobic discourse stigmatised that of the circumcised Jew. The major's fetishisation of Frau Holle's wooden leg thus points once more to the economy of abjection that characterises male desire throughout: woman is the living waste on the border of death; as a cadaver she has to be conquered and then cast aside.

Further evidence of this unconscious libidinal economy is Schulz's relationship with Mira, a survivor of the camps whom he marries for two reasons: she is fat and she does not speak. We are told that Mira is a traumatised survivor of the holocaust who, after the liberation of the camps, cannot stop eating: "Und dann fing Mira zu essen an. Aß von früh bis abends. Kaute sogar im Schlaf. Eine Freßmaschine. Stumm. Eine stumme Freßmaschine." [And then Mira began to eat. She ate from early in the morning until evening. She even chewed in her sleep. An eating machine. Mute. A mute eating machine. NF: 262] This dehumanisation of the traumatised victim of the Nazi crimes is further reinforced when, a little later, Schulz considers marrying Mira and imagines the following dialogue between his mother Minna and Slavitzki:

'Na Anton! Mein Max will heiraten. Mit 40. Was sagst du dazu?'
Und Slavitzki würde sicher sagen: 'Mit 40, da sieht nicht jeder Arsch gleich aus. Da wird man wählerisch.'
Und meine Mutter würde sagen: 'Das stimmt, Anton.'
Und Slavitzki würde sagen: 'Das muss ein guter Arsch sein.'
Und meine Mutter würde sagen: 'Ein Judenarsch! Und obendrein fetter als meiner! Das reizt meinen Max.' (NF: 65)[25]

---

[25] ['Anton! my Max wants to marry. At forty. What do you say to that?' And Slavitzki would most certainly reply: 'At forty not all arses look the same any more. One gets choosy.' And my mother would say: 'You are right, Anton.' And Slavitzki would say: 'It has to be a good arse.'

It is hardly surprising that one critic, Gert Sautermeister, strongly objects to the vulgarity of Hilsenrath's register and the titillation that it engenders here:

> Eine solche Frau ist keine 'Freßmaschine' — ihr Schicksal müßte sie vor derartigen Bezeichnungen füglich schützen. Und sie hat erst recht keinen 'fetten Judenarsch'. Mag der Erzähler diese Gemeinheit auch nur zitieren, er hat sie gleichwohl in Form eines fiktiven Dialogs ersonnen und ist ihr Komplize. Es macht ihm ja auch Spass, Miras Neurose erzählerisch zu verwerten.[26]

Sautermeister's moral outrage at a register that repeats Mira's dehumanisation and degradation linguistically is understandable. It seems to me, however, that Sautermeister fails to see the libidinal economy in Hilsenrath's novel in which loathing is the underside of desire. An illustration of this dynamic is the following aggressive fantasy:

> Sehen Sie, Mira verkörpert irgend etwas für mich, was ich zu kennen glaube und doch nicht recht begreife. Wenn ich an sie denke, dann kriege ich Lust, zuzustossen, zu zertrümmern, aufzufressen, mir einzuverleiben, verliere dabei guten Samen ... und nachdem ich den Samen verloren hab, da möchte ich alles wieder ausspucken, zusammenflicken, streicheln, versöhnen ... aber nicht loslassen, als müßte ich es festhalten, um es wieder zu fressen. (263)[27]

As a speechless "eating machine", Mira points to the semiotic sphere in which somatic and sexual impulses are not yet subsumed under the laws of the symbolic order. Schulz desires and loathes her precisely for this reason: she is a reminder of the repressed other of the symbolic order, the maternal *chora* which threatens to dissolve male identity.

Schulz's sexual fantasies in *Der Nazi & der Friseur* are undoubtedly crude and extremely vulgar. The vocabulary of loathing that characterises his fantasies makes them the final example of a specifically male drama of abjection which projects abjection onto women. In nearly all the narratives from Kafka to Hilsenrath that were discussed in the previous chapters, the reader encounters frightened males who travel through a labyrinthine space

---

And my mother would say: ' A Jewish arse! On top of it fatter than mine! This would turn my Max on!']

[26] Gert Sautermeister, 'Aufgeklärte Modernität', 237. [Such a woman is not an 'eating machine' — her terrible experience should protect her against such low expressions. And she certainly does not have a 'fat Jewish arse'. Even if the narrator only cites this defamation, he is nevertheless the creator of this piece of dialogue and thus its accomplice. He gets a kick out of exploiting Mira's neurosis.]

[27] [You see, Mira represents something for me that I seem to know but cannot quite grasp. When I think of her, I feel like fucking her, hacking her to pieces, gobbling her up, incorporating her — doing this I loose precious sperm, and after losing my sperm I want to throw everything up, to put it back together, to comfort and soothe it but not to let go, as if I had to hold on to it in order to gobble it up again.]

of anxiety. This space is mapped out by the phallic demands of the Law of the Father and a phobic social order.

Summary: A Space of Anxiety

So where did our journey through German-Jewish travel writings from Freud to Hilsenrath take us? Is the travel paradigm really pertinent to the "drama of abjection" which is the theme of this book? Can it be deduced that reality is encoded in a specific way in these texts? And, finally, to what extent is this experience peculiar to German-Jewishness? These are some of the issues that may require a final comment.

(1) At some point in their intellectual journey, all the writers discussed here used the travel paradigm to give voice to the experience of abjection. The travel paradigm lends itself extremely well to foregrounding the unhomeliness of human experience. It entails by definition a severing of the subject's links with the space called "home". Although this is true of much of travel writing from the eighteenth century onwards, the travels dealt with in this study are of a particularly existential nature. They explore the unhomeliness of both the familiar and the foreign and call attention to the frailty of the boundaries between self and other.

A first example of the defamiliarisation of the familiar which is so central to both travel and the drama of abjection is Freud's *Der Mann Moses und die monotheistische Religion*. Here he tells a story of Jewish repatriation which is fraught with problems. We saw that Freud's analysis of the Moses-figure can be read on one level as undermining the very foundations of Mosaic teachings: Freud turns him into a man with personal ambitions rather than a chosen figure with a religious calling. Read in the context of National Socialism there is undoubtedly something disturbing about Freud's interpretation of Moses. However, my analysis attempted to show that Freud's study can also be read as his final response to the Third Reich in that the book challenges the Aryan-Semite dichotomy which underpins Nazism. The choreography of abjection which characterises Freud's *Der Mann Moses* once more underlines a central insight of Freud's: the foreignness of the self.

Kafka and Roth also used a version of the travel paradigm, (enforced) migration, to explore the connection between the abjection of the self and the phobic fear of the other. While Kafka's *Der Verschollene* universalises an unfulfilled want, the longing to belong, Roth articulates this quest in *Hiob* and *Juden auf Wanderschaft* from a specifically Jewish perspective. It is also interesting to note that both authors accentuate their protagonists' desire to belong by engaging them in continued acts of severing social ties. Kafka's and Roth's narratives are thus examples of what one might call the "narrative of separation", adding another version to the drama of abjection which is the central concern of this study. Finally, chapters four and five tried to show, how in Drach's and Hilsenrath's narratives, travel has lost all connection with a positive epistemological appropriation of the world. Here the Enlightenment concept of travel as a learning experience that engenders growth has been completely replaced by the horrific experience of exile and persecution. All the texts discussed here accentuate the negativity of travel from a German-Jewish perspective. From Freud to Hilsenrath, travel is encoded as a disorientating experience in a fragmented and hostile world.

(2) In all the narratives discussed here, the protagonists move through a space of anxiety where their alienation from the outer world is matched by a sense of self-abjection. Many of the narratives therefore represent reality as a frightening labyrinth which traps these modern anti-heroes in a permanent sense of dislocation. This is most obvious in Kafka's *Der Verschollene* and Drach's narratives. The protagonists of these are invariably caught up in a labyrinth *in malo* whose enforced circuitousness, inextricability and disorientation, undermines their attempts at a positive identification with their environment. Here, the horror of the outer world mirrors that of the inner world.

The experience of the world as a terrifying labyrinth also characterises Roth's *Hiob*, Mendel Singer, who perceives both the world at home and later on America as spaces of anxiety. My analysis shows that the abjection articulated in this novel is not caused by the experience of migration but by the erosion of the symbolic order from within. In this case the order referred to is orthodox Judaism. A labyrinth of a different kind was present in Freud's *Der Mann Moses*: rather than mapping the notion of the labyrinth onto the exterior world, Freud turns the labyrinth into a stylistic category and a mode of writing which allows him to choreograph a drama of abjection which defies the common myth of national and racial identity.

(3) From Freud to Hilsenrath, German-Jewish writers had to respond to an increasingly phobic symbolic order which tried to master (in the literal sense of the word) its fragility and lack of foundation through the abjection of "the Jew". Confronting Aryan phantoms and fantasies of Jewish otherness, all the writers dealt with here engage in various modes of "writing back": the deconstruction of the fundamental tenets of a social order whose identity is based on ethnic kinship. In chapter one I argued that Freud's book on Moses is his final expression of the alternative to any form of tribalism, namely a critical engagement with the signifiers of identity as offered by the social order. While this is generally a concern of psychoanalysis which theorises the illusory nature of identity, this critical engagement is also motivated by Freud's personal experience of an increasingly tribal German culture. Freud managed to turn the experience of

abjection into an intellectual advantage that allowed him to question the assumptions of the "compact majority".

Like Freud, Drach also refuses to essentialise his Jewishness in terms of racial traits or religious ties. But unlike Freud, Drach does not embrace the category of Jewishness as an incommensurable quality and a positive alternative to Aryan mob power. For in Drach's view, the category of Jewishness has been too much appropriated by a politicised anti-Semitism. For this reason the author cannot possibly identify with his Jewishness. A powerful examination of this issue is *Das große Protokoll gegen Zwetschkenbaum* where the Eastern Jew emerges within discourses which are mediated by biased parties. Here, the reality of Zwetschkenbaum's life disappears completely behind the competing versions of who he is and what he stands for. He always remains the embodiment of "the Eastern Jew".

(4) This leads me to another point common to all the narratives studied here: from Freud to Hilsenrath, kinship is a highly problematic concept that does not provide a sense of belonging. On the contrary, it undermines identity. Freud's, Drach's and Hilsenrath's narratives all respond in various ways to the Nazis' ethnic interpretation of kinship by highlighting how the phobic exclusion of the other always returns to haunt the self.

Freud tackled the fascist opposition of Aryan and Jew directly in his last book in which he turned Moses, the father of Judaism, into an Egyptian without tribal affiliations, thus refuting the racist equation of ethnicity and (national) identity. Drach's autobiographies show how the suppression of the protagonist's Jewish family ties is a pre-condition of his survival, and yet at the same time, the reason for his continued sense of abjection. While Freud's, Drach's and Hilsenrath's narratives explicitly respond to the Nazis' *völkisch* interpretation of kinship, Kafka challenges the normative assumption that kinship provides a sense of identity by depicting the family in terms of a penal colony that punishes and destroys his protagonists. He highlights the price for the privileging of the phallus as the condition of the symbolic order. Rather than conditioning identity, the paternal metaphors in Kafka's stories are the cause of the protagonists' sense of abjection. The fathers or their representatives in Kafka's universe repress everything that is the antithesis of their rigidly defined and regimented order. In Kafka's stories family and kinship do not foster a sense of identity but the protagonist's interminable sense of abjection.

Chapter three explores the denial of kinship in Roth's auto-narration and Roth's unresolved ambivalence towards his Eastern European background. Here I demonstrated that, although Roth tried to "master" this ambivalence through a celebration of the *shtetl* in *Juden auf Wanderschaft*, his writings continued to articulate a sense of abjection. This was caused to some extent by the negative image of the Eastern Jew in Western discourse. At first sight

Roth seems to reinstate the kinship principle in *Hiob* by ending the novel with the apotheosis of the father's and son's reunion. However, I tried to show that this ending is hardly suitable to uphold a model of identity based on kinship since it only works as a fantasy of a world without women. Roth's resolution therefore unwittingly reflects the crisis of abjection which it tries to overcome.

Chapters four and five show how Drach's and Hilsenrath's narratives call attention to the connection between the kinship principle and the phobic anti-Semitism of National Socialism. Both writers underline how in the fascist order kinship has become an open carrier of abjection, legitimising the extermination of the abjected other, the Jew. In Hilsenrath's novel *Der Nazi & der Friseur* the assumption that an "authentic" sense of identity is based on kinship is turned upside down when the SS murderer Max Schulz mimics a Jewish identity to such a high degree of perfection that he actually begins to develop a Jewish sense of identity.

(5) The authors studied here do not exhaust this topic solely with reference to the individual's identity. They also give expression to the phobic underside of the symbolic order which constitutes its boundaries through the abjection of otherness. While this critique of the phobic social order is most radical in Freud's, Kafka's and Drach's narratives, it is a theme that preoccupies all writers analysed in this study. All the texts included in my book articulate a crisis of belonging. They show that the national body is not a guarantor of a sense of belonging, one of the cornerstones of nineteenth-century nationalism. Instead, in the case of German Jewry, it is the very opposite: the institutionalised expression of a phobic definition of selfhood.

(6) However radical these various critiques of the social order are, the same does not hold for woman as a signifier in the chain of desire: from Kafka to Hilsenrath, women are imagined as fat monsters, badly assembled skeletons, old hags, vampires and eating machines. Schulz's sexual fantasies in *Der Nazi & der Friseur* are only the final example of a general structure which allows the male characters (and their authors) to transfer their experience of abjection onto women. Time and again the reader comes across male protagonists, who, fragile and frightened, try to control their fear of a phobic social order by loathing women. They desire and abject women as the living waste on the border of death. In the body of literature discussed, there is little or no evidence of a second narrative level which creates critical distance towards this "misogynist grammar of desire". The reader is left with the impression that writers from Kafka to Hilsenrath affirm a libidinal economy which turns woman *literally* into the abject other of the symbolic order. It goes without saying that this is not a Jewish problem but one that reflects the position of women within the phallic symbolic order. In the

narratives discussed here the misogynist grammar of desire is encoded in a particularly Jewish way, since it involves the displacement of the abjection of "the Jew" onto woman. Undoubtedly, similar types of displacement can be found in modernist texts by non-Jewish writers.

It seems to me, however, that the misogyny inscribed in these texts could be seen to engage *unwittingly* in a radical revision of the gender system: this literature denotes the genderisation of abjection as the foundation of the symbolic order. In a way this paves the way for a critical re-examination of the phallicisation of the symbolic.

(7) All the writers discussed here deal with the category of abjection on an *imaginary* level. According to Kristeva, writing implies "an ability to imagine the abject, that is, to see oneself in its place and to thrust it aside only by means of the displacements of verbal play."[1] This is, of course, a definition of (post)modernist and avant-garde literature which, in Kristeva's words, is concerned with the "impossibility of Religion, Morality and Law — their power play, their necessary and absurd seeming."[2] The implication here is that contemporary literature ultimately denotes that the symbolic has no ontological foundation. Kristeva continues that the writer is fascinated by the abject, imagines its logic and "as a consequence perverts language — style and content."[3] Writing is a perverse activity because it is indexed against the Law of the Father, "vers le père", by constantly upsetting the boundaries of the symbolic and reintroducing the abject as its repressed other. According to Kristeva, the writer articulates the abject backwards through an overmastery of language. This aspect is particularly prominent in my readings of Drach and Kafka. These underline Kristeva's point that linguistic overmastery is a "fetishist screen" which masks the fear that language hovers over a meaningless void.[4] Ultimately, fear also emerges as the terrifying referent of this literature.

(8) Kristeva's definition of the writer as "a phobic who succeeds in metaphorizing in order to keep from being frightened to death"[5] clearly refers to the modernist and avant-garde writer. My analysis suggests, however, that the problem of modernity and modernism (the artistic reaction to the condition of modernity) was particularly acute for German-Jewish writers before and also after the Shoah. I argued that they turned the trap of ambivalence into a positional advantage that allowed them to address the artificiality of the dichotomy between self and other, homeliness and

---

[1] Julia Kristeva, *Powers of Horror*, 16.
[2] Ibid., 16.
[3] Ibid., 16.
[4] Ibid., 37.
[5] Ibid., 37.

foreignness, Aryan and Jew, pure and impure. Freud, Kafka, Roth, Drach and Hilsenrath can all be viewed as metaphorical borderliners who in various ways challenge the "persistence of tradition"[6] by re-inscribing abjection, contingency, fragmentation and contradiction into the narrative of modernity.

---

[6] Homi Bhabha, *The Location of Culture*, 2.

Bibliography

Abraham, Hilda and Freud, Ernst L. (Eds.) (1965), *A Psychoanalytic Dialogue. The Letters of Sigmund Freud and Karl Abraham 1907-1926*. London: Hogarth Press.

Adorno, Theodor (1987), 'Kulturkritik und Gesellschaft'. In: *Prismen*. Frankfurt am Main: Suhrkamp: 9-26.

Anderson, Benedict (revised ed. 1991), *Imagined Communities. Reflections on the Origin and Spread of Nationalism*. London: Verso.

Anderson, Mark (1992), *Kafka's Clothes. Ornament and Aestheticism in the Habsburg Fin-de-Siècle*. Oxford: Clarendon.

Aschheim, Steven S. (1982), *Brothers and Strangers: The East European Jew in German and German Jewish Consciousness, 1800-1923*. Madison, Wisconsin: University of Wisconsin Press.

Assmann, Jan (1998), *Moses der Ägypter. Entzifferung einer Gedächtnisspur*. Darmstadt: Wissenschaftliche Buchgesellschaft.

Auckenthaler, Karlheinz F. (1994), '"Ich habe mich erst als Jude zu fühlen gehabt, als mich der Hitler als einen solchen erklärt hat." Albert Drachs Beziehung zum Judentum in Leben und Werk.' In: *Modern Austrian Literature* 27: 51-69.

Bakan, David (1969), *Sigmund Freud and the Jewish Mystical Tradition*. New York: Schocken.

Bakhtin, Mikhail (1981), *The Dialogic Imagination: Four Essays*. Ed. by Michael Holquist. Austin: University of Texas Press.

Bauman, Zygmunt (1989), *Modernity and the Holocaust*. Cambridge: Polity Press.

------ (1991), *Modernity and Ambivalence*. Cambridge: Polity Press.

Beicken, Peter U. (1974), *Franz Kafka. Eine kritische Einführung in die Forschung*. Frankfurt am Main: Athenaion.

Bering, Dietz 'Der "jüdische" Name. Antisemitische Namenspolemik'. In: Julius H. Schoeps and Joachim Schlör (Eds.), *Antisemitismus. Vorurteile und Mythen*. Frankfurt am Main: Zweitausendundeins: no year, 153-166.

Beug, Joachim (1991), 'Die Grenzschenke. Zu einem literarischen Topos.' In: Helen Chambers (Ed.), *Co-Existent Contradictions. Joseph Roth in Retrospect. Papers of the 1989 Joseph Roth Symposium at Leeds University*. Riverside, California: Ariadne Press: 148-165.

------ (1999), 'Pogroms in Literary Representation'. In: Anne Fuchs and Florian Krobb (Eds.) (1999), *Ghetto Writing: Traditional and Eastern*

Jewry in German-Jewish Literature from Heine to Hilsenrath. Drawer, Columbia: Camden House, 84-97.

Bhabha, Homi K. (1994), *The Location of Culture*. London and New York: Routledge.

Biale, Rachel (1984), *Women and Jewish Law. An Exploration of Women's Issues in Halakhic Sources*. New York: Schocken.

Binder, Hartmut (Ed.) (1979), *Kafka Handbuch*. Vol. 1. *Der Mensch und seine Zeit*. Stuttgart: Kröner.

Boa, Elizabeth (1993), 'Letters from a Bachelor. Kafka's Letters to Felice and Milena'. In: *London German Studies V*, University of London, Institute of Germanic Studies: 119-140.

Böhme, Hartmut (1977), 'Mother Milena: On Kafka's Narcissism'. In: Angel Flores (Ed.), *The Kafka Debate — New Perspectives for Our Time*. New York: Gordion: 80-99.

Braun, Helmut (1996), 'Erinnerung'. In: Thomas Kraft (Ed.), *Edgar Hilsenrath: Das Unerzählbare erzählen*. Munich: Piper: 43-50.

Bronsen, David (1974), *Joseph Roth. Eine Biographie*. Cologne: Kiepenheuer & Witsch.

------ (1979), 'The Jew in Search of a Fatherland: The Relationship of Joseph Roth to the Habsburg Monarchy.' In: *Germanic Review* : 53-61.

Brown, Gilian and Yule, George (1983), *Discourse Analysis*. Cambridge etc.: Cambridge University Press.

Burgin, Victor (1982), 'Looking at Photographs'. In: Victor Burgin (Ed.) (1994), *Thinking Photography*. Houndsmills and London: Macmillan: 142-153.

Butler, Geoffrey. P. (1988), 'It's the Bitterness that Counts: Joseph Roth's 'Most Jewish' Novel Reconsidered.' In: *German Life & Letters* 41: 227-234.

Carter, Elizabeth A. and McGoldrick, Monica (1980), *The Family Life-Cycle. A Framework for Family Therapy*. New York: Gardner.

Chambers, Helen (1991), 'Predators or Victims? — Women in Joseph Roth's Works.' In: Helen Chambers (Ed.), *Co-Existent Contradictions. Joseph Roth in Retrospect*: 107-127.

Cheyette Bryan and Marcus, Laura (Eds.) (1998), 'Introduction; Some Methodological Anxieties'. In: Bryan Cheyette and Laura Marcus (Eds.), *Modernity, Culture and the 'Jew'*. Cambridge: Polity Press: 1-20.

Chodorow, Nancy (1994), *Femininities, Masculinities, Sexualities. Freud and Beyond*. London: Free Association Books.

Cooper, John (1995), 'Jewish Sexual Attitudes in Eastern Europe 1850 — 1920.' In: Jonathan Magonet (Ed.) (1995), *Jewish Explorations of Sexuality*. Oxford: Berghahn: 181-189.

Decker, Hannah S. (1991), *Freud, Dora, and Vienna*. New York: The Free Press, Macmillan.

Dallos, Rudi (1991), *Family Belief Systems, Therapy and Change. A Constructional Approach*. Milton Keynes, Philadelphia: Open University Press.

Doob, Penelope Reed (1990), *The Idea of the Labyrinth from Classical Antiquity through the Middle Ages*. Ithaca and London: Cornell University Press.

Drach, Albert (1989), *Das große Protokoll gegen Zwetschkenbaum*. Munich: Hanser.

------ (1996), *>>Z.Z.<< das ist die Zwischenzeit*. Munich: Deutscher Taschenbuchverlag.

------ (1988), *Unsentimentale Reise. Ein Bericht*. Munich and Vienna: Hanser.

------ (1993), *Das Beileid. Roman nach Teilen eines Tagebuchs*. Graz: Droschl.

Eco, Umberto (1982), 'Critique of the Image'. In: Victor Burgin (Ed.) (1994), *Thinking Photography*. Houndsmills and London: 32-39.

Emrich, Wilhelm (1957), *Franz Kafka*. Bonn: Athenäum.

Fischer, André (1995), "Der Zynismus ist ein Anwendungsfall der Ironie.' Zum Humor bei Albert Drach'. In: G. Fuchs and G. A. Höfler (Eds.), *Albert Drach*: 31-50.

------ (1992), *Inszenierte Naivität. Zur ästhetischen Simulation von Geschichte bei Günter Grass, Albert Drach und Walter Kempowski*. Munich: Wilhelm Fink: 214-267.

Franzos, Karl Emil (4 ed. 1901), *Aus Halb-Asien. Kulturbilder aus Galizien, der Bukowina, Südrußland und Rumänien*, vol. I. Berlin: Concordia.

------ (1988) *Der Pojaz. Eine Geschichte aus dem Osten*. Frankfurt am Main: Athenäum.

Freud Sigmund (1968), *Sigmund Freud — Arnold Zweig: Briefwechsel*. Ed. by Ernst L. Freud, Frankfurt am Main: Fischer.

------ (1926), 'Ansprache an die Mitglieder des Vereins B'nai B'rith'. In: Sigmund Freud: *Gesammelte Werke*. Ed. by Anna Freud et al. London: Imago, 1941-1952, vol. 17: 51-53.

------ (1909), 'Der Familienroman der Neurotiker'. In: Sigmund Freud, *Gesammelte Werke*, vol. 7: 227-231.

------ (1914), 'Der Moses des Michelangelo'. In: Sigmund Freud, *Gesammelte Werke*, vol. 10: 172-201.

------ (1925), 'Selbstdarstellung'. In: *GesammelteWerke*, vol. 14: 31-96.

------ (1927), 'Die Zukunft einer Illusion'. In: *Gesammelte Werke*, vol. 14: 323-380.

------ (1930), 'Das Unbehagen in der Kultur'. In: *Gesammelte Werke*, vol. 14: 419-506.

------ (1913), 'Totem und Tabu'. In: *Gesammelte Werke*, vol. 9.

------ (1939), 'Der Mann Moses und die monotheistische Religion', In: *Gesammelte Werke*, vol. 16: 101-246.

------ (1969) 'Some Early Unpublished Letters of Freud'. In: *International Journal of Psychoanalysis* 50: 419-427.

------ 'Femininity'. In: James Strachey et al. (Ed.) (1964), *Sigmund Freud: The Standard Edition of the Complete Psychological Works*, London: Hogarth Press, vol. 22: 112-135.

------ 'An Autobiographical Study'. In: James Strachey et al. (Ed.) (1935), *Standard Edition*. London: Hogarth, vol. 20: 7-39.

Fuchs, Anne (1993), 'Laurence Sterne's *Unsentimental Journey* and Goethe's *Italian Journey*: Two Models of the Non-Perception of Otherness'. In: *New Comparison. A Journal of Comparative and General Literary Studies* 16: 25-42.

------ (1996), '"... da Hitler zu Ermordungszwecken nach und nach alle Juden dringend braucht": Labyrinth und Abjektion in Albert Drachs Unsentimentale Reise'. In: *German Life and Letters* 49: 243-255.

------ (1997), 'A Suitcase, Passport and a Photograph: The Iconography of Abjection in Kafka's *Der Verschollene*'. In: Jeff Morrrison, Florian Krobb (Eds.), *Text into Image/Image into Text. Proceedings of the Interdisciplinary Bicentenary Conference held at St. Patrick's College Maynooth in September 1995*. Internationale Forschungen zur Allgemeinen und Vergleichenden Literaturwissenschaft 20. Amsterdam, Atlanta: Rodopi: 193-201.

------ (1999), 'Edgar Hilsenrath's Poetics of Insignificance and the Tradition of Humour in German-Jewish Ghetto Writing'. In: Anne Fuchs and Florian Krobb (Eds.), *Ghetto Writing* : 195-209.

Fuchs, Anne and Krobb, Florian (Eds.) (1999), *Ghetto Writing: Traditional and Eastern Jewry in German-Jewish Literature from Heine to Hilsenrath*. Columbia: Camden House.

Fuchs, Gerhard and Höfler, Günther A. (1995) (Eds.), *Albert Drach*. Graz and Vienna: Droschl.

Fuchs, Gerhard (1995), 'Männer, Mütter, Mädel. Die Funktionalisierung des Weiblichen bei Albert Drach'. In: G. Fuchs and G. A. Höfler (Eds.), *Albert Drach*: 79-121.

Gay, Peter (1993), *Freud. A Life for Our Time*. London: Papermac, Macmillan.

Gelber, Mark H. (1990), '"Juden auf Wanderschaft" und die Rhetorik der Ost-Westdebatte im Werk Joseph Roths.' In: Michael Kessler and Fritz Hackert, (Eds.) (1990), *Joseph Roth: Interpretation — Rezeption — Kritik*. Stauffenburg Colloquium 15, Tübingen: Stauffenburg: 127-135.

Gelber, Mark H. (1996), 'Zur deutsch-zionistischen Rezeptionsgeschichte. Joseph Roth und die Jüdische Rundschau.' In: Mark H. Gelber, Hans Otto Horch, Sigurd P. Scheichl (Eds.) (1996), *Von Franzos bis Canetti*.

Jüdische Autoren aus Österreich. Neue Studien. Tübingen: Niemeyer: 201-209.

Gerstenberger, Katharina and Pohland, Vera (1993), 'Der Wichser. Edgar Hilsenrath — Schreiben über den Holocaust, Identität und Sexualität'. In: *Der Deutschunterricht* 3 (1993): 74-91.

Gilman, Sander L. (1985), *Difference and Pathology.* Ithaca and London: Cornell University Press.

------ (1986), *Jewish Self-Hatred: Anti-Semitism and the Hidden Language of the Jews.* Baltimore and London: John Hopkins University Press.

------ (1993), *Freud, Race, and Gender.* Princeton, New Jersey: Princeton University Press.

------ (1993), 'Zwetschkenbaum's Competence: Madness and the Discourse of the Jews'. In: *Modern Austrian Literature* 26: 1-33.

------ (1993), *Freud, Race, and Gender.* Princeton, New Jersey: Princeton University Press.

------ (1996), 'Hilsenrath und Grass Redivivus'. In: Thomas Kraft (Ed.), *Edgar Hilsenrath. Das Unerzählbare erzählen*: 119-126.

Glasenapp, Gabriele von (1996), *Aus der Judengasse. Zur Entstehung und Ausprägung deutschsprachiger Ghettoliteratur im 19. Jahrhundert.* Conditio Judaica 11, Tübingen: Niemeyer.

------ (1999), 'German versus Jargon: Language and Jewish Identity in German Ghetto Writing'. In: Anne Fuchs and Florian Krobb (Eds.), *Ghetto Writing*: 54-65.

Goldstein, Bluma (1992), *Reinscribing Moses. Heine, Kafka, Freud and Schoenberg in a European Wilderness.* Cambridge, Mass. and London, England: Harvard University Press.

Graf, Andreas (1996), 'Mörderisches Ich. Zur Pathologie der Erzählperspektive in *Der Nazi & der Friseur.*' In: Thomas Kraft (Ed.), *Edgar Hilsenrath. Das Unerzählbare erzählen*: 135-149.

Grosz, Elizabeth (1989), *Sexual Subversions. Three French Feminists.* Sydney, Wellington etc.: Allen & Unwin.

Grubrich-Simitis, Ilse (1991), *Freuds Moses-Studie als Tagtraum. Ein biographischer Essay. Sigmund-Freud Vorlesungen,* ed. by Dieter Ohlmeier, vol. 3. Weinheim: Verlag Internationale Psychoanalyse.

Grunfeld, I. (1972), *The Jewish Dietary Laws.* Vol. 1. London etc.: Soncino.

Henel, Ingeborg (1964), 'Ein Hungerkünstler'. In: *Deutsche Vierteljahresschrift* 38: 230-247.

Herik, Judith van (1982), *Freud on Femininity and Faith.* Berkeley etc.: University of California Press.

Hermand, Jost (Ed.) (1987), *Geschichten aus dem Ghetto.* Munich: Athenäum.

Hermsdorf, Klaus (1961), 'Kafka's America'. In: Kenneth Hughes (Ed.) (1981), *Franz Kafka. An Anthology of Marxist Criticism*. Hanover and London: University Press of New England: 22-37.

Heubach, Helga (Ed.) (1992), *Die Anna O. Sisyphus: Gegen den Mädchenhandel — Galizien*. Freiburg: Kore.

Hilsenrath, Edgar (1995), *Jossel Wassermanns Heimkehr*. Munich and Zurich: Piper.

—— (1996), *Nacht*. Munich and Zurich: Piper.

—— (1996), 'Das verschwundene Schtetl'. In: Thomas Kraft (Ed.), *Edgar Hilsenrath — Das Unerzählbare erzählen*. Munich and Zurich: Piper: 19-37.

—— (1997), *Die Abenteuer des Ruben Jablonski: Ein autobiographischer Roman*. Munich and Zurich: Piper.

—— (1997), *Der Nazi & der Friseur*. Munich and Zurich: Piper.

Höfler, Günther A. (1995), '"Wenn einer ein Jud ist, dann ist das Schuld genug'. Aspekte des Jüdischen im Werk Albert Drachs'. In: G. Fuchs and G. A. Höfler (Eds.), *Albert Drach*, 179-202.

'Holocaust und Unterhaltung: Eine Diskussion mit Edgar Hilsenrath, Michael Komar, Ursula Link-Heer, Egon Monk und Marcel Ophüls'. In: Manuel Köppen (Ed.) (1993), *Kunst und Literatur nach Auschwitz*. Berlin: Erich Schmidt: 107-112.

Horch, Hans Otto (1993), "Im Grunde ist er sehr jüdisch geblieben...' Zum Verhältnis von 'Katholizismus' und Judentum bei Joseph Roth.' In: Hans Otto Horch and Itta Shedlytzky (Eds.) (1993), *Deutsch-jüdische Exil- und Emigrationsliteratur im 20. Jahrhundert*. Tübingen: Niemeyer: 205-235.

Hüppauf, Bernd (1988), 'Joseph Roth: Hiob. Der Mythos des Skeptikers.' In: Bernd M. Kraske (Ed.) (1988), *Joseph Roth — Werk und Wirkung*. Bonn: Bouvier: 25-87.

Jones, Ernest (1965), *Sigmund Freud. Life and Work*, vol. 1. London: Hogarth.

Kafka, Franz (1993), *Der Verschollene*. Ed. by Jost Schillemeit. Frankfurt am Main: Fischer.

—— (1983 = F), *Briefe an Felice und andere Korrespondenz aus der Verlobungszeit*. Ed by Erich Heller and Jürgen Born. Frankfurt am Main: Fischer.

—— (1994 = TB2), *Tagebücher*. Vol. 2: 1912-1914. Ed. by Hans-Gerd Koch, following the Historical-Critical Edition. Frankfurt am Main: Fischer.

—— (1984), *Sämtliche Erzählungen*. Ed. by Paul Raabe. Frankfurt am Main: Fischer.

—— (1992), *Brief an den Vater*. Frankfurt: Fischer.

—— (1982 = A), *America*. Introduced by Edwin Muir, London, Auckland etc.: Minerva.

------ (1974 = LF), *Letters to Felice*. Ed. by Erich Heller and Jürgen Born, translated by James Stern and Elisabeth Duckworth, London: Secker & Warburg.

Kaindlstorfer, Günter (1992), 'Ratzeputz: Der Kanzleischreiber Gottes: Zum 90. Geburtstag des Schriftstellers Albert Drach'. In: Gerhard Fuchs and Günther A. Höfler (Eds.), *Albert Drach*, 270-275.

Kaszynski, Stefan H. (1996), 'Der jüdische Anteil an der Literatur in und über Galizien.' In: Mark H. Gelber and Hans Otto Horch etc. (Eds.) (1996), *Von Franzos bis Canetti*: 129-140.

Klanska, Maria (1990), 'Die galizische Heimat im Werk Joseph Roths.' In: Michael Kessler and Fritz Hackert (Eds.) (1990), *Joseph Roth. Interpretation, Rezepton, Kritik*. Stauffenburg Colloquium 15, Tübingen: Stauffenburg: 143-155.

Kempf, Franz R. (1994), *Everyone's Darling: Kafka and the Critics of His Short Fiction*. Columbia: Camden House.

Kremer, Detlef (1994), 'Verschollen. Gegenwärtig. Franz Kafkas Roman *Der Verschollene*'. In: *Text & Kritik*, special issue VII. Franz Kafka, 1994: 238-253.

Kristeva, Julia (1980), *Desire in Language*. Translated by Leon S. Roudiez. Oxford: Basil Blackwell.

------ (1982), *Powers of Horror. An Essay on Abjection*. Translated by L. S. Roudiez. New York: Columbia University Press.

------ (1984), *Revolution in Poetic Language*. Translated by M. Waller with an Introduction by L. S. Roudiez. New York: Columbia University Press.

Krobb, Florian (1993), *Die schöne Jüdin. Jüdische Frauengestalten in der deutschsprachigen Erzählliteratur vom 17. Jahrhundert bis zum ersten Weltkrieg*. Conditio Judaica 4, Tübingen: Niemeyer.

------ (1996), '"Dina, was sagst du zu dem zuckrigen Gott?" Salomon Kohn und die Prager deutsch-jüdische Literatur des 19. Jahrhunderts.' In: Mark H. Gelber and Hans Otto Horch et al. (Eds.) (1996), *Von Franzos bis Canetti*: 7- 24.

------ (1999), 'Reclaiming the Location: Leopold Kompert's Ghetto Fiction in Post-Colonial Perspective'. In: Anne Fuchs and Florian Krobb (Eds.), *Ghetto Writing*: 41-53.

Kuhn, Annette (1991), Remembrance. In: Jo Spence and Patricia Holland (Eds.) (1991), *Family Snaps — The Meaning of Domestic Photography*. London: Virago: 17-26.

Laermann, Klaus (1993), ''Nach Auschwitz ein Gedicht zu schreiben, ist barbarisch:' Überlegungen zu einem Darstellungsverbot'. In: *Kunst und Literatur nach Auschwitz*: 11-16.

Lamping, Dieter (1998), *Von Kafka bis Celan. Jüdischer Diskurs in der deutschen Literatur des 20 Jahrhunderts*. Göttingen: Vandenhoeck & Ruprecht.

Landsberger, Arthur (Ed.) (1916), *Das Volk des Ghetto*. Munich: Georg Müller.

Le Rider, Jacques (1993), *Modernity and Crises of Identity. Culture and Society in Fin-de-Siècle Vienna*. Translated by Rosemary Morris. Cambridge: Polity Press.

Magris, Claudio (1974), *Weit von wo. Verlorene Welt des Ostjudentums*. Vienna and Zürich: Europaverlag.

------ (1975), 'Der ostjüdische Odyseus — Roth zwischen Kaisertum und Golus.' In: David Bronsen (Ed.) (1975), *Joseph Roth und die Tradition. Aufsatz, — Materialsammlung*. Darmstadt: Agora: 181-226.

Möller, Susann (1996), 'Zur Rezeption – Philosemiten und andere – die Verlagsstationen Edgar Hilsenraths'. In: *Edgar Hilsenrath: Das Unerzählbare erzählen*: 103-116.

Northey, Anthony (1991), *Kafka's Relatives — Their Lives & His Writing*. New Haven and London: Yale University Press.

Oxaal, Ivar (1988), 'The Jewish Origin of Psychoanalysis Reconsidered.' In: Edward Timms and Naomi Segal (Eds.), *Freud in Exile. Psychoanalysis and its Vicissitudes*. New Haven and London: Yale University Press: 37-53.

Politzer, Heinz (1978), *Franz Kafka: Der Künstler*. Frankfurt am Main: Suhrkamp.

Pratt, Mary Louise (1992), *Imperial Eyes. Travel Writing and Transculturation*. London and New York: Routledge.

Preisendanz, Wolfgang (1979), 'Humor als Rolle'. In: Odo Marquard and Karlheinz Stierle (Eds.), *Identität* [Poetik und Hermeneutik VIII]. Munich: Fink: 423-434.

------ (1986), *Humor als dichterische Einbildungskraft: Studien zur Erzählkunst des poetischen Realismus*. Munich: Fink.

------ (1988), 'Die grausame Zufallskomödie der Welt'. In: Gerhard Fuchs and Günther A. Höfler (Eds.), *Albert Drach*: 262-270.

Reed Doob, Penelope (1990), *The Idea of the Labyrinth from Classical Antiquity through the Middle Ages*. Ithaca, London: Cornell University Press.

Rice, Emanuel (1990), *Freud and Moses — The Long Journey Home*. New York: State University of New York Press.

Richter, Matthias (1995), *Die Sprache jüdischer Figuren in der jüdischen Literatur (1750-1933): Studien zu Form und Funktion*. Göttingen: Wallstein.

Robert, Marthe (1977), *From Oedipus to Moses. Freud's Jewish Identity*. Translated by Ralph Manheim. London and Henley : Routledge.

Robertson, Ritchie (1985), *Kafka: Judaism, Politics, and Literature*. Oxford: Clarendon Press.

------ (1988), 'Freud's Testament: *Moses and Monotheism.* 'In: Edward Timms and Naomi Segal (Eds.), *Freud in Exile. Psychoanalysis and its Vicissitudes.* New Haven and London: Yale University Press: 80-89.

------ (1996), "Urheimat Asien'. The Re-orientation of German and Austrian Jews 1900 -1925.' In: *German Life & Letters* 49/2: 182-192.

------ (1991), 'Roth's *Hiob* and the Traditions of Ghetto Fiction.' In: Helen Chambers (Ed.), *Co-Existent Contradiction*: 185-200.

------ (1998), 'Historicizing Weininger: The Nineteenth-Century German Image of the Feminized Jew'. In: Bryan Cheyette and Laura Marcus (Eds.), *Modernity, Culture and 'the Jew'*. Cambridge: Polity Press: 23-39.

Rockman, Hannah (1995), 'Sexual Behaviour among Ultra-Orthodox Jews. A Review of Laws and Guidelines'. In: Jonathan Magonet (Ed.) (1995), *Jewish Explorations of Sexuality.* Oxford: Berghahn: 191-204.

Roith, Esthelle (1987), *The Riddle of Freud. Jewish Influences on His Theory of Female Sexuality.* New Library of Psychoanalysis 4, London and New York: Tavistock.

Roth, Joseph (1924 = W 4), *Hotel Savoy.* In: Joseph Roth, *Werke*, 6 vols. Ed. by Fritz Hackert, vol. 4. Cologne, 1989: Kiepenheuer & Witsch: 147-242.

------ (1927 = W2), *Juden auf Wanderschaft.* In: Joseph Roth, *Werke*, vol 2. Cologne: Kiepenheuer & Witsch, 1990: 827-902.

------ (1927 = W4), *Die Flucht ohne Ende.* In: Joseph Roth, *Werke,* vol. 4. Cologne: Kiepenheuer & Witsch, 1989: 389-496.

------ (1930 = W5), *Hiob. Roman eines einfachen Mannes.* In: Joseph Roth, *Werke* , vol. 5. Cologne: Kiepenheuer & Witsch, 1990: 1-136.

------ (1932 = W5) *Radetzkymarsch.* In: Joseph Roth, *Werke*, vol. 5. Cologne: Kiepenheuer & Witsch, 1990: 137-456.

------ (1970 = B), *Briefe 1911—1939.* Ed. by Hermann Kesten. Cologne and Berlin: Kiepenheuer & Witsch.

------ (1983), *Job. The Story of a Simple Man.* Translated by Dorothy Thompson. London: Chatto & Windus.

Rumler, Fritz (1977), 'Max & Itzig'. In: *Der Spiegel* No. 35 (22. 8. 1977, Reprinted in: Thomas Kraft (Ed.), *Edgar Hilsenrath*: 69-72.

Said, Edward (1991), *Orientalism. Western Conceptions of the Orient.* Harmondsworth: Penguin.

Sautermeister, Gert (1994), 'Aufgeklärte Modernität — Postmodernes Entertainment: Edgar Hilsenraths *Der Nazi & Der Friseur'*. In: Jens Stüben and Winfried Woesler (Eds.), *'Wir tragen den Zettelkasten mit den Steckbriefen unserer Freunde:' Acta-Band zum Symposion 'Beiträge jüdischer Autoren zur deutschen Literatur seit 1945'.* Darmstadt: Häusser: 227-242.

Scheible, Hartmut (1982), 'Joseph Roths Flucht aus der Geschichte.' In: *Text & Kritik: Sonderband Joseph Roth*: 56-66.

Schlant, Ernestine (1993), 'Albert Drach's *Unsentimentale Reise*: Literature of the Holocaust and the Dance of Death'. In: *Modern Austrian Literature* 26, 35-62.

Schobel, Eva (1995), 'Albert Drach oder das Protokoll als Wille und Vorstellung'. In: Bernhard Fetz (Ed.), *In Sachen Albert Drach*. Vienna: WUV Universitätsverlag: 8-13.

------ (1995), 'Albert Drach: Ein lebenslanger Versuch zu überleben'. In: Gerhard Fuchs und Günther A. Höfler (Eds.), *Albert Drach*: 329-372.

Segal, Naomi (1988), 'Freud and the Question of Women'. In: Edward Timms and Naomi Segal (Eds.), *Freud in Exile*: 241-253.

Settele, Matthias (1992), *Der Protokollstil des Albert Drach — Recht, Gerechtigkeit, Sprache, Literatur*. Frankfurt am Main etc.: Peter Lang.

Shedletzky, Itta (1996), 'Ost und West in der deutsch-jüdischen Literatur von Heinrich Heine bis Jospeh Roth.' In: Mark H. Gelber, Hans Otto Horch et al. (Ed.) (1996), *Von Franzos bis Canetti*: 189-200.

Smith, Anna (1996), *Julia Kristeva. Readings of Exile and Estrangement*. Houndsmills: Macmillan.

Sontag, Susan (1989), *On Photography*. New York: The Noon Day Press, Farrar, Straus and Giroux.

Spira, Leopold (1981), *Feindbild 'Jud'. 100 Jahre politischer Antisemitismus in Österreich*. Vienna and Munich: Löcker Verlag.

Sprengnether, Madelaine (1990), *The Spectral Mother. Freud, Feminism and Psychoanalysis*. Ithaca and London: Cornell University Press.

Stach, Rainer (1987), *Kafkas erotischer Mythos. Eine ästhetische Konstruktion des Weiblichen*. Frankfurt am Main: Fischer.

Starobinski, Jean (1971), *Jean-Jacques Rousseau: la transparance et l'obstacle*. Paris: Gallimard.

------ (1990), *Psychoanalyse und Literatur*. Translated by Eckhart Rohloff. Frankfurt am Main: Suhrkamp.

Steinlein, Rüdiger (1993), 'Das Furchtbarste lächerlich? Komik und Lachen in Texten der deutschen Holocaust-Literatur'. In: Manuel Köppen (Ed.) (1993), *Kunst und Literatur nach Auschwitz*. Berlin: Erich Schmidt: 97-106.

Stenberg, Peter (1982), 'Memories of the Holocaust: Edgar Hilsenrath and the Fiction of the Genocide'. In: *Deutsche Vierteljahresschrift für Literaturwissenschaft und Geistesgeschichte* 56 (1982): 277-289

Sterne, Laurence (1984), *A Sentimental Journey through France and Italy by Mr. Yorick*. Ed. by Ian Jack. Oxford: Oxford University Press.

Thornhill, Chris (1996): "Grenzfälle': Galician Jews and Austrian Enlightenment.' In: *German Life & Letters* 49: 171-181.

Timms, Edward (1994), 'The Wandering Jew — A Leitmotif in German Literature and Politics'. Professorial Lecture given at the University of Sussex on Tuesday 26 April 1994.

Toury, Jacob (1982), 'Die Sprache als Problem der jüdischen Einordnung im deutschen Kulturraum.' In: *Jahrbuch des Instituts für deutsche Geschichte*, Tel Aviv, Beiheft 4 (1982): 75-84.

Unterman, Alan (1991), *Dictionary of Jewish Lore & Legend.* London: Thames & Hudson.

Wassermann, Jakob (1994), *Mein Weg als Deutscher und Jude.* Munich: Deutscher Taschenbuch Verlag.

Watzlawick, Paul; Beavin, Janet Helmick; Jackson, Don D. (1968), *Pragmatics of Human Communication. A Study of Interactional Patterns, Pathologies and Paradoxes.* London: Faber & Faber.

Weininger, Otto (1906), *Sex & Character.* Authorised translation from the 6th German Edition. London: William Heinemann.

Wistrich, Robert S. (1982), *Socialism and the Jews. The Dilemmas of Assimilation in Germany and Austria-Hungary.* Rutherford etc.: Fairleigh Dickinson University Press; London and Toronto: Associated University Press.

------ (1989), *The Jews of Vienna in the Age of Franz Joseph.* Oxford: Oxford University Press.

Yerushalmi, Yosef Hayim (1991), *Freud's Moses: Judaism Terminable and Interminable.* New Haven and London: Yale University Press.

Young, Robert (1989), *White Mythologies. Writing History and the West.* London and New York: Routledge.

Zborowski, Mark and Herzog, Elizabeth (1970), *Life is with People. The Culture of the Shtetl.* New York: Schocken.

Zweig, Arnold (1920), *Das ostjüdische Antlitz.* Berlin: Welt-Verlag.

Index

Abraham, Karl, 28
Adorno, Theodor, 98, 166
Amenopis IV, 36
Anderson, Benedict, 129
Anderson, Mark M., 51
Asch, Schalom, 99
Aschheim, Steven S., 9, 130-132
Bakhtin, Mikhail, 141
Bateson, Gregory, 104
Bauer, Felice, 77
Bauer, Ludwig, 96
Bauman, Zygmunt 2, 3, 11, 123, 128, 158
Beicken, Peter U., 56
Beug, Joachim, 151
Bhabha, Homi K., 13, 15, 20- 21, 122, 137-139, 141, 152, 170-171
Binder, Hartmut, 57
Börne, Ludwig, 123
Braun, Hermann, 167
Brentano, Bernhard von, 86
Bronsen, David, 81-82, 101
Buber, Martin, 136
Burgin, Victor, 66-67
Butler, Geoffrey P., 102-103
Carter, Elizabeth A., 105
Céline, Louis-Ferdinand, 7
Dallos, Rudi, 105
Darwin, Charles, 39
Drach, Albert, 2, 8, 10, 12, 13, 15, 123-162, 171, 178-182
Emrich, Wilhelm, 61, 76
Fischer, André, 135, 142
Fluss, Emil, 24
Foulkes, Peter, 57
Franzos, Karl Emil, 9, 87-88, 93

Freud, Jakob, 22, 36, 37
Freud, Sigmund, 2, 8, 13-14, 19-47, 57, 171, 177, 178-180, 182
Fuchs, Gerhard, 145
Gay, Peter, 22
Gerstenberger, Katharina, 172
Gidon, Blanche, 81, 99
Gilman, Sander L., 11, 19, 21, 22-23, 26-27, 125, 172
Glasenapp, Gabriele von, 12
Goldstein, Bluma, 41
Graf, Andreas, 165, 169-170
Grass, Günter, 165
Grice, H. P., 54-55
Grimm, Jakob and Wilhelm (brothers), 163-164
Grosz, Elizabeth, 5, 55
Grubrich-Semitis, Ilse, 35
Grunfeld, I., 110
Grün, Isaac, 99
Herik, Judith van, 19
Hermsdorf, Klaus, 62-63
Herzberg-Fränkel, Leo, 87
Herzog, Elizabeth, 103, 106
Hilsenrath, Edgar 2, 7-8, 10, 13, 15, 163-176, 178-180, 182
Hine, Lewis, 49-50, 79
Höfler, Günther A., 136
Hoffmann, E. T. A., 144
Hohenlohe-Langenburg, Max von, 96
Horkheimer, Max, 98
Jones, Ernest, 23
Joseph II, 149
Jung, Carl Gustav, 28, 31
Kafka, Franz, 2, 7, 8, 10, 13-14, 49-80, 175, 177-182
Kaszynski, Stefan H., 89
Kiepenheuer, Gustav, 82, 84
Kompert, Leopold, 87
Kuhn, Annette, 49, 66, 121
Kraus, Karl, 28
Kremer, Detlef, 75

Kristeva, Julia, 2, 4-7, 45-46, 55-56, 59, 61, 66, 70, 75, 81, 85, 94, 100, 113, 148, 160, 162, 181
Krobb, Florian, 10, 137
Laermann, Klaus, 166
Landauer, Gustav, 96
LeRider, Jacques, 20, 22, 31
Magris, Claudio, 94, 102
Mann, Thomas, 141
McGoldrick, Monica, 105
Mendelssohn, Moses, 12
Nathanson, Amalie, 22
Nietzsche, Friedrich, 56
Ottla (Kafka's sister), 77
Pappenheim, Bertha, 92-94
Pohland, Vera, 172
Politzer, Heinz, 61, 76
Pratt, Mary Louise, 1
Preisendanz, Wolfgang, 135
Rank, Otto, 44
Reick, Theodor, 57
Reifenberg, Benno, 86
Rice, Emanuel, 41,
Richter, Matthias, 11-12
Robert, Marthe, 19, 22, 36
Robertson, Ritchie, 43, 61-62, 76, 77, 104, 111
Roith Esthelle, 19, 22, 23, 112-113, 120
Roth, Joseph, 2, 8, 10, 13, 14, 81-122, 136, 177-180, 182
Roth, Nachum, 81
Rousseau, Jean-Jacques, 142
Samuely, Nathan, 87
Salten, Felix, 77
Sautermeister, Gert, 166, 175
Schlant, Ernestine, 124, 159
Sellin, Ernst, 38
Smith, Anna 7
Sontag, Susan, 65-66, 121
Stach, Rainer, 75, 77

Steinlein, Rüdiger, 166
Sterne, Laurence, 154-155
Wassermann, Jakob, 11
Watzlawick, Paul, 104
Weininger, Otto, 25-26, 28, 75-76
Weizmann, Chaim, 98
Wistrich, Robert S., 8-9
Yerushalmi, Yosef, 36-37
Zborowski, Mark, 103, 106
Zweig, Arnold, 10, 30, 32-33, 34, 42, 136
Zweig, Stefan, 84, 96, 97

Amsterdamer Publikationen zur Sprache und Literatur

Band 100: **Peter Delvaux**: *Antiker Mythos und Zeitgeschehen. Sinnstruktur und Zeitbezüge in Gerhart Hauptmanns Atriden-Tetralogie*. Amsterdam/Atlanta, GA 1992. 342 pp.
ISBN: 90-5183-424-1   Hfl. 110,-/US-$ 61.-
Band 101: **Kerstin Schoor**: *Verlagsarbeit im Exil. Untersuchungen zur Geschichte der deutschen Abteilung des Amsterdamer Allert de Lange Verlages 1933- 1940.* Amsterdam/Atlanta, GA 1992. 281 pp.
ISBN: 90-5183-385-7   Hfl. 100,-/US-$ 55.50
Band 102: **Nico Unlandt**: *... E si fetz mantas bonas chansos ... Techniques romanes dans le Minnesang allemand du treizième siècle*. Amsterdam/Atlanta, GA 1992. 444 pp.
ISBN: 90-5183-428-4   Hfl. 150,-/US-$ 83.-
Band 103: **Lambertus Okken**: *Kommentar zur Artusepik Hartmanns von Aue. Im Anhang: Die Heilkunde und Der Ouroboros von Bernhard Dietrich Haage.* Amsterdam/Atlanta, GA 1993. 564 pp.
ISBN: 90-5183-440-3   Hfl. 230,-/US-$ 127.50
Band 104: **D.G. Bond**: *German History and German Identity. Uwe Johnson's Jahrestage*. Amsterdam/Atlanta, GA 1993. 232 pp.
ISBN: 90-5183-459-4   Hfl. 80,-/US-$ 44.-
Band 105: *Niederländische Autoren über Franz Kafka, 1922-1942.* Hrsg. von Cor de Back und Niels Bokhove. Amsterdam/Atlanta, GA 1993. 168 pp. ISBN: 90-5183-543-4   Hfl. 70,-/US-$ 38.50
Band 106: *Ulrich Füetrer. Flordimar. Aus dem Buch der Abenteuer.* Hrsg. von Heinz Thoelen. Amsterdam/Atlanta, GA 1994.76 pp.ISBN: 90-5183-594-9   Hfl. 40,-/US-$ 22.-
Band 107: **Anthonya Visser**: *"Blumen ins Eis". Lyrische und literaturkritische Innovationen in der DDR. Zum kommunikativen Spannungsfeld ab Mitte der 60er Jahre*. Amsterdam/Atlanta, GA 1994. X,422 pp. ISBN: 90-5183-662-7   Hfl. 140,-/US-$ 77.50
Band 108: **Jakob Koeman**: *Die Grimmelshausen-Rezeption in der fiktionalen Literatur der deutschen Romantik*. Amsterdam/Atlanta, GA 1993. 638 Seiten einschl. 38 Bildseiten.
ISBN: 90-5183-513-2   Geb. Hfl. 240,-/US-$ 132.-
Band 109: *Helvetien und Deutschland. Kulturelle Beziehungen zwischen der Schweiz und Deutschland in der Zeit von 1770-1830.* Hrsg. von Hellmut Thomke, Martin Bircher und Wolfgang Proß. Amsterdam/Atlanta, GA 1994. 298 pp.
ISBN: 90-5183-655-4   Hfl. 100,-/US-$ 55.50
Band 110: **Peter Delvaux**: *Leid soll lehren. Historische Zusammenhänge in Gerhart Hauptmanns Atriden-Tetralogie*. Amsterdam/Atlanta, GA 1994. 383 pp.
ISBN: 90-5183-709-7   Hfl. 120,-/US-$ 66.50
Band 111: **Helga Stipa Madland**: *Image and Text: J.M.R. Lenz.* Amsterdam/Atlanta, GA 1994. 166 pp.
ISBN: 90-5183-726-7   Hfl. 50,-/US-$ 27.50
Band 112: **Helga Schiffer**: *Die frühen Dramen Arthur Schnitzlers. Dramatisches Bild und dramatische Struktur*. Amsterdam/Atlanta, GA 1994. 182 pp. ISBN: 90-5183-667-8   Hfl. 60,-/US-$ 33.-
Band 113: *Deutsche Literatur im Exil in den Niederlanden 1933-1940*. Hrsg. von Hans Würzner und Karl Kröhnke. Amsterdam/Atlanta, GA 1994. 254 pp.
ISBN: 90-5183-649-X   Hfl. 75,-/US-$ 41.50
Band 114: **Priscilla A. Hayden-Roy**: *"A Foretaste of Heaven". Friedrich Hölderlin in the Context of Württemberg Pietism.* Amsterdam/Atlanta, GA 1994. 308 pp.
ISBN: 90-5183-784-4   Hfl. 90,-/US-$ 49.50
Band 115: **Margrit Verena Zinggeler**: *Literary Freedom and Social Constraints in the Works of Swiss Writer Gertrud Leutenegger.* Amsterdam/Atlanta, GA 1995. VI,169 pp.
ISBN: 90-5183-763-1   Hfl. 80,-/US-$ 44.-
Band 116: **Colin Barr Grant**: *Literary communication from consensus to rupture. Practice and Theory in Honecker's GDR.* Amsterdam/Atlanta, GA 1995. VII,244 pp.
ISBN: 90-5183-785-2   Hfl. 75,-/US-$ 41.50
Band 117: **Dennis Tate**: *Franz Fühmann: Innovation and Authenticity. A study of his prose-writing*. Amsterdam/Atlanta, GA 1995. 263 pp. ISBN: 90-5183-805-0   Hfl. 75,-/US-$ 41.50
Band 118: **Christoph Lorey**: *Die Ehe im klassischen Werk Goethes.* Amsterdam/Atlanta, GA 1995. XVI,308 pp.
ISBN: 90-5183-865-4   Hfl. 95,-/US-$ 52.50
Band 119: **Erika Langbroek**: *Zwischen den Zeilen. Untersuchungen zu den lateinischen Kommentaren und den deutschen Glossen der Edinburgher Handschrift Adv. Ms. 18.5.10.* Amsterdam/Atlanta, GA 1995. 274 pp. + 27 Abb.
ISBN: 90-5183-893-X   Hfl. 95,-/US-$ 52.5
Band 120: **Cristina M. Pumplun**: *"Begriff des Unbegreiflichen". Funktion und Bedeutung der Metaphorik in den Geburts betrachtungen der Catharina Regina von Greiffenberg (1633-1694)*. Amsterdam/Atlanta, GA 1995. VII,344 pp.
ISBN: 90-5183-920-0   Hfl. 120,-/US-$ 66.50
Band 121: **Charles W. Martin**: *The Nihilism of Thomas Bernhard. The portrayal of existential and social problems in his prose works*. Amsterdam/Atlanta, GA 1995. 277 pp.
ISBN: 90-5183-886-7   Hfl. 90,-/US-$ 49.50
Band 122: **Frank Finlay**: *On the Rationality of Poetry: Heinrich Böll's Aesthetic Thinking.* Amsterdam/Atlanta, GA 1996. 284 pp.
ISBN: 90-5183-989-8   Hfl. 90,-/US-$ 49.50
Band 123: **Marieke Krajenbrink**: *Intertextualität al Konstruktionsprinzip. Transformationen des Kriminalromans und de romantischen Romans bei Peter Handke und Botho Strauß*. Amsterdam/Atlanta, GA 1996. XII,352 pp.
ISBN: 90-420-0016-3   Hfl. 110,-/US-$ 61.-
Band 124: **Karl Tax**: *Das Janota-Officium. Geschichte und Sprach eines ripuarischen Stundenbuches*. Amsterdam/Atlanta, GA 1996 VIII,506 pp. ISBN: 90-420-0018-X   Hfl. 160,-/US-$ 88.50
Band 125: **DAGMAR WINKLER**: *Die neo-kybernetische Literatur* Amsterdam/Atlanta, GA 1996. XLIV,168 pp.
ISBN: 90-420-0030-9   Hfl. 75,-/US-$ 41.50
Band 126: **PAUL O'DOHERTY** *The Portrayal of Jews in GDR Prose Fiction* Amsterdam/Atlanta, GA 1997. 348 pp.
ISBN: 90-420-0158-5   Hfl. 110,-/US-$ 61.-
Band 127: **VALENTIN UND NAMELOS**. *Mittelniederdeutsch unc Neuhochdeutsch*. Hrsg., übersetzt und kommentiert von Erika Langbroek und Annelies Roeleveld. Unter Mitarbeit von Arend Quak. Amsterdam/Atlanta, GA 1997. VIII,190 pp.
ISBN: 90-420-0384-7   Hfl. 65,-/US-$ 36.-
Band 128: **ULRICH MEHLER**: *Marienklagen in spätmittelalterlicher und frühneuzeitlichen Deutschland. Textversikel und Melodietypen Darstellungsteil.* Amsterdam/Atlanta, GA 1997. 319 pp.
ISBN: 90-420-0305-7   Hfl. 100,-/US-$ 55.50
Band 129: **ULRICH MEHLER**: *Marienklagen in spätmittelalterlicher und frühneuzeitlichen Deutschland. Textversikel und Melodietypen Materialteil.* Amsterdam/Atlanta, GA 1997. 319 pp.
ISBN: 90-420-0315-4 - Bde 1-2   Hfl. 100,-/US-$ 55.50
Band 130: **STUART TABERNER**: *Distorted Reflections: The Public and Private Faces of the Author. The Fiction of Uwe Johnson Günter Grass and Martin Walser, 1965-1975.* Amsterdam/Atlanta GA 1998. 141 pp.
ISBN: 90-420-0353-7   Hfl. 50,-/US-$ 27.50
Band 131: **JULIA SCHMIDT**: *Karneval der Überlebenden Intertextualität in Arno Schmidts Novellen-Comödie "Die Schule de Atheisten".* Amsterdam/Atlanta, GA 1998. VII,187 pp.
ISBN: 90-420-0661-7   Hfl. 65,-/US-$ 36.-
Band 132: **BIRGIT A. JENSEN**: *Auf der morschen Gartenschaukel Kindheit als Problem bei Theodor Fontane.* Amsterdam/Atlanta, GA 1998. VIII,178 pp. ISBN: 90-420-0413-4   Hfl. 65,-/US-$ 36.-
Band 133: **LITERATUR UND GESCHICHTE**. *Festschrift für Wul Koepke zum 70.Geburtstag*. Hrsg. von Karl Menges Amsterdam/Atlanta, GA 1998. 363 pp.
ISBN: 90-420-0443-6   Hfl. 120,-/US-$ 66.50
Band 134: **MIT DEN AUGEN EINES KINDES**. *Children in the Holocaust. Children in Exile. Children under Fascism.* Hrsg. von Viktoria Hertling. Amsterdam/Atlanta, GA 1998. 317 pp.
ISBN: 90-420-0623-4   Hfl. 100,-/US-$ 55.50
Band 135: **MANFRED KERN**: *Edle Tropfen vom Helikon. Zu Anspielungsrezeption der antiken Mythologie in der deutscher höfischen Lyrik und Epik von 1180-1300.* Amsterdam/Atlanta, GA 1998. VIII,567 pp. ISBN: 90-420-0379-0   Hfl. 175,-/US-$ 92.-
Band 136: **ALBRECHT CLASSEN**: *Deutsche Frauenlieder des fünfzehnten und sechzehnten Jahrhunderts. Authentische Stimmen in der deutschen Frauenliteratur der Frühneuzeit oder Vertreter eine poetischen Gattung (das Frauenlied)?* Amsterdam/Atlanta, GA 1998. 228 pp.
ISBN: 90-420-0442-8   Hfl. 80,-/US-$ 44.-